THE MAN BOOK

Becoming a Man in the Twenty-First Century

STEVE CLARKE

Balboa Press books may be ordered through booksellers or by contacting:

Balboa Press
A Division of Hay House
1663 Liberty Drive
Bloomington, IN 47403
www.balboapress.com
1 (877) 407-4847

Print information available on the last page.

ISBN: 978-1-9822-0783-0 (sc)
ISBN: 978-1-9822-0785-4 (hc)
ISBN: 978-1-9822-0784-7 (e)

Library of Congress Control Number: 2018908049

Balboa Press rev. date: 08/14/2018

CONTENTS

To my son,
Richard.
He is authentic and curious.
In short, he is a
Man.

IMPORTANT CAUTIONS

I AM NOT A LICENSED PHYSICIAN or therapist in any discipline. In a book of this type, I can't deal with your particular needs, so it's important that you engage a licensed physician, therapist, or other appropriate professional to assist you with any treatment you might need for a psychological or physiological condition.

I am not offering specific medical, psychological, or emotional advice. Similarly, I am not diagnosing any condition from which you may be suffering or prescribing any treatment for any problems related to your condition.

Consult your physician or therapist before you make any changes to your prescribed treatment regimen, which you should follow as prescribed until your treating provider amends it.

If you suffer from any type of genital illness or disease, not only should you consult a physician, but you *must* inform any potential partner of your condition before you become sexually involved with her or enter into a relationship with her.

ACKNOWLEDGMENTS

I HAD MUCH HELP IN THE preparation of this book from an incredible group of people.

Mr. Rich Clarke, my son, was the major inspiration for this book. As I watched him living his life, I had an epiphany. He was doing exceptionally well but I could tell there was something missing. He saw it too and began the work to become a rock-solid Man. There is nothing missing from his make-up now but he is still learning, growing and evolving.

Rich is a gifted writer in his own right, and he was generous with his time as he gave overall directional guidance on the ultimate shape of the finished work. In addition, he provided thousands of detailed observations and corrections as the book progressed. Rich was free with his time and with his heart as he told me about his own journey from being a young boy to becoming who he is now. He introduced me to many of the young men in his world; they are all good men. This book is for them and for the tens of millions of adult males like them.

Ms. Karin Goodwin, my editor, deserves enormous credit for putting up with my quirky content and style. As I put pen to paper, what appeared on the page looked like the pieces of a jigsaw puzzle that had been thrown up in the air. Karin helped me sort it all out. She is a woman with a strong feminist view of the world. She argued with me for hours as we navigated the tricky waters of feminism and its role in driving adult males to where we find ourselves today. She resigned the job of editor multiple times because she found what I was saying offensive. Every time she resigned, I explained my position, and she signed on again. The fact that she hung in with me is a testament to her staying power and the power of what I have to say in this book.

A wise and highly developed group of friends, male and female, read the drafts and gave valuable feedback about what I had written, as well as pointing out other issues I needed to address. I benefited in ways large and small from contributions made by Susan Coates, Taj Moore, and Chris Katsaounis, who were present when the seed that became this book first germinated. Thank you for helping birth this book and for your ongoing support. I extend special thanks to the following people who were particularly important to the development of the book and The Men's Workshop:

Dr. Helen Chen came into my life at a perfect time and has inspired me to grow and become a better adult male every day since I met her. Her enthusiasm for this project was a constant companion on the road to its completion, and my discussions with her gave me the focus I needed to complete the work.

Ms. Susana Fernandez brought deep spirituality, support, and magical insights to my early writing efforts and made valuable contributions to the Men's Workshop, many of which found their way into the pages that follow.

Mr. Luis Sosa is the most masculine man I know. He embodies a perfect balance between his deep masculine and powerful feminine essences. He helped me see further into the spiritual world of masculine men. His insights into how he grew to become the adult male he is now are scattered throughout this book and informed much of the Men's Workshop.

Mr. Simon Goodway (Goodway Group), provided the illustrations of female genital anatomy you will find later in the book. He was patient as I made numerous revisions to his work product. Each of the revisions was the result of my inadequate initial instructions. His work was exemplary throughout. I used images I purchased from Adobe as the raw material for Simon to improve.

Ms. Karen Lucas Clarke, my incomparably serene lover and colleague, was by my side when I needed it most throughout this book's gestation and eventual birth. Her detailed challenge of my work caused me to reconsider, carefully, every single word. Although much of my original writing survived her critical eye, the finished product would not be anything like the book you hold in your hands without her contribution. She read and re-read my crazy scribbles and generally kept me going for the past three years. I could not have done it without her. She is a woman with a capital W, but that discussion will have to wait for the next book. Karen (nee Lucas) and I married after I finished writing this book but before its publication. It was her choice to change her name to Lucas Clarke after the wedding.

Karen, Susana, Helen, and Luis teach elements of the Men's Workshop, and each helped me create what is a truly remarkable experience for all who attend.

If errors or omissions remain in the finished work, they are all mine. I own every word in these pages.

—Steve Clarke

LATE ADDENDUM

SINCE I BEGAN TO WRITE this book, there has been an avalanche of complaints of sexual harassment by what the media often describe as *powerful men* (my emphasis). The behavior these men engaged in, or are alleged to have engaged in, is appalling. Some have been charged with crimes as a result of their exposure. Whatever else they got, these men suffered public humiliation as well as loss of fortune. In virtually every case, the supposedly powerful man lost his employment, at which point he no longer appeared so powerful. Other perpetrators reached monetary settlements with their victims that limited their personal losses by using various legal maneuvers (such as confidentiality agreements). The fact that these men are as yet undiscovered does not mean that they are any less guilty of inappropriate or illegal behavior than those who were unable to buy their victims' silence.

Why am I writing this here? My complaint is with the media's use of the word *powerful* to describe these men. Make no mistake, these perpetrators are bullies and especially weak men who were able to use their powerful position to pressure victims into satisfying their demands. The Men I reference in this book do not need to pressure others to force them to do something. Forcing someone into action is bullying, plain and simple. As I will explain further, bullying is a sign of weakness not strength. Nothing I say in this book is supportive of any criminal activity or inappropriate pressure exerted by any male against any person. A Man would never do such a thing.

I hope we are able to remember that it is vital to the health of our community (and that includes our nation, our culture, and our way of life) that males not be afraid to 'flirt' with females. They just have to do so responsibly, without exerting any pressure or demanding any quid pro quo other than mutual attraction. I hope this book sheds some light on how all adult males can safely flirt with women. What follows is designed to empower men to become Men who know who they are, who can stand in their own power, and who are not afraid of doing what is right in all aspects of life: at work, at play, with women generally, and with lovers in particular.

INTRODUCTION

What is a Man?

As with all things human, an adult male lives his life across a spectrum of possibilities, from childlike behavior as a young boy to the highest level of masculine behavior in his finest hour. I don't believe you, or any other adult male, is broken or that you need fixing, no matter where you lie on that spectrum. In the text, I use the word "Man" (i.e., Man with a capital 'M') to refer to an authentic, resilient, centered, adult male who knows who he is, and where he is going. Rich Clarke and Luis Sosa, two adult males who helped me with this book, are two such Men.

A Man is broadly developed and comfortable with who he is. He is not afraid or ashamed to behave as a Man. He is constantly growing, expanding, learning, and accepting risk. He is open and vulnerable in affairs of the heart, and remains calm under duress. He accepts that other people may not like him, but he does not change himself just to please them; he only changes because *he* chooses to change. This book is about becoming a Man.

I use the word "man" to refer to an adult male who lacks some of the characteristics that would make him a Man. He may not yet be a Man because he suffers from an imbalance in his emotional or mental characteristics. For example, a Man is capable of a degree of aggression, which he may express when defending himself. However, if a male's aggression is out of control, his behavior will be inconsistent and may even be dangerous to those around him. The imbalance means he is not yet a Man. There is no shame in being a man. Nobody ever taught you to be a Man. As I point out in the book, being a Man will make your life richer, and easier to understand. Once you become a Man, the world will make much more sense.

I adopted the term "inner Man" to refer to the real Man who exists inside you. Your inner Man is the Man you will become when you eliminate the overbearing programming other people plastered over your natural self in an attempt to control you. The main goal of this book is to free your inner Man so you can become the Man you were always meant to be.

This book puts into words what it means to be a Man. It's not prescriptive, nebulous, or scientific. It's not cloaked in barely fathomable parable, nor so technical that you will be unable to decipher its meaning. It highlights the skills, qualities, and traits of a Man and does so in plain English. I squeezed every drop of scientific jargon and nebulous language out of the finished product. Even mature teenage boys will be able to understand what remains. In fact, I hope you give a copy to your son (and your daughter when she is ready for it).

A Man's Train

An adult male is always headed somewhere; he has a direction. I use the idea of a *train* to describe an adult male's direction (i.e., his mission, goal, or focus at any time). To qualify as *your* train, you must have fired up the train's boiler and be thundering down the track to a destination you have chosen. It's not your train if someone else chose its destination. The train concept marries the masculine tendency to focus on one objective at a time with the singularity of a railroad track that only goes from A to B.

When a Man has either achieved what he set out to do or abandoned the effort, he fires up the next train and heads off again to a new destination. A Man may have many trains running down different tracks all at the same time. A man, on the other hand, is unlikely to have decided where his train should go, so it goes around in circles in the rail-yard. A man may also be toying with so many possible destinations for his train that he never leaves the station.

Exemplars

Throughout the book, to illustrate various points, I write of people doing things well and, sometimes, not so well. Where my exemplars are real people, the facts I state are generally accurate, although they may only represent a part of the whole story. I have changed the names and facts to mask the parties' identities where appropriate.

All of my exemplars are good people. If the specific behavior I describe shows them in a bad light, don't think poorly of them. At the time, they were trying their best to live the life fate had dealt them. Wherever I have no real example, I created vignettes to illustrate a point, and make that clear in the text.

I use the construction "his woman" or "your woman" to denote that there is a relationship of some kind between the male and the female involved (e.g., husband/wife, lover/beloved, friend/sex-partner). I do so to save reiterating all of the possible relationships that might exist between a couple. I am not using this possessive terminology to diminish the humanity of the woman, and it certainly does not signify any degree of *ownership* by the male, as I make quite clear in the text.

Although I have written the book in the context of a relationship between a heterosexual male and a heterosexual female, much of what I write will apply to you no matter what your sexual expression may be. Of course, the applicability of any element of the book's message will vary, based on your life experience and your personal sexual expression. As you read, I believe it will generally be obvious what will work for you and what won't.

So What is This All About?

There are few Men under the age of 50 for reasons I explain later. The other adult males, the men, seem lost, often pushed around by each passing fad or whim, without the masculine underpinning needed to cope when life takes an unexpected turn. Wracked by doubt, especially in regard to women, many men don't know what to do unless someone pushes them, and then many of them resent the push. While I specifically address many of the problems men face, it is impractical to reiterate all the problems throughout the book, so I use one word to describe the entire range of problems from which men suffer – confusion. Enough of this preamble, let's get started.

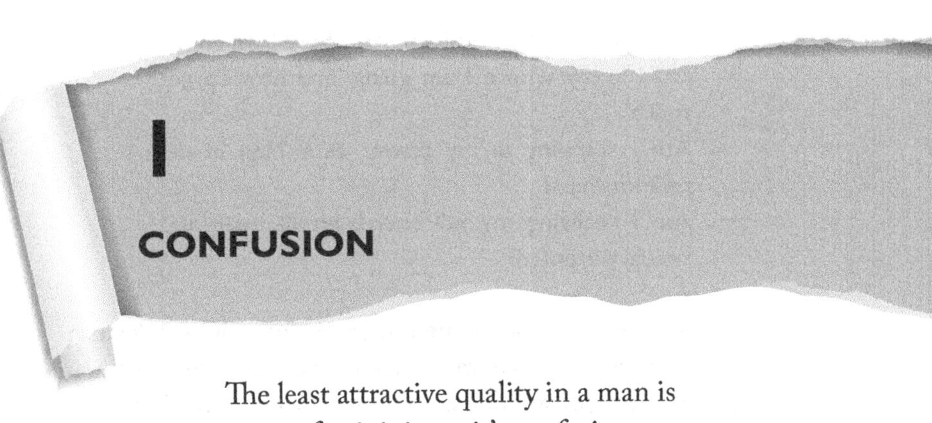

1

CONFUSION

The least attractive quality in a man is
not femininity— it's confusion.
Karen Lucas Clarke

A Letter to Every Adult Male:

Dear John,

I can hear you thinking: "Wait a minute Clarke. I am an adult male. Being a man comes naturally to me. How is it even possible for me—a successful, mature, adult male—to be anything other than a Man in the fullest sense of the word?"

I'm sorry, John, but the sad fact is that if you are like many adult males, you are *confused* about your role as protector, husband, lover, parent, and provider. You are also *confused* about women and by women: how to relate to them; how to love them; and how to live with them. The confusion seeps into your work life too, where you probably lack the direction, focus, and commitment to be as successful in your job as you could be.

If you doubt me, look around, or better yet, ask all the men you know how their lives are going. My observation from asking that very question is that young men are unhappy, lost, or drowning in doubt. I challenge you to ask yourself:

- Am I happy with who I am and where I am going?
- Do I know where I am going, and how to get there?
- Am I standing in my power as a Man in my relationships?
- Am I realizing my full social, intellectual, and sexual potential?

If you are like millions of other men in the industrialized Western world, your confusion makes it impossible to reach your full potential as a Man. Take heart; you are not alone. You are a member of the man club that grows bigger every day if any of these descriptions fit:

- You feel trapped by your work, family, friends, or location.
- Your reality leaves you cold.
- You have lost your spark.
- Your relationship has no juice but you are afraid to leave it.
- You have no direction and no purpose.
- You avoid relationships because you fear losing your identity.
- You dislike the thought of providing income and security for a woman.
- You are a 30-year old still living with your mother.
- You thought life as an adult was going to be great, but now you know it's not.

If any of these descriptions fit, you are not odd, unusual, or flawed. You are in good company. Almost every young man you know is in the same boat with you.

To become a Man, you must take the difficult first step and accept that you, an adult male with a good job and no shortage of sex partners, might not yet be the Man you are capable of becoming. There is a Man inside you, no matter how confused you are. As I discuss further later, he is your inner Man, and you soon will free him from the prison cell in which you have held him all your adult life.

While the process of becoming a Man is simple, it's not easy. It's simple because you don't have to dedicate a lot of time to the task or pay lots of money to shrinks or counselors. You can continue to work, enjoy sports, hang out with your friends, and date women. You can grow and become a Man as an undercurrent to your normal daily life. Nevertheless, becoming a Man is not *easy* because you have to grow into the role, which means you must decide that you need to change. You will have to shake off years of doubt about who you are and where you are going. You will have to replace all those years of shame and blame others have heaped upon you with your own view of who you really are and how you will live your life. Once you are a Man, you will never again say, "It's not my fault. I'm doing what you told me to do. So, don't blame me." Once you become the Man you were always meant to be, you will be playing out your life with *your* deck of cards. You won't be outplayed by other Men playing their game with their cards—and, quite possibly, your woman.

As soon as you embark on this journey, your friends will notice a difference in you immediately. They may not understand what has happened to you, but they will notice that you are brighter, and more interesting. I have known numerous men who have taken the first step on their journey to become Men, and the change in them is stunning. Some who took that first step found it was too challenging and gave up. If you give up because of the challenge, realize that a Man does not give up because his goal is too challenging.

If you get nothing else from this book, stop worrying about the past or the future. Take joy in the moment—yes, this very moment— and be fully present whether you are pleasuring your lover, or yourself for that matter. Once you are present, you won't be worrying about the fence that needs painting or the report that is due next week. When you are present in the now, your life will become simpler, and so much better. Presence is so important that it has a section of its own later in the book. Here is a start on being present: if reading *The Man Book* right now is not the best thing you could be doing, please go do whatever it is you believe is better.

I am not going to turn you into something you are not. There is no one-size-fits-all solution. I am going to describe the attributes of a Man, and you can decide how to use the information to set your inner Man free. There is no recipe. I am not going to tell you to "follow this ten-step program" to become a Man. Would you feel better if I told you how to become the Man *I* think you should be? If you are yelling, *"Hell, no!"* Congratulations on a good answer.

You already have the tools to become a Man. Trust me; this is not superhero material. You don't need a PhD. You don't need to learn a new language. You don't need to spend a lot of money. There's no age limit. There are no prerequisites. If you are quiet and introspective, you can become a Man and still be quiet and introspective. If you are an all-action charger with a brash approach to life, you can retain all your fire and still become a Man. When you set your inner Man free you will finally become *you*—the only *you* who has ever existed. The only *you* who will ever exist. The world needs *Men* like you. Become one.

If your life is great, and you have goals and a plan to achieve your goals, and you have strong relationships with male and female friends, congratulations. Keep doing what you are doing. You may already be a Man. Even so, you will find things in this book that will make you a better Man; that struggle to be better never ends. Take a chance, and set off on a journey to your future as a Man. You have nothing to lose.

If you are still with me, focus on being right here, right now! You feel brighter and easier already! You just tested out of Man 101.

Steve Clarke

So What Do You Want to Be? Media Model or Man

In spite of the wide degree of sexual, cultural, and political freedom we enjoy, many adult males are struggling to be authentically themselves. Until 50 years ago, males found out about being masculine Men from other males who were already Men. Now, there are too few Men capable of teaching boys and young men how to become Men. If you search for a role model in movies or on television, you will only become more confused. Movies and TV shows put impossibly beautiful men and women in equally impossible situations, unfettered by the realities of living a life. Unfortunately, if you become beguiled by the way these actors and models appear, your efforts to emulate them will prevent you from being authentically yourself. You will be forever jumping through hoops trying to become *them* instead of becoming *you*. Once you realize your effort is doomed to fail no matter how hard you try, you can relax. Keeping up with the Joneses is a terrible way to live; keeping up with the media Joneses is impossible.

Mass marketing shows women in the thrall of men who have applied the right cologne, driven the right car, or worn the right clothes. The message is clear – it's *things* that make men successful, and if you don't have those things, you are failing. On the other hand, film makers and advertisers show us that women can use their bodies and sex to manipulate and control males without repercussions (most of the time). Fortunately, these manipulations will fail once you become a Man because you will have no need of cologne or a woman with impossibly shiny hair to validate you. Baubles matter not to a Man. It is his character that matters.

Hollywood has capitalized on the rise of newly empowered women by turning gender roles on their heads. Strong women and weak male leads are the new normal. In the last twenty-five years, female TV and movie characters win all manner of fights that, in reality, would get them killed. Xena may cut it in her skimpy outfit, but she would never cut it in a fight. Angelina Jolie,

Jodie Foster, Uma Thurman, Sigourney Weaver, Glenn Close, and Demi Moore portray powerful female characters as *actually* tough, while Steven Seagal, Sylvester Stallone, Arnold Schwarzenegger, Bruce Willis, and Mel Gibson portray men who are *cartoonishly* tough—think movies like *Under Siege, Rocky, Terminator, Die Hard, and Lethal Weapon*. In these movies (all of which I enjoyed), the characters have a comic book feel. They are fun to watch but they are so divorced from reality that they make a mockery out of what being a *Man* is all about. Gone are the TV characters of old, like Marshal Matt Dillon (*Gunsmoke*), Rowdy Yates (*Rawhide*), Sergeant Joe Friday (*Dragnet*) and the eponymous *Kojack*, who were fighting for justice as Men. Even comedy shows are not immune. Many involve men who are inept or just plain stupid, while the show's women save the day. It was only a few years between the female klutz in *I Love Lucy* (1957) and the powerful female leader in *The Mary Tyler Moore Show* (1970).

The move to heroic female roles happened at a time when women in the industrialized Western world were taking a far more prominent role in society as governments legislated equality among the sexes. Unfortunately, what began as a fight for equal rights under the law, soon became a demand for fundamental changes in the *character* of adult males. Adult males were criticized for their manly traits and were pressed to become gentler, more heart-centered, and emotionally available (i.e., more feminine). It was as if women and the media assumed that males did not have feelings, when the reality is that males feel just as much as females. However, in the same way that wounded wolves hide their weaknesses from the pack, males hide their emotions and wounds so as not to appear weak. This has been a masculine trait for millennia, and criticizing the trait betrays a lack of understanding of masculine biology. For fifty years now, women have berated adult males for their masculinity, and the mass media lost no opportunity to highlight the sins of the masculine (uncaring, unfeeling, unemotional, egotistical, one dimensional, and so on). During that time, adult males lost the guts of their masculinity as the tidal wave of feminism and the mass media squeezed it out of them.

The result was a revolution with—as with all revolutions—unintended consequences. Adult males suffered multiple major setbacks: The media tore down everything masculine. Many males were slow to adapt to the rapidly changing environment caused by the feminist revolution and, as a result, lost their sense of manhood, their dignity, and sometimes their jobs. Any male who complained was branded a Neanderthal. The most damaging effect of these changes was that boys failed to become Men because older Men stopped showing them how (even the older Men began to doubt what appropriate masculinity looked like). Males also suffered in the workplace, as hiring preferences changed to meet gender-based staffing goals.

I am fully aware that men have been fired for harassing or otherwise inappropriately treating women in the workplace. The culprit is usually a predatory senior male using his position of authority to draw a woman into a sexual relationship of some kind. I absolutely abhor such behavior because it has created the false narrative that all males engage in such predatory practices.

Of course, some men do commit violent crimes against women, including rape, molestation, and beatings. What is lost in the sensationalist media coverage is that these crimes are committed by a tiny minority of men. Therefore, I am going to focus on non-criminal men and let someone else deal with the criminals and predators. As a result of the feminist revolution, males have grown ever more confused. The confusion I am referring to causes many men to feel unsatisfied, unfulfilled, and even lost. If you have ever had thoughts like these:

- Nobody wants to be with me.
- Women are crazy.
- I never have enough money.
- I have great plans, but they never seem to work out.

- I'm a loser.
- Is this all there is?
- My work sucks, my life sucks; what is the point.
- I give everything I have, and it's never enough.
- I have no idea what I want to do or where I want to go.
- My boss doesn't like me, my girlfriend doesn't like me, *I* don't even like me.

then you have probably fallen victim to confusion. If that is the case, then you are like many men who are no longer anchored to a reality they can understand. For them, reality moves like a shifting fog as they are pushed wherever the wind blows them. Because they don't know what they want, they never find it. Because they don't know where they are going, not only do they never know when they have arrived, where they actually *are* never feels right either. Scorned by the media and by women as misogynistic, oafish, or clueless, men seem to have no idea where to go or what to do if they ever *arrive*. These men are not stupid. They are well aware that their lives and their relationships with women are unsatisfying. They even know they have no direction, no purpose, and—if they don't sort themselves out—no future. If they ever had a train, it lies cold and rusting, its fire snuffed out long ago. Under attack from all directions, their performance, manliness, and energy level are all targets for their critics. If you ask them, they may tell you they hate women, their boss, or their government (maybe all three) because they have to blame somebody for their confusion. Is it any wonder they give up?

If any of this seems to fit you, *it's not your fault*. Please let that sink in. Roll it around in your mouth, and say it out loud. Then feel the truth of it in your body. It's not your fault because nobody ever taught you how to be a Man. Repeat, and scream it out:

It's not *my* fault because nobody ever taught me how to be a Man!

Make no mistake though. It will be your fault if you do nothing about it now that you know. So what is it to be a Man? Are Men supposed to be soft and gentle or strong and tough? Should they be tender and heart-centered, or should they fight to protect their families, friends and way of life? Should they be singularly focused on a mission (a masculine trait), or should they be diffused and unfocused (a feminine trait)? For decades, feminists have required Men to shoehorn their behavior into a revised model of masculinity, and it has not worked. Many males under 50 years of age lost sight of their naturalness as their masculinity slowly seeped away. Paradoxically, as adult males yielded to the feminist demands, women have grown more dissatisfied with them. If you need confirmation of this, just ask women how they feel about the men in their lives. All the women I know who are in a relationship with the man they thought they wanted (i.e., because he was kind, gentle, heart-centered, and emotionally available), are dissatisfied with him because what these women really *needed* was a relationship with a Man. Sadly, as my real life example below shows, young Men are few and far between.

Audrey is a wonderful young woman, beautiful on the inside and the outside. She is intelligent, beguiling, and witty. She would have no trouble attracting a Man, if she could find one. I asked her why she was not with a Man, and she said, "Introduce me to one who is not attached already. I don't know any." Audrey is not looking for a perfect Man; she just wants a Man who is single and available. Of all the adult males I know, I could not think of one who fit the bill. Audrey's inability to find a Man is a fact of life for millions of other women too. This book is an attempt to give Audrey—and women like her—a chance at finding a Man.

Where Are the Men?

Where have the Men gone? Have I imagined their disappearance? I looked for the answer everywhere—from practitioners, online, in books, in seminars, and in workshops dealing with males in general, and their relationships with women in particular. I hosted discussion groups (Salons) that focused on sex and relationships. There is no doubt that Men are hard to find.

I came to realize that a wide cross-section of adult males, and most of those under the age of 50, are having trouble with their women, their work, and their lives. The tragedy is that Men are becoming extinct in our society and throughout the developed Western world. Boys become adults by the passage of time, but they are not becoming Men. How can they? Boys don't become Men without years of training by other Men. Too many of the fathers who *could* help their sons become Men are not close enough or available enough to teach them. Mothers raising boys have no idea how to help their sons become Men. Paradoxically, the more a mother lavishes her feminine care on her son, the more difficult it will be for him to become a Man. A boy may learn from his mother how a woman lives and loves, but he will not learn how a Man lives and loves.

Consider the questions below. Be honest as you answer them. Don't try to give a "right" answer to each question.

- Do you really know what you want out of your life?
- Do you have a plan to achieve what you want?
- Are you consistently the person you believe you are?
- Do you have at least one train and know where it's going? How do you feel about your train's direction and progress?
- How many adult males (include yourself) do you know who are happy with their lives?
- When did you last talk to an adult male who was appropriately self-confident?
- Are you appropriately self-confident?
- If you suffer a setback or a loss, do you bounce back quickly?
- When you try to befriend someone, do you often fail?

- Are you always yourself, no matter what others think of you?
- Do you lose your temper easily, or often?
- Do your friends know who to expect when you show up?
- Do you care about other people, your country, the world, nature?
- If a driver cuts you off, do you honk the horn, or chase after him?
- Are you supporting yourself or anyone else?
- Do you have satisfying romantic relationships with women?
- Do you have solid friendships with women who are not romantic interests?
- Do you make most of the decisions in your life? If you don't, who does?
- Have you ever told a lie when trying to get a woman to have sex with you?
- Do you manipulate people to get them to do what you want?
- Would you risk your life to save your child's life?
- Would you risk your life to save your woman's life?
- Would you risk your life to save a stranger's life?
- Do you follow your own path or the path of the nearest alpha male?
- Do your friends rarely (never) accept your ideas or suggestions?
- Are you unsure how to relate to the Men you know?
- Do you think women are all the same, or that they're crazy, or that they only want you for protection and provisioning?
- Are you afraid of being open because you always get hurt when you open up?
- What would a satisfying life look like for you?

- Do your friends seem to have more satisfying lives than you do?
- Are you trying to feel better through alcohol or drug use?

Of course, I could write many more questions similar to these. The purpose of asking yourself these questions is to help you determine whether you are confused. If you did not like your answer to more than a handful of these questions, the chances are that you are confused. If you are confused, you are not weak or a failure. You did not forget how to be a Man. If anybody tried to teach you how to be a Man, the teaching was quite likely wrong, especially if the person who taught you was a woman.

You can be a Man and be big and strong, or weak and frail. You may be young, old, or middle-aged. You may consider yourself intellectually, artistically, or athletically gifted or feel you lack any worthwhile gift. You may be film-star handsome or not. You may be thoughtful and kind or a boastful oaf. You may have a relationship with a beautiful woman or be unattached. So be honest with yourself, and carefully consider your answers to the questions above. Then decide for yourself whether you are confused.

If you are confused, you may realize that there is not enough joy in your life; that your future is uncertain, bleak or even hopeless; that your brain is so overwhelmed by your confusion that other feelings are numbed out of you. You may no longer feel pleasure, happiness, or satisfaction. When you feel such negativity, it's impossible to feel love or connection. You keep other people at arm's length for fear they will hurt you, leading to isolation and even more confusion. Nevertheless, your masculine biology still pushes you to have sex with women, so you fake it as you make it through another episode of empty sex. The result of all this confusion is the certain knowledge that this is no way to live your life.

2

HOW DID WE GET HERE?

Back to Basics

For between one hundred thousand years and two hundred thousand years (estimates vary), people (Homo sapiens) have roamed this planet. Modern and early humans are so alike that if you adopted a baby from one of these ancient couples, you could teach it to speak like you, or write a book! They are us. We are them. Obviously, these ancient Men were driven to mate (the drive is innate, so they couldn't help it, and neither can you) and their women managed to keep them around with all kinds of attractions, like 24/7 sex, long enough to provide for and protect their families until the children matured. Over the centuries, Men who best protected and provided for their families were able to choose the best women and so were able to pass on their genes. Therefore, the genes of good providers and protectors won the battle of biological selection over the millennia, and our species prospered.

Given these realities, a relationship with a woman in which she gives you many benefits (such as children, companionship, support, and sex), while you provide for and protect her and your children is natural and much more satisfying than the blogosphere suggests. If you are wondering why you should provide for and protect a woman who makes more money than you do, I don't blame you. It's a logical question. You may also be asking why you should do anything that benefits a woman at your expense, especially if you feel undervalued by her. Fortunately, the answers are simple. When you are providing for and protecting your family, you are living out your human destiny, consistent with your biology. Ignoring your biology means losing your humanity and raises the inevitable question, "What's the point … of anything?" If that is how you are living, you are confused and likely heading for a miserable future. Don't fight your biology; if you do, you will lose the fight. When you free your inner Man, it will all make sense.

In the last ten years or so, there has been a growing body of male discontent in the internet-based "manosphere." A significant element of the discontent is the suggestion that men need to disconnect from their biological inheritance of providing for and protecting their women and their families. In his book, *The Rational Male* (see Resources), blogger and podcaster Rollo Tomassi coins the term *spinning plates,* which is a brilliant term to describe a male who is dating multiple women (serially, or at the same time). There is nothing wrong with a male spinning plates (provided he is honest with the women he dates). Unfortunately, if he is spinning plates to *avoid* providing for and protecting a family, he is denying his human biology, which means that if he isn't already confused, he soon will be. You ignore 100,000 years of biological selection at your peril.

Rites of Passage

In tribal society, your life depends on the Man standing next to you. Therefore, you have to *know* he is prepared to die for the tribe and for you, as you would die for him. Tribes train and educate their boys in the ways of Men, and how to provide for and protect the tribe and their own families. The transition from boy to Man begins when the elders separate a boy from female influences at puberty. He then spends years in the company of

Men, learning how to hunt, fight, and behave as a Man, including how to relate to a woman as a husband/lover/provider/protector. A tribal boy will also undertake arduous rites of passage as he grows. These rites are difficult, usually extremely painful, and sometimes deadly. The tribes make these efforts because they know that their continued existence as a tribe depends on the tribe's Men.

For at least fifty years, Western society has failed to teach boys how to be Men. We are now living with the results of society's failure. In the Western world, the tribal style of educating boys was abandoned centuries ago. However, as long as the boys continued to work with their fathers and other Men, they became Men by watching Men relate to each other in the workplace. Sadly, structural changes in Western society (factory work, farm mechanization, etc.) eliminated that practice too, and separated boys from Men to an ever greater degree. For the last fifty years, it has been predominately mothers, female teachers, and other female caregivers who have raised the boys of the industrialized Western world.

As I stated previously, women have no idea how to help a boy become a Man. Any efforts women do make are often counterproductive. These days we seem to think a boy will become a Man by osmosis; that if he has a pulse, he will become a Man. What many people think of as rites of passage are nothing more than events that fail to test a boy's character, bravery, or endurance. For example, at sixteen years of age a boy can get a driver's license; at eighteen he becomes an adult; at twenty-one he can legally drink alcohol. These are mere events that teach a boy nothing about becoming a Man. Some Native American tribal groups have rites of passage for boys, and some of these may require strength and courage. Unfortunately, outsiders know so little about what goes on within the tribal rites that they remain an unhelpful mystery for those outside the tribe.

Some commercial organizations offer rites of passage for boys, men, and women, and these are probably helpful (see Resources).

I can't recommend them because I have not done them myself, but my reading of their promotional literature suggests that some involve tests of an attendee's endurance and tenacity. In today's litigious society, it's unlikely any organization would risk exposing boys to true rites of passage at an appropriate age. As a result, the advertising and focus of these groups is mature adults. Just be aware that these modern rites lack the years of education and training by people who have known you since birth. While these rites of passage groups are the best we have in today's society, you will still need to work to become a Man.

To help your son, spend as much time with him as possible, and include him in events where other Men are present. Talk to him about Man stuff like sex, relationships, his direction (his train), and courage; in short, talk about the contents of this book. Give your son this book when he is ready for it (which will probably be long after he actually *is* ready for it; try not to wait too long).

You may be asking yourself whether military service helps men to become Men. While initial military training puts men (and women) under intense pressure, one of the main purposes of initial training is to weed out those who won't make it through later training, which focuses on specific skills (radio use and repair, engine maintenance, marksmanship, and so on). Therefore, even though military service includes many dangerous activities (active duty under fire is a severe test of courage for anyone), it's not a rite of passage designed to make a boy into a Man. Military training provides opportunities for a male to test himself on important masculine traits, such as courage, tenacity, and teamwork, but such training omits a broad range of activities (sexuality, relationships with women, living in civil society, and so on) that he will have to master to become a Man.

If you can find a "tribe" of brothers to join you on your quest to become a Man, even if your tribe is just one other male, you will have an enormous advantage over those operating alone.

Rest assured, though, that you can become a Man by yourself. I have added some resources at the end of this book that may help you in your quest and outlined some exercises that might get you started on the journey to becoming a Man. These exercises are simple (not necessarily easy) in their execution because I won't be there to supervise you while you do them. They are designed to test your resolve without putting you in danger. Although you don't have to make ritual sacrifices, suffer genital mutilation, or put your life at risk, doing these exercises will sharpen your sense of self as a Man because they will ask more of you than you are accustomed to giving.

My main fear is that without a correction soon, there will be no Men left alive to teach the next wave of boys how to become Men. The result will be a disaster for our society. We *must* find a way to develop Men. It's a daunting task because the damage men have suffered is so extensive, and the time for action is almost over.

A Case Study in Confusion

What follows is an example designed to illustrate man behavior. Peter is an amalgam of three real men, and the key elements of the story are real:

Peter is big and strong. He is highly educated, articulate, and intelligent. He has a great smile and a gentle demeanor. In short, he looks like a perfect specimen of a Man. Peter holds the door open for his date, takes her to great restaurants, and buys expensive wine with dinner. Afterwards, Peter takes his date back to his house in the ritzy part of town and makes her feel like he is highly attracted to her. She appreciates his tanned body and his toned physique. She looks forward to a relationship with him, so she agrees to have sex with him when he makes the appropriate overtures.

So what is the problem? Well, Peter has many problems, but here are just three: (1) he has no idea who he is; (2) he has no idea what he wants; and (3) he has so far proved himself incapable of loving anyone. As a result, he does not even love himself. He is inauthentic most of the time, and he often slips into characters that confuse women and his colleagues at work.

While Peter sounds like a great catch to many women, he chases women for one thing: sex. He never dates them more than five times so he never has to commit to them. Of course, the women often figure Peter out before they reach his five date maximum. They are not sure why, but they quickly feel uneasy about him, even after spending only a short time in his company. They are uneasy because they don't know who he really is. He is afraid to tell them how he feels because he assumes they will reject him (Peter the Reject) or attach themselves to him (Peter the Project).

When the women realize Peter is faking his affection for them in order to get sex, they walk out, slamming the door as they leave. Their actions make Peter feel terrible but he has no idea what he is doing wrong. He shows the women a great time and he gets commitment-free sex, which all sounds perfect to him. He thinks it's a fair exchange even though his actions look a lot like a business transaction; like those of a customer engaging a prostitute.

Peter used to have a train that was going somewhere, but for the last few years, he knows he has been "mailing it in" at his work. He has made no effort to change his situation, even though he is bored with the work. Peter has a few weak relationships with other males but even they sense there is something not quite right about Peter. They are unable to explain why he wants so much sex while at the same time pontificating about women being a *pain in the ass*. They are also fed up with his complaints about lack of promotion because they all know he puts no effort into his work. Because so much of Peter's self-image is tied to his highly paid job, he would be lucky to survive losing his job.

Peter is circling the drain and could slip down it at any time. His life is a constant round of empty sex and slamming doors but he has no idea how to behave differently. He has rendered his life meaningless and is only surviving by breathing in the intoxicating fumes of empty sex. Those fumes have already consumed the joy he used to feel when he made love to a woman, and they are now eating away what remains of his soul. Obviously, Peter is not yet a Man, and his apparent addiction to empty sex is only one of his personal difficulties. To become a Man, he will have to:

- Change the way he feels about women.
- Treat women as human beings instead of objects to pick up and drop on a whim.
- Forgive himself for his past.
- Do better in future.
- Find his train and get it started down the track.

Even this short list of changes may not be enough to put Peter back on track but it's certain that anything less will mean failure. If he learns how to behave like a Man, everything about his life will become clearer, and his confusion will begin to evaporate. He will be able to enjoy his life instead of floundering around in his misery. Peter is the poster child for what this book is about.

Peter also provides an object lesson: you can't know what a person is like on the *inside* by seeing how they look on the outside. Peter is tall and handsome. He has a wonderful smile that can light up a room (even though he has been faking it for at least the last few years). To the women he meets, Peter looks like he has it all, and his gentle voice suggests he will be kind as well. In fact, Peter has nothing other than trinkets, like his big house and a nice Mercedes. Even while the women in his life are raging at him, Peter's ego won't allow him to accept that he is the cause of his own pain.

Parts of Peter's life may seem appealing. Perhaps you would like his financial success (even though he is mailing it in at work, he is highly paid). Maybe you would like to bed as many women as he does, as if notches on his bedpost mean anything. The reality is that Peter has settled for Faustian bargains, none of which has made him happy. If you are even slightly jealous of Peter's life, you are confused!

I am not saying that Peter needs to propose marriage to every attractive woman he sees. But he does have to regain some integrity by being honest with the women he dates or beds. To calm his emotional roller-coaster, he needs to have sex only with the women he actually cares for. Meaningless sex, which is what Peter has been doing for at least the last five years, will only make him more despondent, and ever more confused. Last time I saw Peter, he was crying and I feared he may be suicidal.

Your Inner Man

Don't let the noise of others' opinions
drown out your own inner voice.
Stanford University, June 12, 2005
Steve Jobs

How do you drop the confusion and become a Man? The answer is not the traditional advice: to love yourself. Loving your confused-self won't work. Panaceas don't work either because no matter what they tell you to do, they are designed to "fix" you. You don't need to be fixed. Here is the reality:

All you have to do to eliminate your confusion is to set your *inner Man* free!

Even though your inner Man is the real you, it may be hard to access him because as a child, you locked him away to shield him from everyone who tried to control you. It was the only recourse you had to protect yourself from the powerful forces that surrounded you. In a well-run family, those forces are gradually loosened so a boy can grow into adulthood at a pace he can manage. Sadly, in the last 50 years, a boy's freedom and independence have been severely curtailed as helicopter-parenting became the norm. This phenomenon has slowed the development of boys so much that they are ill-prepared to become Men as they grow. This is not the boy's fault. These shifts in parenting style have occurred because more and more mothers were forced into work, and sensational journalism made everyone afraid to let their children outside to play.

While your parents were the greatest influence on you as you were growing, they had a lot of help from clergy, teachers, and friends as they tried to control you. Their controls may now be so hard-wired in your brain, that you believe there is no other way to live. But, if you are going to be a Man, you have to test everything others put in your head and decide whether those controls are right for you now. Your friends and foes may have called you mean, dumb, weird, or similar put-downs, and some of those criticisms are alive and well inside you. Recall when your parents and teachers called you lazy, selfish, rude, or any one of many other criticisms. Those criticisms have stuck with you too. Your clergy may have told you that you were a *sinner* even when you were still a child, and threatened you with eternal damnation if you defied them. These criticisms hurt you at the time, and every one added another layer of the foundation upon which you built your *story*. Unfortunately, these criticisms may be so baked into your brain that you live your life as if they are true. Meanwhile, the real you is locked away, adding more scars to your embattled psyche. Although you may have forgotten these scars, they have not forgotten you. If you have ever said or thought the words, "I can't help it. That's just who I am," that was your scars talking. If you have ever wanted to do something legal and legitimate but declined to do so because of a thought planted in your head years ago, that was your scars talking again.

With your inner Man locked away and out of reach, you lost much of your naturalness without even noticing what was going on. Your "advisers" appropriated your life, and decades later what they did is still controlling you. Your inner Man has been imprisoned for so long that you no longer remember a time when he was free. The good news is that as an adult, you don't need to protect your inner Man any longer. Set him free and start living your life. He is strong, and he knows where your train should be going. Your inner Man is not a devil who makes you do "bad" things. In spite of what your parents and clergy told you, you now know that pleasuring yourself did not make you go blind or grow hair on your palms. You may also have shed the idea that consensual sex before marriage does not mean you are headed straight to hell.

Fortunately, you don't have to learn a set of rules or behave in a prescribed way to set your inner Man free. You don't have to be someone you are not, and you sure as heck don't have to do what I tell you to do. Your inner Man has been inside you since you were born. He knows what to do without any help from me. All you have to do is set him free and choose the life you want. Think the thoughts that you want to think. Be the Man you want to be. Then stand back; life is about to become much more interesting!

The first step to freeing your inner Man is to answer some tough questions and be honest about the answers:

- Do I have at least one train?
- Did I decide where my train is going? Is it actually going there?
- Am I authentic, centered, resilient, and calm?
- Am I living my life on my terms?
- Do I manipulate other people?
- Can people rely on me to do what I say I will do, when I say I will do it?
- Do I play games with myself?
- Is my ego under my control or does my ego control me?
- Am I curious, growing, learning, and stretching?

- Do I have strong relationships that I can rely on?
- Am I developing greater understanding of myself and others?
- Have I learned to be 100% present in whatever I am doing?
- Do I establish strong and deep connections with my sexual partners?

The number of questions to which you answered *yes* is less important than your awareness of them as valid reflections of where you are in life. If you are trying to improve on all of these elements of your character (and more), then you are on the way to a life well lived, and if your inner Man is not already free, he soon will be. When you eliminate the programming imposed on you by others, you can just be you. The real you. You may still have some work to do to eliminate all of your confusion, but you can't do that until you are choosing to live the life you want to live.

When you become the Man you were always meant to be, you won't be perfect. You don't even *want* to be perfect. What does a perfect human being even look like? You may be a Harvard PhD, or a high-school dropout. You may have a large family or live alone. You may be tall or short; large or small; weak or strong; pale or dark. Whoever you are, once you control your life, you will choose how to live and how to love, and next time you receive unsolicited advice, you will say, "Thanks," and ignore it if you choose. For the first time in your life, meet your imperfect, honest, vulnerable, authentic self. Oh! That feels good!

3

MYTHS VS. REALITIES

Women Are from Venus

When you stop expecting people to be perfect,
you can like them for who they are.
Donald Miller

When he is chatting with the guys at a bar, Bart says things like, "Women are stupid," and "Women only want a man for protection and provisioning," or "I don't want a relationship; I want sex without strings." The reality is that Bart finds it impossible to sustain a relationship. When Bart wants sex, however, he will chase *stupid women* for all he is worth. The fundamental contradiction in what he says and what he does is striking, yet I have witnessed this exact scenario play out many times with men like Bart.

Myths: Women are from Venus. Women are all the same. Women only want a man for provisioning and protection. Women are never satisfied. It's impossible to understand a woman. Women are irrational. Women only give sex in order to get love, and it is bad sex.

Reality: If you believe these myths about women, you are confused. Women behave the way they do because they are women. Let them be women, and delight in their amazing complexity. Women will be delighted to let you be a Man, *once you become one.*

Reality: A Man does not believe any of these myths about women. Women are not aliens from another planet. Women are human beings who are similar to you but deliciously different in many ways. Treat a woman well, and she will be easy to love. Treat her like a goddess, and she will become one (hint: she may already be a goddess, but she won't behave like one until you treat her like one).

Reality: It's not difficult to understand a woman. Start learning about women, and see whether you understand them better a year from now. Interestingly, when a woman tries to teach you about life, she likely will make you more confused. Women generally don't have the masculine language to teach you what you need to know, and much of what they say may sound critical or condescending. To really learn about life and women in particular, you need to read extensively and attend at least a few workshops (see Resources). Also, do your own research by talking to as many women as you can to learn what makes them different. It's a great journey of discovery and a never-ending quest. Enjoy it!

Reality: A woman wants a Man who understands her and knows how to satisfy her.

Reality: Many women can't find a Man.

Reality: The women you meet may be suffering from their own confusion after fifty years of feminism. Help women by being a Man and standing in your power. When you do, the women in your life will find it easy to regain their femininity, at least while they are with you.

Reality: When you are a Man, standing in your power, you know who you are, you know what you want to do, and you know where you are going. As a result, you know whether to say yes when opportunities arise. You recognize that other people have free will and may exercise it without your control. You are centered and able to hold your center, even under verbal or physical assault. Not only do you know what you want, but you know how to ask for it with understanding and humility. You are always trying to learn.

Reality: As a Man, you are always aware of what is happening around you. You recognize your anger, jealousy, or other negative emotion for what it is, and you may choose to ignore it because your emotions no longer control your behavior. You control your behavior now.

Reality: Striving to improve yourself in areas of personal weakness allows you to stand in your power more often throughout your life. A by-product of working on one area of weakness is that you will probably improve across the board as your strengths grow stronger and your weaknesses grow weaker.

Reality: You don't have to be a good fighter to be a Man, but you must be prepared to die for your cause. When you can look death in the face and accept it, other people will see something in you that sets you apart. They will recognize a confidence, a *knowing*, in you, even if they can't say what it is.

Men Are from Mars

A man might lurch from one meaningless relationship to another, blaming his female partner for what went wrong—she always did this; she never did that; she was crazy. It is never *his* fault the relationship failed or became unsatisfying. Escape from a marriage can be difficult, especially if children make it emotionally, culturally, and economically difficult to walk away. Even if a male gets out of a bad marriage, he will often find himself with no partner, no house, and child support payments. And what do most males do after a failed marriage? They repeat the same sorry saga. Until they eliminate their confusion and become Men, life is always going to be difficult and unsatisfying.

Myth: Whether you are married or single, once the first rush of lust dies down, your sexual interactions with the same woman will not be satisfying.

Reality: Untrue. It's not only possible, but it's delicious to discover that you can keep your sex life juicy, even after you have been in the same relationship for many years. You just have to keep growing and be willing to take chances. Curiosity is your friend; embrace it, and your sex life will become much more interesting. It takes effort, but what delightful rewards you and your woman will reap.

Reality: The whole idea that men and women are from different planets is preposterous, but the title sure sold a lot of books. Men and women are not the same, but you would not want them to be the same. Savor those differences.

Reality: The main reason your marriage will fail or become mediocre is your confusion. There is nothing inherently wrong with the institution of marriage, and there may not be much wrong with your woman (even if she is flawed, just like you). The way to create a solid relationship is to become a Man and behave like one. When you are a Man, your woman can relax and be a feminine woman instead of testing you or, worse, trying to fix you (which is always a disaster).

Validation by Sex

I didn't leave because I stopped loving you.
I left because the longer I stayed, the less I loved myself.
Milk and Honey
Rupi Kaur

As early as your teenage boyhood, your hormones drove you to desire women, so you learned (from your peers, the media, society, and, if you were lucky, your parents) to pursue women for sex. You probably also learned that there was something wrong with you if you were not chasing women and having sex. By now, you have realized that sometimes when you have sex, all you gain is momentary pleasure. Why? Because another round of empty sex in a meaningless relationship means fleeting pleasure … at best. If you later conclude that she was *no good in bed*, join the throng of men who blame their partners when sex leaves them feeling empty. The next thing you will do is jump to the conclusion that if you could only find a woman who knew how to satisfy you, everything would be fine.

Myth: All you need to make sex feel wonderful, even magical, is the right woman.

Reality: You can't validate yourself (or your sexual performance) by using a woman to improve your rating on the Man spectrum. You are a Man because of who you are and how you behave, not because a woman sprinkles fairy dust on you.

Reality: No woman can make you feel better about yourself or validate your status as a Man. If you even think a woman can validate you, you are confused, and when you are confused, no amount of sex is going to help you feel better. Sadly, bad sex will make you feel worse. Great sex can happen, but your role in creating great sex is paramount. It's not your woman's job to make you a sexual superman.

Reality: Sex is not a rite of passage, and if you think a sexual relationship will make you a Man, you are going backwards in your quest to become a Man.

Reality: Having sex twice a day every day, will not make you a Man. Having sex with a different woman every day will not make you a Man either. Sex cannot validate your Man ticket.

Myth: If you feel unsatisfied after sex, it must be the woman's fault.

Reality: It's not the woman, and it's not the sex. Unless you are a Man, it's you! Until you know where you are going, and your train is going there, not much will work out the way you would like. This is especially true about sex and relationships. Even if she decides to have sex with you, a woman will sense your confusion and lack of direction. Don't blame your lover for your confusion. She did not do this to you.

Reality: If a woman recognizes your confusion and chooses to stay with you anyway, beware! She probably thinks she can fix you, and—*just like that*—you become a project.

Reality: When you become sexual with a woman, you must give her your most expansive, masculine self. Your role is to create the overall experience for her. Bringing focused masculine energy to your interaction will generate much more satisfaction than an empty-sex tussle and may even allow you to uncover parts of her you never would see otherwise. Sexual technique can't make up for a weak connection with your woman.

Reality: If you are present and deeply connected to your woman during sex, your sexual technique will not matter too much.

Reality: Learning a woman's anatomical geometry and pleasure zones will be a magical journey you can take together. Mmmm!

Reality: Great sex comes with a wonderful bonus. When your sex life is firing on all cylinders, your work life and your friendships will all become better too. By always striving for new ways to be a better lover, you will continue growing and expanding your horizons, so your already full life will become even more interesting.

Manipulation Hurts Everyone

Love comes when manipulation stops;
when you think more about the other person
than about [her] reaction to you.
When you dare to reveal yourself fully.
When you dare to be vulnerable.
Elle, May 14, 2013
Dr. Joyce Brothers

If you manipulate a woman to have sex with you, your confusion will intensify. Why? Because when you act without honor or integrity, you lose a piece of yourself in the process. Later, when you fail to maintain your pretense, she will reject you. If you are a serial manipulator, other women will have rejected you too, which means even more confusion for you. To protect your ego, you will no doubt have concluded that these failures were all caused by crazy, unfathomable women because it couldn't be your fault, could it?

Myth: It's better to manipulate your way into bed than be yourself and have a woman turn you down.

Reality: Finding a woman to have sex with you is not difficult (even if you think it is). There is no need to manipulate a woman into your bed. Even a clueless, undeveloped male can find a woman willing to have sex without having to manipulate her. But, when you are a Man, you will be much more attractive to a woman than the manipulator you think you need to be. Being the real you all the time is a major step to becoming a Man.

Weak Bullies; Strong Men

When a boy learns to stand up to tyranny and injustice, he takes a big step to becoming a Man.
Ms. Susan Coates

When you bully others, especially if they can't strike back, you are displaying weakness, not strength. A bully lacks decency and honor (a Man never bullies anyone). I have worked for a few bullies, and I had no respect for them. Rather than admire them for their strength, I pitied them for their weakness.

Myth: Intimidating other people makes you strong.

Reality: A bully never attacks someone stronger than himself. Even if the bully is physically bigger and more powerful than his victim, a bully is always temperamentally and emotionally the weaker party. He only *appears* to be stronger and will back down if you stand up to him. He does not want to take the chance that his weakness will be revealed.

Reality: A Man stands up to bullies and works to right injustices. It may be frightening, but you must find the courage to take a stand. While there may be times when the consequences of standing up to a bully will hurt you in the short run, those effects are outweighed by the satisfaction you feel when you stand up for yourself (or someone else).

I Am Defenseless against Women

That women are "the weaker sex" is a cliché. Like most clichés, it contains a grain of truth, but just because it's an old saying does not make it right. While women may not win a physical confrontation with you, they have other ways of making you toe the line. They do it with subtle (or not so subtle) cajoling, shaming, wheedling, and more. Happily, you are not defenseless when a woman pressures you or attacks you in some way.

Myth: When a woman attacks you or abuses you, there is nothing you can do about it.

Reality: You don't have to accept bad behavior from anyone. If your woman behaves badly toward you, especially if she continues to do so after you have explained how her behavior makes you feel, it's time to say goodbye to her. No matter how good-looking she is, no matter how good the sex is, no matter how much money she makes, she is not for you. Cut your losses and leave. If your boss treats you poorly, you do yourself no favors by remaining in your job. If you are using your employment as a springboard to a better destination for your train, you might choose to accept the pain of your boss's behavior for a while. Don't stay too long though; a bad boss or a bad job will drain your spirit and your energy. If someone tries to bully you into a course of action you don't feel is right, assert yourself; choose your own path. If you stay in your family home, and the price you have to pay is accepting your parents' oppression, then the same advice applies—move out! The longer you stay, the longer it will take to shake off the effects of their oppression. You *must* make your own decisions.

I Never Do Anything Right

It doesn't take much for a woman to make you feel like you have been stupid or that you have failed. The *look* can do it. You know the look—the one that hits you right where it hurts. You might be choosing a restaurant for dinner or choosing a wine to have with your meal, and then, out of left field, there it is—the look that lets you know you screwed up. Again! Even if you don't know what you did to displease her, the look says you are *supposed* to know. Like all males, you hate to fail, especially when a woman witnesses your failure! The feeling of having failed can drain the life out of you, and affect how you feel about yourself for a disproportionate length of time.

Myth: Women put you down to keep you off balance and in your place.

Reality: Putting someone down is not an honest attempt to resolve an issue or improve a situation. If her put-down is designed to *fix* you, it's time to move out. You are not broken. If you have done something stupid or unhelpful, you may deserve a sideways glance or some rolled eyeballs, but don't sweat this small stuff. We all deserve a well-placed eye-roll from time to time. If you did screw up, just say, "Oops. Sorry. Won't happen again." If her put-down goes beyond small stuff, you have some serious talking to do. If she continues to put you down, it's time to let her try to fix some other poor guy. Leave.

Myth: You do *everything right*, and your woman still does not appreciate it.

Reality: You almost certainly don't do everything right, so let's begin there. The first step is to figure out what you did, and own it. Don't blame anyone else. If this issue has arisen before, it's a clue that you may have some learning to do. You must figure out why she is complaining and exactly what she's complaining about. Are you deliberately sabotaging yourself or the relationship, or are you too lazy to be aware of what you are doing? When you have explored these issues, tell her with calm honesty how her behavior affects you (I write about how to have these honest discussions later).

Reality: If she is putting you down or fixing you, you must address that issue before you can repair the relationship. If this is not possible, the relationship is dead and you leave.

I Have No Idea What Women Want from Me

Why does a woman work ten years to change a man,
then complain he's not the man she married?
Barbra Streisand

Ask yourself if you have ever heard the following words in your head:

- I can't do anything right.
- I have no idea how to please a woman.
- I feel stupid when a woman treats me like this.
- I am a failure when it comes to women.
- I never know whether to help a woman. When I do, they get angry; when I don't, they get angry.

If these words have rattled around in your head from time to time, you're not alone. Most men have thought such things at some point, even highly successful Men. You may even have heard these comments directly from your woman's lips. In your efforts to figure out what your woman wants, you probably have tried all kinds of things to see if something will work. The problem then is that you appear to be unsure of yourself, and unsure men are not appealing to women. When you appear to be unsure, you can rest assured that your woman will attempt to make you more *sure* by telling you what you should be doing and thinking. Having your woman deciding for you is a terrible way to live. If you have no idea what women want, try not to worry about it. Here is the dirty little secret that you will *never* read in *Cosmopolitan*: Women don't even know what they want! Worse, when you give your woman what she asks for, it won't make her happy for long. What a woman really wants is for you to be a Man so she can relax and be a woman.

Myth: You are an idiot if you can't figure out what your woman wants.

Reality: You can deliver what your woman wants, even if she can't tell you what it is. She wants *you*. That is the straight scoop. She wants *you*. Not 98 percent of you, not the man who is distracted about the ball game, and definitely not the man who is thinking about another place, another time, or another woman. She wants you to be fully present. All. The. Time! This does not mean you are at her disposal or that you can't drive your train down the track. It means that whatever you are doing, you do all-in. Driving your train, talking to her, making love to her, or fixing the drain—all-in, all the time.

Reality: If you are a Man, many women will find you attractive. They may not know why. Attraction is notoriously difficult to explain, but if you are a Man with a train, many women will want to get on your train and go with you wherever you are going.

Reality: Even if you are a man, there is a woman who will like you (there are millions of women who will like you, actually). Together, you will be happy for a time. Take that time to become a Man, and watch her grow ever closer to you.

Reality: If you are a man, especially if you are making no effort to grow, improve, or become a Man, your woman will eventually tire of you. If you stay with her, you may be in one of those sad relationships that is not bad enough to quit and not good enough to satisfy either of you. Such relationships eventually become a prison in which neither partner is happy. The phenomenon of relationships and marriages that are not good enough to satisfy but not bad enough to leave is described in Pamela Haag's book, *Marriage Confidential.*

My Woman Does Not Appreciate What I Do for Her

On a recent trip to a large hardware store to buy some garden materials, I asked for help from a customer service assistant ("Xavier"). His face had cuts around the eyes, and he had bruises all over his face. I asked him what had happened, and he told me he had intervened when he saw a man beating a woman in the parking lot. The man had stopped beating his girlfriend and beaten Xavier instead.

This is an example of what a Man does even though he recognizes that any time he intervenes there is a possibility that he may get hurt. Xavier was prepared to take that chance rather than watch a man beat a woman.

Myth: Women don't want masculine strength and protection anymore.

Reality: If you are a Man, a woman will find you attractive because she will know she can trust you. She will appreciate the protection you bring to her, instead of being of afraid of your strength. Even if she earns more than you, she will appreciate the provisioning you bring to the relationship because it allows you both to live better than you could separately or with just one income. If she earns a lot more than you, what you provide may not be money.

Your care and support may be perfect for her. In the increasingly common case where the male stays home while the woman works, she will appreciate that too—and yes, you can be a stay-at-home Man. You will have to work extra hard to maintain your status as a Man though, so remember to create the space for yourself to do so.

Reality: If your woman makes more money than you do, she may be the breadwinner in the family. But, if she tells you to your face that she is the family's breadwinner, it will be hard to be a Man around her. Make no mistake—she is not being honest or accurate when she says this—she is emasculating you. You must make her understand that her comments have no place in your relationship. You may also point out that keeping score in a relationship spells doom for the relationship. You can bank on the fact that if she uses such terminology, she will use her breadwinner status to trump whatever you say or do. If she does it more than once, whether by speaking those words or by her actions and demeanor, she already has your balls in her pocket. You will have to get your balls back where they belong or surrender your status as a Man.

Reality: A woman wants healthy, mind-blowing sex as much as you do and will love the passion you bring to a sexual interaction when you are fully present. Don't simply go through the motions when you are sexually engaging with a woman. Be creative. Be curious. Be spontaneous. And above all, be present.

Reality: If your woman lies inert while you have sex, in spite of your efforts to bring her really good sex (or mind-blowing or earth shattering sex), it will not be good sex. If your woman is not into sex with you, it is a good indication of what she thinks of you. It is time to leave unless you are happy to be a statistic in Ms. Haag's book.

I Don't Understand My Role in Society Any Longer

Society and the relationship between the sexes, have changed more quickly than male biology can accommodate, and the pace of change over the last fifty years has been astonishing. The United States now has women in combat situations, which was the last bastion of a man's biological predisposition to protect his family and his way of life. In addition, many men find it difficult to reconcile providing for a woman when she can provide for herself.

We still have no idea how society will respond to these changes over the next century or two. What we can be sure of is that until society figures out how to accommodate the new relationship, the feminist agenda will continue to cause more of the confusion I write about in this book.

Myth: Since the feminist revolution, Men have no place in society anymore.

Reality: Actually, there are two revolutions in progress: In the first revolution, women fought for—and won—numerous changes in the law to address the legal inequities between men and women. As women succeeded in their quest, they gained freedom and independence. While women were claiming their rights, changes in the working environment, the home, and society closed many of the natural pathways to becoming a Man. When the natural connections between fathers and sons withered away, few boys had someone to teach them how to become Men. The second revolution is a counter-revolution, in which Men are beginning to claw back their personal sovereignty and reestablish their natural masculinity, while relating more forcefully to the newly powerful women they know. We can't tell yet how these two revolutions will proceed or how they will end. We do know one thing you can do in the meantime; become the best Man you can be.

Reality: The feminist movement stirred up the first revolution, and that resulted in a long list of unintended consequences. While you might think such sweeping changes take hundreds of years to transpire, the feminist revolution happened much faster than that, and most of the unintended consequences occurred in the last fifty years.

Reality: You can become the Man you were always meant to be. Alternatively, you can remain confused for the rest of your life. It is your choice.

Women Have All the Power These Days

Have you ever felt the longing for someone you could admire?
For something, not to look down at, but up to?
Ayn Rand

Many women are in positions of power now. Companies have female senior executives, and women hold many professional leadership roles. Certain career paths that were once exclusively male are now populated by highly educated women. Women of cabinet rank have been in government for decades, with numerous women running for the office of President of the United States. While it's true that women are still underrepresented in the most prestigious and highest-salary jobs, women are making major inroads in occupations and roles formerly dominated by males.

Myth: Women have all the power these days.

Reality: Most politicians, corporate "suits," investment bankers, lawyers, and other highly compensated people are male. This imbalance is even true in the performing arts (e.g., theater, film, music), where men, on average, enjoy longer careers and earn more per show than women. So forget the idea that women have all the power.

Reality: While males wield most of the power in Western society, men are not standing in their power in their relationships. They have no idea how to be strong and powerful without, at the same time, becoming domineering or aggressive. Instead, their confusion renders them clueless about what to do.

Reality: Throughout human history, Men have protected and provided for their women and children. While rarely being called upon to make such sacrifices, this role is fundamental to who Men are. In an age when so many males have heard nothing positive about themselves from society, it would be good for them to hear from the women in their lives that they are admired for what they do. To test this concept, in one of my Salons, I asked the males what they most wanted from the women in their lives. The women were shocked to learn that these Men all wanted to be *admired* for who they are and what they do.

Myth: When women are stronger, men are weaker.

Reality: As a Man, you know who you are, so none of this male/female tension matters to you. You know that your woman is capable, and you admire her for her abilities. Your woman's superiority in formerly manly pursuits does not threaten your masculinity. If she is an electrician, mechanic, fighter pilot, or chief executive, you are happy to let her do her thing, while you concentrate on being you and doing your thing. What your woman does in no way diminishes you. One major step on the road to eliminating your confusion is to let go of your need to make her feel *less*, so that you can feel *more* (a fruitless battle, if ever there was one).

It's All about Me

I am not conceited because I'm better than I think I am.
Comedian and impersonator, Mike Yarwood

Even if you agree with Mr. Yarwood and believe that you are actually better than you think you are, it's not all about you. While other people may care for you in some way (filial love, fraternal love, romantic love, friendly affection, etc.), nobody likes that care to be a one-way street. In the last year alone, I have had conversations with people in which I hardly spoke a word. These people simply had no interest in what anyone else might say. The conversation had to be about them.

Reality: You were born selfish. It takes social awareness and a desire to connect with others to wean yourself off your innate selfishness. Making yourself the center of attention is especially caustic to friendships. If this describes you, don't search for a new audience for your boorish behavior. Become a curious Man and find out about others. As you learn about *them*, you will lose the habit of making everything about *you*.

Reality: If you don't get the attention you crave, you may crave attention even more, and the vicious spiral tightens until you are talking to yourself. Next time you meet someone new, focus your attention on them, and see how much you can make them talk about themselves. It's not—and never will be—all about you.

Reality: People who think it is all about them will often take over a conversation someone else began. Like this:

You: I used to play football, but I broke my leg in a game and had to stop playing.

Tom: I know what you mean. When I played basketball at college, I broke my ankle and broke my wrist twice. I don't play sports anymore. I watch on television. Did you see that game between the Warriors and Cavs last week? Great game. LeBron was incredible!

Tom topped your story with multiple fractures and then took over the conversation. He diverted a conversation about the end of your football career into one about a televised basketball game. Tom hijacked the conversation because he needed it to be about him. I know many people who do this. Whatever their intent, at best these people are living their lives unconscious of those around them. Do you want to be a friend to someone like this? Thought not!

Reality: When your friends figure out that it's all about you, they will leave your circle and let you continue your self-centered ego trip alone.

Reality: It is about you … *a little.*

Everyone gets noticed now and then, unless
of course, that personage should be
invisible, inconsequential me.
You can look right through me, walk right
by me, and never know I'm there.
Mr. Cellophane from the musical Chicago
John Kander and Fred Eb

Give yourself permission to hold center stage from time to time. You have life experience, and you have stories to tell, and it's okay for you to tell your stories—at the right time, to the right person, in the right place. Take the following illustration as an example:

Jeremy was walking down a boulevard in Paris with his wife when he saw a male (his name turned out to be Etienne) collapse to the ground. Jeremy recognized that Etienne's heart had stopped beating and began CPR that got it beating again. He stayed with Etienne until an ambulance arrived. Etienne made a full recovery and still sends Jeremy a letter every year on the anniversary of the event.

Reality: Jeremy is quiet and reluctant to talk about himself, but his prompt action saved a man's life, an action about which he can be rightly proud. Many people would find Jeremy's story interesting. Although he does not often tell the story, if others are talking about related subjects, he shares his experience of this event. It's okay to share information about your life experience at appropriate times.

Reality: If you think that what you say or do is unimportant, you are wrong. What you say may not have the impact it could have because of the way you speak or the way you behave, but what you have to say is important at the right time and in the right place, so learn to be a conversationalist.

Reality: Your reticence to think it might be about *you* is that you don't attach enough importance to what you want. Your desires may relate to your career, your relationships, and your sexuality. Try this experiment: Compare the choices you made in your life to what you actually desired at the time. If those two don't line up, ask yourself why that happened. Did you pursue your desires? If not, why not? The disconnects between your choices and your desires may surprise you. Was it because you did not work hard enough to make what you desired actually happen or because you thought you were not worthy. If there is a meaningful difference between what you wanted to do and what you actually did, you may be responding to restrictions that others put in your mind. Most of these preprogrammed strictures sound like, "Don't talk to strangers," or "Don't have sex except how I tell you to have sex."

Programming put there by someone else can lead you to conclude that:

- You are not worthy of someone else's time.
- You are stupid, naïve, or immature.
- You are unable to make decisions for yourself.
- What others think is more important than what you think.
- You are okay with people being rude to you or other variations of *poor me.*

Programmed advice might sound like, "Get a good job. Marry a nice girl. Buy a nice house." While such advice is not meant to hurt you, it can contaminate your life. You must decide for yourself what to do.

Reality: If your childhood programming is controlling your adult life, you need to figure out where the real you begins and ends. If you find it too frightening to let your desires, hopes, and dreams take flight, then congratulations—you have recognized your programming and taken the first step toward eliminating it. Programming from someone else is not who *you* are. Once you eliminate your programming, to paraphrase a Southwest Airlines slogan, "You are now free to move about the world." Go ahead, live your life how you want to live it. Sweet!

4

MAN

We're not afraid of God's blade,
or of being chained up, or
of having our heads severed.
We're burning up quickly, tasting a little hellfire as we go.
You can't imagine
how little it matters to us
what people say.

Rumi, thirteenth-century poet
Birdsong, English translation by Coleman Barks

MY INTERPRETATION OF THIS POEM is that it's all about Men (the *"We're"* in the poem's first line). These Men are living life with hellfire in their veins, unafraid of what people might say about them, and happy to die for a cause. When I read it, I stopped and marked the page because it describes how I strive to live my life.

Some combination and balance of personality, character, education, spirituality, virtue, knowledge, and wisdom will allow you to live as a Man. Which combination and balance is right for you is your choice. Study the list of the major traits of a Man below, then consider which balance of these traits will allow you to live your life as you want to live it. While the list is not meant to be exhaustive (a Man is too complex to cover all the bases in one book), it does include many traits that are essential if you are to become a Man. If you already have a firm grasp on these traits and embody them in your daily life, you are probably already a Man (or you are about to become one).

Authentic

Authenticity is the heart of a Man. That is how important authenticity is! In fact, you can't be a Man unless you are authentic at all times. For a Man, authentic means:

- You know who you are.
- You don't change who you are to please someone else.
- You are open and honest.
- You don't manipulate others.

You are authentic when you are your most basic, unspoiled, natural self, the self you are when nobody else is looking. I am guessing that you already consider yourself authentic at all times. If so, you probably say, "I'm just me." Unfortunately, being authentic is not as easy as you may think. Although it should be simple to be your authentic self, most of us are pressured into being someone else some or all of the time. Of course, you behave differently at work from the way you are when you are home relaxing. You also behave differently when you meet the guys at the game, from the way you behave when you visit your parents for the weekend. You are not being inauthentic when you behave in a socially appropriate manner consistent with your location and the company you are keeping. On the other hand, being authentic means you never play a role that betrays who you really are, especially one role for Jack and another for Jill. You are always honest to yourself about who you are.

Others may pressure you to change who you are. For example, if you are an extrovert, others may tell you to rein in your exuberance. If you are an introvert, others may push you to be more outgoing. If you are like most people, you will reluctantly try to do what these people (e.g., parents, bosses, friends) ask, especially if they have power over you. The pressure to change makes it difficult to know yourself. You may not even know what it feels like to be your natural self because you are so rarely able to be natural. If you don't do the work to figure it out, you may never learn who you really are. If this is confusing, ask yourself if you have ever had thoughts like these:

- I couldn't do that because my mother/wife/friend would disapprove.
- If I say no to my woman, she becomes angry.
- I know who I am. I am just me. I don't need to do any work to figure that out.
- I keep a part of me hidden.
- If I said what I really wanted, people would not like me.
- If my friends knew what I really think, they would not be my friends anymore.

If so, you are playing a role and you are not authentically yourself.

Growing

If you feel that you are living your life on a not-so-merry-go-round of wake up, work, sleep; wake up, work, sleep, it will be hard to be authentically yourself because there is no room in your life to let the real you shine. If you are not trying to grow mentally and spiritually, if you have not done something new in years, if you have not challenged yourself to push your own boundaries of possibility, then you are not yet a Man. A Man never stops growing and challenging himself—*never.* You do the work to figure out who you are and where you need to do more work. Then you go and do that work. Your self-knowledge means you are not afraid to be yourself while you continue growing and evolving.

Driving Your Train

You can't always wait for the perfect time.
Sometimes you must dare to jump!
Anonymous

Life won't suddenly grab you by the scruff of the neck and demand that you live it. To live as a Man, you must have at least one train that you are driving to a destination you chose. When you are steaming down the tracks, you will feel the exhilaration of purpose and meaning that make life worth living. You can be a passenger on someone else's train occasionally, but don't become too comfortable there or you may never get off. When you are driving your train, you can never fall asleep, and you cannot give up until you reach your destination. If you fall asleep or give up, you will hurt someone important to you, and that someone may be you.

If you have not learned anything new in years and have no train and no direction, you are just warehousing yourself while waiting to die. You may go to a ball game, the pub, or a party with friends. You may spend hours watching TV and then go to bed after an evening doing precisely nothing. If so, you may wonder, "Is this it?" If you continue as you are, the answer is "Yes. This is all there is for you." If you want to become a Man and get more out of your life, you have to put more into your life. Don't waste another precious moment!

Some time ago, Ivan said to me, "I am going to retire in three months." I was excited for him. I had known for some time that he no longer enjoyed his work as a lawyer. I asked him, "What are you going to do once you retire? What will your purpose be for the rest of your life?" Ivan's reply stunned me. He said, "I don't know. I've provided for my family for fifty years, and now I want to do something for me. I don't know how to do that. I have enough money to last the rest of my life, so that is no problem, but I have obligations to my family. I can't just walk away."

Ivan is a fine man—intelligent, talented, kind, gentle—yet he had consigned himself to the scrap heap by pulling his train into a siding and shutting off the boiler. As I listened, I realized that he was about to become one more man in the warehouse of the dying. He did not know how to follow his passion in retirement (free legal services for people who could not afford a lawyer) and still be a good husband and father. You probably know other men like Ivan. They have many years of life remaining but no train, so their lives have no meaning. Even if they know where they *want* to go, they decline because it would be disloyal to someone (wife, family, parents, or friends). You are a Man, so you are free to do whatever you want at any time, but you have to choose. This is your life, and only you can live it. Here is another reality to avoid:

Andy is talented and smart, big, strong, handsome, witty, and full of fun. He has a gorgeous girlfriend. All the time I have known him, he has been aimless. He has had a series of nothing jobs that did not stretch his talent or abilities. He has just wandered around going nowhere. When I look at Andy, he appears to be lost. If he ever had one, his train has fallen off the tracks. Maybe he can start it up and find a new destination; more likely, he will continue to wander around aimlessly. Interestingly, Andy has not *chosen* the life he is leading. He has simply not made a choice to do something else. With no direction and no purpose, Andy's life has little meaning. Sadly, when he reflects on his life, he is likely to feel it was all just a waste of time.

Many other men I have spoken to are lost, like Andy. Being lost is one of the badges of confusion. These men have no idea what to focus on or what to do. Some of them say they will choose their direction later, but as yet, *later* has not arrived. These men are decaying in the warehouse of the dying.

If the idea of planning a future for yourself seems difficult, start by finding one train and one destination, and then climb aboard and go there. The beauty of having a train is that you don't have to stop once you reach your destination. You don't even have to stop at one train; you can have many trains. Maybe you want to learn to play the piano; maybe you want to live or work abroad; maybe you want to father a child; maybe you want to pursue all three. If you have the bandwidth to do more, find another train, and set off somewhere else, belching smoke and spewing sparks as you roar down the track. That is living!

If you are struggling to make a start on creating a direction for yourself, here is a tip to try: break up the future into a number of time slots. For example, you could decide what you are going to strive for in the next hour, the next day, the next week, and even the next decade. What you choose is up to you. What matters is that you *decide* instead of letting your life just happen.

Your direction will give your life purpose and meaning. Once you point your train down the track, follow your direction until *you* change it. Don't let anyone hijack your train. The choice of where you go is yours and yours alone. If people try to pressure you to change your direction or purpose, tell them you are grateful for their advice but you decline. Be especially aware of the word *should*—that is someone (male or female) telling you that they know where you should go better than you know yourself (it's actually an attempt to control you, and it happens all the time).

If you have no train, you may blame others for your situation. Maybe you think all women are angry and hate men. Maybe you think your boss is unfair. Maybe you think your parents did not help you enough as you were growing up. In other words, it's not *your* fault that you have no train. Having no direction is a sad place to find yourself, but it's nobody else's responsibility to find you a train; it's *your* responsibility. All you can do in this life—the only thing you can control—is *your* direction. Don't wait. Once you find your direction, you will become lighter, shinier, and happier. Sweet!

If you are struggling to find a train, here is a suggestion: Make a difference in someone else's life. Help children on a sports team. Help someone with grocery shopping or yard work. Help at a soup kitchen. Help a colleague win a promotion to a better position. You can hold doors open, smile, or simply talk to people. If you go out of your way to give more than you receive, you will be delighted to discover that the more you give away (with no expectation of anything in return), the more you gain. When you try to make a difference, your purpose will become clearer, and your direction will logically follow. Hey presto, you have a train. That feels so much better.

Centered

One of the hallmarks of a professional is that he seems to have all the time in the world in which to act. In basketball or football, a professional has time to pass the ball to a player in a better position. In a business meeting, a professional senses the mood of a meeting before others and takes action to move the meeting in the right direction. Professionals do this by maintaining their centers. You can't act with composure when you have lost your center. Using your mind to analyze a situation will slow your reaction time because your mind is so easily distracted.

In the movie *Unforgiven*, Clint Eastwood stars as an aging gunslinger named Munny, who sets out to avenge a wrong. Not much action occurs as the film winds its way to its stunning climax but the climax is a wonderful illustration of what being centered means and how having your mind out of the way is priceless.

Munny walks into a saloon where ten men and the town's crooked sheriff are waiting to kill him. When Munny shoots the sheriff, the other men reach for their guns but fear causes them to lose their center. In their panicked state, some can't draw their weapons, and even when they do, they can't take proper aim. As a result, their shots go wide. Meanwhile, Munny maintains his center and methodically shoots them.

In this illustration, the men are all thinking too much while Munny allows his body to make the moves it needs to make. I know this is just a movie, but it's a good illustration of how to stay in your body and out of your head. Your head/mind will second-guess a course of action so often that you may end up taking no action at all. Remaining in your body will also help you deal with life when things start to go wrong. Your body does not make mistakes. Once you let your mind into the decision-making process, you are playing Russian roulette with a bullet in *every* chamber. The answer is to keep your mind out of the way and *feel* what action is appropriate. Even if some thought is required to make a decision, let your body (i.e., what you feel) be the final decision-maker. Of course, your mind will play its role (seeing, hearing, etc.), but it will be under your control, instead of dithering as it considers myriad alternatives. No matter how dire a situation may seem, stay present in your body, as Munny did. Never give up. Keep trying until you succeed or you are incapacitated. If you go into your head, you will lose your center and likely lose the fight with your circumstances.

There are great examples of maintaining your center in the field of sports, where feats of incredible mental focus are common. Ask yourself how you would perform if you were the field-goal kicker for your favorite NFL team, with the ball on the forty-yard line, your team one point behind, three seconds on the game clock, and the Super Bowl on the line. A place in history for your club, your coaches, and your teammates is all on you. Professionals who perform in situations like this learn to keep their heads out of the action. If they start thinking about winning or losing—or anything except kicking the ball—they will miss. All the thinking takes place before the game, so that when it's time to perform, they keep their minds on silent and let their bodies do the job.

I realize you are probably not a Super Bowl kicker, so let's bring this example closer to home. You have probably lost your composure when someone trespassed on your *territory* (your woman, your car, your place in line). If you lose your center, you will be out of control, and anything can happen. If someone cuts you off in traffic, count your blessings that you are safe; and forget it—it's not worth responding. If someone takes your parking space, find another. If jealousy is coming up in your gut because your woman danced with another man, focus on the fact that she is a free agent. If she wants to dance with the other man, that's her decision. You don't own her. Of course, you get to decide whether to stay in the relationship with her, but all you can control is yourself. When you lose your center, you first lose control of yourself, and then you lose control of your situation. Maintain your center at all times.

The next time you feel your anger rising, focus on where you feel it coming from. You will probably find that it flows upward from a place very low in your abdomen in the area of your anus; this is your trigger point. When people use the phrase *pucker up* to describe what happened when they were severely stressed, they are referring to tension in their trigger point. Maybe you have felt that too. As your anger (or fear) builds, it rises from your trigger point and flows rapidly up your body in a wave of tension. Your heart races, you begin to shake, and your voice goes to a higher pitch until you are unable to speak at all. These sensations are almost identical to the panic you might feel when your life is threatened. With both anger and panic, the effects on the body are similar—shaking, loss of speech, loss of sphincter control in extreme cases, and worst of all (yes, worse than loss of sphincter control), an inability to act rationally that can get you or someone else killed.

To take the most common source of anger, you are a Man behind the wheel of a car when another driver cuts you off. Do you flip off the driver? Do you lean on the horn? Do you chase the other car down the street? You are a Man so here's what you do: nothing! You simply ignore the other driver and carry on about your business; you know that bad things can happen in a traffic altercation, and nothing good ever comes out of one. What do you want the other driver to do? Write a letter of apology? Similarly, when someone pushes ahead of you in a line at the supermarket or at a bar, again ask yourself what you would do. Would you push back? Would you adopt an angry tone and tell them to wait their turn? As a centered Man, you are no pushover, but you don't react in anger. If you wish to register a protest of some kind, remain centered and quietly (to preserve some dignity for the other person) say to the cashier, "Excuse me, but I was next in line." Most people called on jumping ahead of a line will yield. Some won't, but at least you will have made your point and maintained your center. It isn't worth going any further with such a minor issue.

The best way to find your center is to *feel* it. It's the center of your body after all, so you are intimately familiar with it, even if you have never named it before. It's easy to feel your center when you are under stress. The feeling of tension begins deep in your pelvis. When you feel the tension rising from where it begins, remain conscious of it as it reaches your navel, that is your center. Pay attention next time it happens to you. When the anger reaches your center, you may feel that you are about to explode. The slightest additional provocation or increased fear at this moment will send you into a paroxysm of rage or a frozen panic. This is the last moment that you can regain control of yourself before you melt down. To regain control of yourself, push the anger (or fear) back down to where it originated (as I describe in more detail below). If you don't stop the rising tension here, you will feel the need to *do* something. Unfortunately, what you choose to do is quite likely to be something stupid.

When you next start losing control, keep your awareness on what is happening inside your body, and you might learn a valuable lesson. You will feel your anger moving upward from its origin, through your belly, and overwhelming your center as adrenaline floods into your bloodstream to prepare your body for fight or flight. This is the time of red faces, bar-room brawls, and road rage. The reality is that you are not confronting a wild animal that wants to eat you. It's highly unlikely you need to react at all. If you must, allow yourself to roll your eyes and relax. You're fine.

So what can you do when your anger or panic begins to overwhelm you? You have two options: (1) give in to it and lose control of your mind and body, or (2) push the anger back down where it came from. I know this sounds a little strange, but you really can stay in control of your body by pushing the anger or panic back down deep into your gut.

The military spends a great deal of time training its people to prevent anger or panic from taking over when things are not going well. The military leaders know that an angry or panicked soldier can jeopardize a team and its mission. So, they train their people to manage anger and fear by exposing them to it over time. You can do it quickly by pushing your anger or panic back to where it came from by constricting your abdominal muscles and forcing the rising tension back down into your lower gut where it began. It may feel like you are trying to overcome a bout of constipation – yes, seriously. Once you know how to do this, you can reduce your anger or panic to a quick stomach churn. Here's what I did when my jet caught fire:

I was a raw Royal Air Force student pilot with little instrument flying experience, so I was only allowed to penetrate a few thousand feet of cloud cover. On a solo flight in my jet trainer, as I climbed through clouds at about two thousand feet above ground level, smoke and hot engine gases poured into the cockpit. I remained calm and informed air traffic control (ATC) in my uber-cool Chuck Yeager drawl, that I had a problem and might have to eject. Ten seconds later, my situation grew much more serious as my oxygen supply was cut off, which meant I was immediately choking on hot gases. At the same time, the smoke blinded me and I could no longer see my flight instruments. I became so disoriented, I had no idea whether I was right side up or upside down. I was certain the airplane was about to explode or spin into the ground. Needless to say, adrenaline flooded my system and panic began to rise toward my center from deep in my gut. Seconds later, I felt panic's powerful tentacles begin to wrap around my throat. My next call to ATC was an incoherent babble (not my finest hour), as panic obliterated my power of speech. My entire body was shaking uncontrollably.

When I was on the verge of pulling the ejector seat handle, I *decided* to regain control of myself and the situation. Somehow, my reptilian brain found a way to push the panic back down into my lower abdomen, where I had felt it begin. In a few seconds, my panic evaporated as I regained my center. I was once again calm enough to speak to ATC in a coherent manner. I closed off the hot gases at their source (a fractured engine unit caught fire), opened the canopy to blow out the smoke, then returned to base for an uneventful landing.

As I reflected on the incident, I realized that regaining my center allowed me to save the airplane and eliminate the possibility of injury to people and property on the ground when several tons of airplane and fuel returned to earth. Staying with the airplane, also saved me from the obligatory broken back (an occupational hazard of the old-style ejector seat).

When you can hold your center, your confusion will diminish because you have control of your body and your mind. You also will find that the external things that happen to you, large or small, will no longer rule your life. *You* will rule your life. If you can change the way you react to panic and anger, you can change anything.

In future, when you feel your anger or panic rising, simply force it back down into your lower abdomen. It's easy to do when you are angry with your partner and just a little harder when your life is in danger. Once you learn to maintain your center, you will better understand your own physical and emotional condition and be able to take appropriate action no matter what the circumstances. Learning how to remain centered will be a great step on your journey to becoming a Man.

You don't have to suppress your emotions and feelings in order to stay centered and calm. To enjoy life in all its glory, you need to feel what is going on around you and connect with what you experience. Remaining centered allows you to connect with other people more easily, and more clearly feel your emotions instead of being overwhelmed by them. As a Man, you have no need to wall off your ego to protect yourself. Such a wall prevents you from feeling anger, disappointment, sadness, and other distressing emotions, but it also prevents you from feeling love, affection, joy, and pleasure. President Ronald Reagan, standing near the Berlin Wall, famously demanded of the Soviet Union's leader, "Mr. Gorbachev, tear down this wall!" It's now time to tear down *your* wall. When you are no longer hiding behind your wall, you will feel your emotions in your body and be able to choose how to respond to what you are actually feeling instead of being bowled over by a mental tsunami. Phew! What a relief! Another example:

I was admitted to the Royal Air Force College (a British institution similar to the US Air Force Academy) when I was eighteen. On the day I arrived at the academy for a few weeks of introductory activities, there was the usual reception committee of about a hundred senior students, who were determined to haze the group of about fifty incoming freshmen. The senior students and their ringleader, Ronald, formed a ring around our group and told us what they were going to do. It was to be a classic hazing, with all manner of humiliating and dangerous stunts.

I am just an average sized male, but after Ronald made his speech, I walked to the front of the freshmen and, with my face about three inches from Ronald's face, said, "We are new here, and we don't want any trouble. But if you think we are just going to let you do this, you need to think again. There is not going to be any hazing. If you make one move, I will drop you right where you stand." I called Ronald's bluff, and he did not move a muscle or say a word. I then broke the tension by saying, "OK, then. Let's all go to the bar for a drink. The new guys are buying." (In case you are wondering, the officer's mess at the RAF College has a great bar, and we were all old enough to drink there).

Throughout the encounter, I kept my center. There was no question of an empty threat or an argument. I simply rejected Ronald's plan, and left him in no doubt what would happen if he tried to carry it out. Not one of his 'gang' stepped forward to take his place either. They had no idea what to do. My restraint allowed our would-be assailants to reconsider their position without losing too much face, and the whole event was over in less than forty-five seconds. We all went to the bar and enjoyed a drink with our new colleagues.

It takes courage to stand up to someone like Ronald in such circumstances, but someone had to take that stand. Hazing is bullying, and I was not prepared to let it happen. Like I said earlier, bullies always back down when challenged because they are weak.

When you are centered, you don't allow yourself to be drawn into arguments or even heated discussions. You may excuse yourself from the fray or simply remain silent, but if you must say something, try this: "I am not ready to discuss this right now," or "That's unfortunate." Then refuse to be drawn in. The argument will usually wither and die at that point. After all, a protagonist needs an antagonist to gain any satisfaction from an argument. If you don't make yourself available to be their punching bag, your tormentor will usually quit.

You may ignore any problem that's not worthy of your attention. If you do decide to address an issue with an antagonist, do so calmly, with no attachment to an outcome. When you have no attachment to an outcome, you can't lose an argument. Deal with a situation in the best possible way, even if the result is not what you want. Once the outcome is determined, accept it with all the grace you can muster.

Once you are conscious of your own anger, you will be able to control it before it ever sneaks out of its dark and venomous hole. Henceforth, you can safely save the adrenaline rush for when you fall into the lion's enclosure at the zoo.

Courageous and Determined

I learned that courage was not the absence
of fear, but the triumph over it.
The brave man is not he who does not feel
afraid, but he who conquers that fear.
Nelson Mandela

What does it mean to be courageous? First of all, it does not mean being macho or pugnacious. You don't become a Man because you are good in a fight. Being capable and willing to beat a person to a pulp may allow some temporary bragging rights over the bloody mess lying on the floor, but it won't make you a Man. Courage is not about throwing your weight around. Some acts that require courage are not in any way life-threatening. It takes courage to ask a woman for a date because she might say no, bruising your ego in the process. Showing up every day for work, taking care of your family, living a meaningful life—these all take dedicated courage because the effort never ends. Accepting the challenge of growing every day requires courage, as anyone who ever has been on a growth path can tell you; baring your innermost secrets to others (or even to yourself) can be terrifying.

You don't have to be physically tough to be courageous. You can be gentle and kind and still be courageous. Being the opposite (rough and cruel) is certainly no indicator of courage. You can be a strong and powerful protector of your family and yourself, and still be gentle and kind. There is a time and a place to exercise your physical strength (when under attack by an intruder, for example) and a time to be tender (when taking care of your children). Physical stature and a gentle nature are not indicators of courage either, as the following example so perfectly illustrates:

Ted awoke from a deep sleep when he heard someone moving in the corridor outside his bedroom. He peered through the open bedroom door and saw a man a few feet away. While his wife and children were sleeping, Ted confronted the intruder. As he struggled with the man, his daughter awoke and came to help. Together, they subdued the intruder and held him until the police arrived.

Even though Ted is quite possibly the gentlest man I have ever met, just the opposite of a macho man, when the time came for him to protect his family, he was courageous and took down a much younger man. Ted risked his life to protect his family; that is what a Man does.

Resilient

Bad things happen to everyone; it's how you
deal with those things that matters.
John Kent

Nobody is immune to the vicissitudes of life. Disappointments and tragedies happen all the time, and sometimes they will happen to you. When you are resilient, you take whatever life throws at you without allowing it to defeat you. For example, you lose your job; you have a terrible fight with a close friend; you suffer a debilitating injury; a deal you worked on for two years falls apart. These are all setbacks that you take in stride. I know people (and you may too) who are bothered by everything: It's too hot or too cold. It's too soon or too late. It's too bright or too dark. If you stop work because it's too hot or too cold, you have allowed the weather to divert you from your goal. As a Man, you don't let minor irritations stand in your way. You just get on with what you were doing. When you focus on the task at hand, you will find that all those minor irritations disappear because you are no longer thinking about them. Stay focused on your goals and you will be better able to ignore the external pressures. Your resilience will open you up to possibilities that you might otherwise miss.

Curious

He not busy being born is busy dying.
It's Alright, Ma (I'm Only Bleeding)
Bob Dylan

When you were a child, you exercised your spirit and curiosity boldly. You were exploring the world, falling down, taking chances, skinning your knees, and generally living all-in, all the time. You did not second-guess yourself when thinking about climbing a tree or playing with the bigger boys. Whether it was safe did not enter into your thinking too much. You climbed trees and sometimes you hurt yourself, but you went right back to climbing trees as soon as you recovered. This is the spirit that makes Men who they are: adventurous; fearless; curious; growing.

Elliot is a wonderful child, about seven years old. He is brave, curious, and willing to try anything—climbing on high rocks, swimming in cold mountain streams, playing games with the grown-ups. Elliot lives all-in, all the time. He and children like him are true treasures for the world. There are millions of children just like Elliot.

As I watched Elliot play, I realized that by the time he is eighteen years old, society will have crushed much of his wonderful spirit by telling him:

- Don't do that. It is sinful!
- Stop that, you'll hurt yourself!
- Don't go there, you'll get lost!
- No you can't take the bus, it's dangerous; I'll come for you!
- Don't play with those boys, they're too rough!
- Be home by eight, or you'll be grounded!

By the time Elliot is an adult, he will probably have learned to conform to the wishes of parents, friends, teachers, and pastors. As a result, boys like Elliot will find it difficult to become curious, adventurous Men. When boys replace their natural spirit with fear, and are content to wallow in the safety of their iPhones or empty sex, their train—if they ever had one—is going nowhere. If you conform, you will end up in a rut, which, like a forty-foot python, can swallow you whole.

Whenever you say to yourself, "I could never do that," stop and ask yourself, "Why not?" Is it because your teacher/parent/friend said, "If you do that, you will be ____!" (You fill in the blank). If so, you are allowing someone else to run your life. As a Man, you are constantly reinventing yourself. You are curious about the world around you, the people in it, and the myriad opportunities you have to grow. Curiosity leads to opportunity, and opportunity leads to growth. Make *Yes* your default response to new opportunities, and your intellectual, emotional, physical, and spiritual development will naturally follow. Searching is great fun too. If you keep searching, you will be growing and learning. Why not meet new people, go to the symphony, attend a sexuality workshop, learn a new sport, develop a new skill, travel to a foreign country? There is no shortage of things to do and they are all just waiting for you to discover them. Take a chance and cancel the cable subscription; you *can* live without it (I do). If you fear change, your fear may be so powerful that you will even stay in a dangerous or miserable situation rather than chance something new and you will be, as Mr. Dylan so eloquently stated, *busy dying*.

Want to know how curious you are? Ask yourself these simple questions:

- Do I shy away from new ventures because I think I'll look naive when I begin?
- Have I ever decided against joining a new club because I would feel uncomfortable?
- Do I avoid international travel because airplanes and foreign countries are too dangerous?
- Have I done nothing new in the last week, month, or year?

If you answered *no* to these questions, please congratulate yourself; you still have some of your childhood curiosity. Kids get many things wrong before they figure anything out. It does not stop them from trying new things. Don't let it stop you. If you fear looking awkward or inept when you do something new, let that fear go; everybody was new once! Keep the fire in your belly stoked so you can *boldly go where you have never gone before* (with apologies to *Star Trek* producers and fans everywhere). Don't stop growing until you run out of ideas as you take your last breath. If you can't recall the last time you did something new, put this book down right now, and go do something you've never done before. If you ever balk at taking a chance, just ask yourself, "What would Elliot do?"

Courteous

Your development as a Man includes treating everyone in a polite and courteous manner. This is particularly true of service people (e.g., a waiter, a grocery store clerk). A Man treats service people like human beings rather than functionaries. If you are rude to waiters or junior members of your team, it's a sure sign that you are a bully. It costs nothing to be kind, and the positive effect of your kindness on its recipient will be significant. A Man treats everyone with respect.

It's paradoxical perhaps, but if you are condescending or demeaning to people in subordinate positions (whether their subordinate position derives from your superior rank, such as a CEO talking to a vice president, or your status as a customer when ordering in a restaurant), you are not demonstrating personal strength. Your *apparent* strength derives from your position, not your character. If you are a Man, you are dignified, fair, and respectful of others, even in the midst of a disagreement, especially with loved ones. If you find it difficult to be dignified when you are fighting with your lover, I understand. In Chapter 7, I will explain how to de-escalate confrontations with your lover and avoid the horrors of passive-aggressive separation.

Present

When you become a Man, you are always 100% present. By definition, you cannot be *present* unless you are 100% present (henceforth, I use the word *present* to mean 100% present). Have you ever noticed how often you are physically present, but your mind is elsewhere? Maybe you are in a business meeting, but you are thinking about last night's ball game. Maybe your mind was somewhere else during a sexual interaction. Think about that for a moment: you had a magnificent woman in your arms but thoughts of another place, another time, or (heaven forbid) another woman, pulled you away. The instant you notice that you are not present, you must snap your attention back to the here and now. Put all of your attention into *this* moment. Let everything else wait, and become present again. You will be better at everything you do once you are present with whatever it is you are doing. (I will give you some tips on how to be present in Chapter 17).

While it takes only a little practice to refocus your mind once you recognize that your attention has wandered, it's harder to realize that you are no longer present. Like billboards on the freeway that distract you from driving your car, little attention stealers can worm their way into your brain unnoticed. By maintaining your awareness, you will recognize their arrival and dismiss them so you are able to regain your presence.

Radiating

As Man, you know who you are. Your comfort in that knowledge radiates like a beacon for all to see. People simply recognize an inner glow emanating from you that begins with your lack of pretense and continues with knowing that you are living your life your way. After all, once you are a Man, you are always just *you*! You never have to figure out which role you are playing because you never play roles. You radiate a positive, nonthreatening demeanor that makes everyone around you feel better. My wise friend Christoforus said, "There are some Men who, by their demeanor or their actions, raise up the people they interact with and make them better." This is the very concept I am writing about here. When you raise other people up instead of trying to impress them, or making them feel inferior in some way, you will find that both you and they are brighter and happier, and that together you can accomplish much more.

Relaxed

Emotions are a necessary and wonderful part of your humanity but they can overwhelm you if they are not under your control. Loss of control, anger, or blind rage are unbalanced emotions that frequently precede violence. When your emotions are out of balance, you may cry for no reason. You may become upset at the slightest thing. You may be elated one moment and depressed the next. In other words, your life is a drama or a disaster. The overwhelming stress of living like this will fray your nerves as you register every little blip on your radar screen as a threat. If your emotions flow through you like an ever-present tidal wave, pulling and pushing you this way and that, you really have no idea what you might do in the heat of the moment. Living under the control of your emotions is hard work—for you and for those around you. You will feel much better throughout your day if you can control your emotions.

If you "feel miserable today, as usual," it may seem that you have no choice but to feel that way. When you are unhappy, you are unhappy, right? Wrong! Emotions are a choice; a choice you often allow your mind to make instead of listening to your body. It may sound impossible, but you can simply choose to feel how you want to feel. Trust your body to make that choice, and see what happens. Get your head out of the way, and you can change the way you feel about anything, at any time, because you are in control of your life, not that argumentative committee in your head. Establish control of your emotions by simply *choosing* the emotion you want to feel. Like most things you do, you need to practice until you have your emotions under control but keep trying. Peace for your body and soul is the goal. In the following example, Dave makes a great choice when he gains control of his emotions:

Dave was on his way to a marriage counseling session. As usual, he was angry as he drove to the meeting. He ruminated on how to use the session to get one-up on his future ex-wife. As he drove, Dave realized that scheming before the counseling session was counterproductive. In that moment, he chose a new approach. He realized that he could not do much about how his wife felt, but he could change how he felt. So, he decided to be happy. Instead of going into the session angry, once he chose to feel happy, he was able to relax because he became happy. Dave had no idea where his new approach came from. He had never before tried *choosing* to be happy; the very idea seemed ridiculous. Nevertheless, he was able to feel genuinely happy and became brighter, and more comfortable in his body. He was amazed that choosing to be happy actually made him happy. He knew his marriage was doomed, but he now felt able to give it a decent ending.

Dave reports that he has had only momentary lapses into anger or unhappiness since the day he chose to feel happy. He stresses that he is not pretending to be happy; he *is* happy.

Once you realize that emotions are a choice, you can control them. Try it. Choose to be happy (or content, or ecstatic), and see what happens. At a minimum, you should be able to sense the lightness that comes with having your emotions under *your* control instead of you being under *their* control. In the realm of emotions, you are striving for balance. When you have your emotions under control, you are able to live a life free of an emotional helter-skelter. With a strong emotional balance, you may feel pleasure or sadness, or any other emotion. Your emotions are not numbed out of you. When you control your emotions, you gain control of your life, so you won't do something stupid while celebrating your good fortune or fighting your despair.

Calm

When something bad happens to you, or someone behaves poorly toward you, as a Man, you maintain your center. If you really feel the need, give yourself thirty seconds to do an internal eye roll, and then go about your business. If someone else is involved, there is no need to raise your voice. There is no need to threaten anyone. Just ask yourself how to prevent such an event from happening again, and forgive the person who did it. When things have calmed down, consider your role in creating the event (it rarely will be entirely the other person's fault). If someone rejected you or your idea, they did so for a reason. Even if you disagree with the rationale, accept the rejection as an opportunity for growth. Don't retaliate, whine, or cry. Once you accept that such rejections are a normal part of life, you can let it go. *Poof*—it's gone.

Honorable

Honor is a prerequisite to being a Man. It's a quality of spirit that you feel in your body. Being honorable also means you have standards of behavior that you won't compromise. Honor means doing the right thing, no matter what. It also means there are things that are more important to you than your own life. As an honorable Man, you accept that your life is forfeit when your woman, your child, or your friend is in danger. For you, losing your honor would be far worse than dying while doing the right thing. Like a man who stands for nothing, a man who has nothing worth dying for is, in many ways, a lost soul. When you act honorably, people around you will recognize that you are different from many other people they have met.

As an honorable Man, you may not always do the right thing, but you always do what *feels* right at the time. There may be instances when doing the right thing is onerous, and a shortcut would go unnoticed. It doesn't matter. You can't act in a way you know to be wrong or is anything less than your best. That is a fundamental element of your basic character as a Man. When you are prepared to risk your life to save someone precious to you, your friends will recognize you as a Man, even though they may not know why.

For thousands of years, males have done the most dangerous jobs—going to war, hunting, putting out fires, and fighting to defend a way of life, to name just a few. In a sense, a man's life has always been forfeit to the good of his community. When duty demands a call to arms, there is never a shortage of willing male volunteers. In spite of all the changes in societal structure, to this day males do the vast majority of the dangerous jobs. For example, using the last year of available data, 93 percent of the people who died on the job in the United States were male.

The era of males deciding what women can and can't do is over. There is a strong push from many quarters to have women play more prominent roles in the military combat arena. Therefore, if women choose to put themselves in harm's way they are now free to exercise that choice. Putting women in harm's way is contrary to a Man's biology, which may mean that in the future, society will pay a high price for taking this new direction. We won't know the final outcome of such a huge societal shift for many generations. One thing I am certain of is that if society continues to undermine masculinity as it has for the last 50 years, the results will be disastrous for our civil society and, ultimately, our way of life.

Lead

You don't have to be a Man to be a leader, and you may be a Man and never become a leader. When you are a Man interacting with other people, you may be able to provide leadership to the group in a manner that does not pressure them to do something against their will or leave them out of the decision-making process. Leadership is not about making people do what you tell them to do, although it may sometimes include such action, especially in a military or business setting. Instead, leadership is about identifying a goal, creating a plan to achieve the goal, and then leading others toward the goal by direction, instruction, or example. Leadership, therefore, is about completing a mission not about controlling people. To lead other people without controlling them, do the following:

- Have a goal and a vision of how to achieve it.
- Share your vision with others in your group.
- Let others know that they are as important as you are.

- Solicit ideas at appropriate times, and then make a plan and offer it to the group.
- Accept rejection of your plan if it happens. It's not about you.
- Help the group find an alternative plan, if necessary.

Here is an example of a common leadership problem: When you and five friends decided that it would be a good idea to see a movie, the following conversation occurred:

You say, "Let's go see *Ben Hur*." Bobbi says, "I'd prefer *The Graduate*." Joanie jumps in with "I think *101 Dalmatians* would be better." Everyone continues to throw out ideas. Obviously, nobody can force a decision on the group in this situation. When you say, "Let's take a vote. If it's a tie, we'll flip a coin" your leadership offers a way to stop the endless debate. You realize that the group vote might not favor the movie you would like to see, but you accept that seeing the movie the majority wants will maximize the group's pleasure. Instead of trying to manipulate the group, your suggestion allows for a solution, even if you don't personally like the group choice. That is often how leadership works; leadership is not about what *you* want. Leadership may mean suggesting that the group go for a walk as an alternative.

Some people seem to have a natural flair for leadership, so they often take leadership roles in group settings and, most of the time, manage to lead a group to a good outcome with minimum fuss. Occasionally, there will be pushback from others in the group.

Freddie has a fertile imagination and solid leadership skills. He is often the de facto leader of a group of friends. He was on vacation with three other people, the "Rebels." The Rebels told Freddie that they would not accept his leadership that day. The four of them set off walking, with Freddie assuming his assigned role of follower. None of the Rebels wanted to assume the role of leader, so they just wandered around aimlessly for an hour. Eventually, they found themselves in a housing complex with rows and rows of identical condominiums in every direction. They were lost. One of the Rebels sheepishly asked, "Freddie can you get us out of this maze?" Once out of the maze, the group continued to wander aimlessly for another hour until they arrived back at their starting point, having gone nowhere.

The rebellion put Freddie in the role of follower, but with no leader, the group became a ship without a rudder. Their meandering showed that somebody (not necessarily always the same person) had to provide direction and cohesion if the group was to achieve anything.

Fearless

Many men don't know how to take a calculated risk. Asking a woman to dance is one example of a risk many men find difficult to take.

Andrew went to his favorite music haunt. He desperately wanted to ask one of the many women on the dance floor to dance with him. Andrew kept his seat all night and just watched, torn between his desire and his fear.

Asking a woman to dance is not a dangerous activity but it is an up-close-and-personal interaction that carries a risk of rejection. As a result, many men can't pluck up the courage to ask a woman to dance. Have you ever heard this thought in your head as your ego jumps up to protect you? "Don't ask her. She is sure to say no." It is much worse if the woman you want to dance with is particularly attractive. Her beauty turns up your ego's amplifier so it screams at you, "She's way too good for you buddy. She'll reject you for sure. Save yourself. *Don't* ask her." If you take a chance and she declines your request, your ego plays a familiar tape in your head: "I told you she'd say no! You shouldn't have asked her. Listen to me next time." Of course, her choice is not a reflection of your value as a person. She just didn't want to dance with you.

Next time you see a woman with whom you would like to dance, invite your ego to go to hell and ask her to dance. Just trust your body and keep your mind out of the calculation. It's your privilege to ask a woman to dance, and it is her prerogative to decline your invitation. Cool?

Let's take this common scenario further and suppose the woman accepts your offer, and you dance with her. Now your ego identifies new perils. Do any of the following sound familiar?

- What will she think if I walk away after one dance?
- Shall I talk to her while we're dancing?
- Will she be angry if I touch her?
- What if I hold her close?
- If the next song is a slow dance, shall I thank her and sit down?
- Shall I ask her to join me for a drink?
- Is it too soon to ask her for a date?

These are not life-threatening matters, but your ego is in crisis. If you don't know how your dance partner will answer these questions, it is a sure sign that you have been *thinking* instead of paying attention to what her body has been telling you. If you have been present with her, you will already know the answer to all these questions. You can't *think* this through. If you are thinking what to do, your ego will tell you to walk away. But now that you control your ego, let it warn you of danger and then *feel* whether to ignore it. If you make decisions when you are present and conscious, you will be fine. Send your ego back to his watchtower to take a nap! Don't refuse to act because there's a risk, and don't allow yourself to be pushed into taking a risk simply because someone else told you it was okay. Weigh the risks, and decide for yourself.

Here's a tiny tip for the situation in which you've danced with a woman you are attracted to: instead of showing doubt by asking her whether she would like to join you for a drink, be more confident and say, "Let's go and sit down over there. I'd like to get to know you better." Most women will admire a Man who is confident enough to take the lead, and will often respond, "Yes, that would be nice." If she doesn't agree, it's her choice and not a reflection on you. She might be out with her girlfriends. She might be another male's fiancée. She might be ready to go home. It's all OK. Accept her answer with good grace.

5

man

If you wanna find out what's behind these cold eyes
You'll just have to claw your way through this disguise.
In the Flesh?
Pink Floyd

Pretzel Man

A man will often twist himself into whatever shape he thinks will get him what he desires (especially sex). When he does, he loses his authenticity and becomes a pretzel. If you are a pretzel, you are wasting everyone's time. Even if your subterfuge works, your gains are temporary and will backfire later. Your inauthentic behavior will scare people away (especially women) because it destroys the trust that is a prerequisite for a solid relationship.

Jamie wants the life he thinks he should be living, which means he desires the warm body of a woman in his bed. He knows from experience that he feels "owned" when he has a relationship with a woman. For example, if he watches the game on Sunday, she will complain; if he sees his friends on Thursday night, she will go crazy. Jamie is stuck. He desires a woman but does not like how he feels when he is in a relationship with one. In the constant maelstrom of his conflicting desires and his inability to give and receive graciously, Jamie is blown this way and that as his confused thoughts go round and round in his head. Of course, Jamie blames women for his difficulties (because women are "crazy" and "all the same").

So let's see how Jamie is going to get a woman into his bed:

When Jamie meets Annie, she lets him know right away that she has a conservative approach to life, a great job, and is in a book club with her girlfriends. Therefore, Jamie plays the role of the "socially acceptable" male. He tells her that he does not drink much and that he likes reading. He smiles at her expositions on marriage, children, and politics. Although Jamie drinks every night, hates politics, and is an avid football fan, he hides behind a mask and plays the man he thinks Annie wants. What *he* wants is sex, but he assumes he has no chance with her if he is honest. He figures that he can sweet talk her into bed if he plays the character he thinks she wants.

Obviously, Jamie is a pretzel. People make mistakes about other people, so if you are a pretzel, you occasionally will find a woman who likes you enough to go on a date with you; let's call her a *pretzel lover.* If the date goes well, you become Mr. Happy Pretzel, at least for a while. As Mr. Happy Pretzel, you may get sex, but afterward you realize that the experience has left you unsatisfied (dare I say, confused?). Why do pretzels feel this way after they get what they want? Because *manipulated* sex is a calculated betrayal in which you play a role to get what you want at your partner's expense. You know you are faking it. As a result, you feel worse after your sexual interaction than you did before, and your manipulation adds to your confusion. Unfortunately, there is worse to come. If you enter into a relationship with a *pretzel lover,* you will find that your troubles are only just beginning. Keeping up appearances is hard. At first, you give her only tiny glimpses of who you really are, but little by little, and more and more often, the real you emerges from behind your disguise. Tension and fights ensue. So you have make-up sex and peace reigns until the next time *you* emerge. Eventually, the woman rejects you, and you become Mr. Miserable Pretzel and feel worse than you did before your relationship began.

As any pretzel can confirm, this date-sex-rejection routine happens repeatedly. You blame the woman, but the reality is that you are the cause of your own pain. You can't fake it and be happy. Fakery leads to empty sex and empty sex will drain the life out of you. Because you know you have had one meaningless relationship after another, your confusion deepens, and your downward spiral grows ever tighter. If this is you, you are doomed to hide behind one façade after another. For you, Mr. Pretzel, a miserable life is inevitable.

We all do the wrong thing occasionally and feel bad afterward. What is different about Mr. Pretzel is that he sets out to do the wrong thing, so his actions immediately turn on the acid drip of deceit in his brain. Deceit has been the basis for many plays, films, and books that focus like a laser beam on the guilt that flows from a deliberate, deceitful act. Don't become a guilt-ridden mess. Do the right thing. Act with integrity; it's what a Man does and what Jonathan did in the following real example:

Jonathan had a fun first date with Julie. They got along well and he really liked her. After their fifth date, Julie called and told him, "I am only interested in an exclusive partner. I want a commitment from you." Jonathan really liked Julie. She was interesting and fun to be around. He certainly did not want to stop seeing her and was actually looking forward to developing a strong relationship with her. Even so, he would not lie to her about his future intentions, which at that point did not include exclusivity.

Jonathan did not tell Julie what she wanted to hear. Had he done so, he would have been lying, which he knew would turn their spirited and satisfying sex life into another round of empty sex. Then, inevitably, the acid drip would have started to eat away his brain. Instead, Jonathan went to her house for a chat. Over a glass of wine on her patio, he told her that he was not the Man she was looking for. He then went a step further and told her that if, after a couple of dates, any man said, "Yes, I want to commit" he would probably be lying in order to manipulate her into continuing their sexual relationship. Sage advice, indeed. Julie and Jonathan parted on good terms and have been friends ever since.

"Getting lucky" is not so lucky when it leads to failure and rejection. If you are playing roles to get sex, when your woman figures you out, she will cut you off at the knees (and you'll deserve it). If this is your pattern, many women will have already cut you off at the knees. Pathetic, yes? Why would any man want to keep going on this track?

I often see inauthentic behavior when an attractive woman joins a group of men. As soon as she arrives, the group dynamics change to focus on her as the men try to impress her. They laugh more and speak louder. They also put down other men in the group to make themselves appear to be the more alpha male. This is all pretzel behavior. Many women have told me that such inauthentic behavior does not impress them at all because they view it as a weakness, not a strength. Most women know inauthentic behavior when they see it, probably because they see it so often. And, they all figure out a pretzel eventually.

If a male joins your group at a party and focuses on *your* woman, you may slide into inauthenticity as jealousy rears its ugly head. If you are not solidly authentic, you may try to monopolize her attention so she has no time to talk to the stranger. Any woman worth your time will see right through this behavior. Although she will notice what you are doing, like most women she will be too kind to tell you to stop. She will quietly give you a low score on the Man scale. Make sure she is safe, and stand back while she talks to other men. It will do you both good. When you behave as a Man, she will admire you even more. The moral here is that you don't change because someone else, even an attractive woman or a powerful male, joins your group. If they become the focus of the group for a while, relax. Just be yourself.

If many people seem to dislike you, don't look to them to find out why; look inside yourself. You may be living out a story (more about your story in Chapter 11) or carrying baggage of another kind that cripples your interpersonal connections. There is nothing wrong with being the way you are—unless, at the same time, you complain that all the people you know are mean (no, people are not all mean); that the women you meet are all crazy (no, women are not all crazy); and that people won't accept you as you are (maybe they just don't like you as you are).

If you are comfortable as you are, be happy being yourself. If *you* choose to change some aspect of your personality, congratulations. Choosing is half the battle. Changing yourself may take years, and it may be difficult, but neither is a good excuse for quitting, or never even starting. Rest assured that if you are a Man with a train and an authentic personality, many people will like you just as you are.

Empty Sex

> It's good to love as many things as one can,
> for therein lies true strength, and those who love much,
> do much and accomplish much,
> and whatever is done with love is done well.
> *Vincent van Gogh*

Does sex without strings (i.e., empty sex) sound good to you? Does it sound like it would be a painless way to get sex? If so, you are in danger of falling into a trap. Empty sex is, at best, only briefly satisfying and it can hurt you.

To illustrate the damage empty sex can do, consider Derek's encounter with a woman he just met:

Last night at the gym, Derek saw Sarah, an athletic young woman in a happy mood. He didn't know anything about her, but he thought, *Why not? She's gorgeous and looks ripe for the picking.* When he talked to her, he let her know he drives a new sports car and lives in the *right* part of town. When he touched her low on her back and made suggestive remarks, she did not recoil or flinch. Half an hour later, she accepted his invitation to a bar, and from there she agreed to follow him home. After a nightcap, she wound up in Derek's bed. The sex was okay, and she spent the night, but she left before Derek awoke in the morning. She did not leave her contact information. Derek put her behavior down to her being a typical, ungrateful woman. Surely, she owed him *something.*

Even if you had never heard of empty sex, it would probably sound like an apt description of Derek's interaction with Sarah. He has not figured out that he never feels better after empty sex no matter how many women he manipulates into his bed. If Derek wants to feel better about women and sex, the answer is not more empty sex. Although he does not need to propose marriage or swear undying loyalty to a woman he beds, he *does* have to feel some kind of connection where it matters, and that is not his groin! Derek's fear of commitment means he can't treat his partner as a human being, so the acid drip caused by his serial deceit, leaves him feeling worse after every encounter.

I'm not saying that a quickie lovemaking session is a bad thing; but a quickie and empty sex are not the same thing. A quickie with your lover can be just what the relationship doctor ordered. In the days when wives tended to stay home during the work day, Men could pop home at lunchtime for a "Nooner." We could always tell when a colleague had more than soup and a sandwich for lunch! A quickie can be exciting, spontaneous, and fun. If you are present with a woman you care for, it won't be empty sex even if you only have half an hour to spare. Quickies are a wonderful element of a healthy sex life.

A sexual interaction with someone based on simple physical attraction is not a problem either, provided you both go into the interaction with no pretense. It's not empty sex when you are honest with each other about your desires and your intentions, and you feel a degree of affection and respect for each other.

Provided the interaction is a mutual exchange to satisfy a sexual hunger, there is nothing wrong at all. If you give the relationship a chance, you may actually grow to love each other. Empty sex, on the other hand, will leave you and your partner feeling "blah" about yourselves and about each other. Even if it lasts for hours, empty sex is still just empty sex. Avoid empty sex like the plague.

Tongue-Tied

Being tongue-tied is often a problem when you are looking to connect with a woman you just met. Many women have rolled their eyes while telling me about the dopey things men have said to them during a date, especially before they have calmed down. When connecting with a new partner, you may be nervous and unable to find something to say. But you want to sound interesting, so you talk anyway and end up digging yourself into an ever-deeper hole. Your nervous behavior is obvious (though your date will usually be too polite to say so). You are thinking too much and trying to be cool, so you don't have enough brain cells left over to form a coherent sentence. The solution is simple; take your mind out of the process. Settle back into your body. *Feel* the right thing to say. The awkward silence is not as awkward as you think. If you are witty, be witty; if you are intellectual, be intellectual; if you are quiet, be quiet. Being your authentic self and trusting your body will untie your tongue. If a woman rejects your authentic conversation, you lose nothing. It's her choice to conclude that you are not her type.

Manipulative

In the book *The Game (Undercover in the Secret Society of Pickup Artists)*, journalist and author Neil Strauss chronicles the exploits of a group of men who learn from the "Master" how to pick up women. These men went out to clubs and bars in Los Angeles and were able to make dates with lots of women (how many is not clear). The following example is an illustration that I created, based on my understanding of the approach described in *The Game* (this is not a quote from Mr. Strauss's book):

Vinnie walks into the hotel in downtown LA and sees three women sitting in a group at the bar. They are chatting happily, but Vinnie is struck by the beauty of the redhead (Red), who is sitting in the middle of the group, in a dress that shows off her ample breasts and twelve inches of tanned thigh. He moves in, saying, "Hey, Red, who did that crazy color thing in your hair? Bet it wasn't your mom!" All three women giggle, indicating they are interested in this confident male. Vinnie has them hooked. In the vernacular of the Game, the mild put-down about Red's hair was a "neg" (a term created by the Master), and it establishes Vinnie as the *one-up* player at the outset; Red goes one down. Later, Vinnie negs the other women too ("Hey, Blondie, did you borrow those shoes from your kid sister?" and "So, Ms. Wild Afro, did your mother choose that blouse?"), which keeps them off balance, laughing, and on the hook.

When he looks at his watch after about thirty minutes, he says, "Oops. Sorry to break up the party, ladies, but I have a hot date, so I've gotta run. Don't want to keep my sweetie waiting. [His comment indicates he has a romantic interest and that he cares about being late, both of which make him even more attractive.] This has been fun. Hey, give me your numbers so we can stay in touch." They all do. He puts an asterisk next to Red's number.

In spite of their success (make no mistake; these guys were good), it appears the pickup artists (PUAs) eventually gave up the Game. The book is not clear why they gave up, but the answer is right here in the preceding paragraphs. The PUAs were involved in pseudo-relationships—playing a role and following a script given to them by the Master. By playing the Game, each PUA was a crash-test dummy in someone else's experiment. These men probably got lots of sex but the book suggests they found it difficult to enter into relationships, which is not surprising. What they were doing was premeditated manipulation and a perfect recipe for empty sex, which almost certainly resulted in the PUAs becoming more confused. A man may be clueless, but at least he is not following a script someone else gave him. Of course, to the PUAs, these women were little more than lab rats to be picked up then discarded.

Who Are You?

Watch out now, take care
Beware of the thoughts that linger
Winding up inside your head
Beware of Darkness
George Harrison

Do you know—*really know*—who you are? This is not a trick question. The answer should be easy. After all, you live inside your own mind and body. Interestingly, inside you there are many versions of you, all fighting for supremacy. If you doubt me, consider an adult male, William, who may be all of the following at different times:

- Billy the Buddy, who engages in bawdy locker room banter with the guys, watches sports on TV, and drinks beer at a different bar every night.
- Will the Pretzel, who worries about what other people think of him, so he changes his behavior to get them to like him.
- Bill the Brilliant, who tells everyone about his conquests, how his project at work saved the day, how he never loses a bet, how tough he is, and how good he was at sports (at least back in his glory days).

- King William the Domineering Parent, who might have his children under control but only by squelching their spirit and their natural curiosity.
- William at different times may be a Kindly Boss, a Tantric Guru, a willing Suitor, Nervous Nelly, Stud, Jester, Orator, and on and on and on.

Do you recognize yourself in any of these characters? These and many other versions of you may exist in your head, and you may appear as any of them, depending on the situation. If characters like these are all versions of you, are you really *any* of them, or are you someone else? Will you recognize your true, unadorned self when you take the time to look?

You may believe your body knows nothing because it can't think and that it can't possibly tell you what to do. But your body can say, "I'm tired. Let's go to sleep now." You also know that when a pedestrian steps off the sidewalk in front of your car, your body hits the brakes long before you have time to *think* about braking. Your body can even sense danger before there is anything to see (you have felt that sensation in your gut, haven't you?). Your body knows which woman to approach, and what she is going to do before she does it. Your body is amazing; trust it. Feeling what is going on with your body is far better than analyzing every puff of wind that blows your way. Trust your body to know the difference between an exciting opportunity, and a dangerous possibility. Let your body be part of your decision-making process. Try to *feel* more and *think* less. When your mind is racing from one possibility to the next, give it a rest, and feel what your body is telling you to do. Give your ego the night off. Yes, you feel better already!

Envious

Who are you? I really wanna know. I really
wanna know. Who are you?
Come on tell me, who are you? 'Cause I really wanna know.
Who Are You?
Pete Townshend

Do you think your life would be better if:

- You were as good as that other guy?
- Your boss would realize how good you really are?
- You *were* the boss?
- You were more handsome, slimmer, taller, wittier?
- You were more tanned, more outspoken, or more interesting?
- Your woman was cuter, easier, sexier, sane?

If so, then you are a prime candidate to play roles. This is all man-thinking. When everyone else seems to have it better than you, it may seem to make sense to try to become more like them. Happily, I have good news for you. It's much easier than that. All you have to do to make your life better is to become *you*. Forget that fantasy male you wish you were. Just be happy being you, then do the work to make yourself better. Once you know who you are, you will no longer have to figure out what to do; you will know what to do. Perhaps for the first time in your life, you won't be playing games or pretending. You can banish your envious self and just be *you*.

My wonderful teacher, Amara Charles, told me, "Who you actually are is far greater than who you wish you were." What a magical observation! Imagine that you already *are* more than you can ever imagine becoming! Repeat this axiom to yourself every time you doubt yourself until you finally accept yourself just as you are—a growing, centered, authentic male whose inner Man is about to be free.

6

MORE ON RITES OF PASSAGE

THE RITES OF PASSAGE THAT boys experience in tribal culture around puberty are orchestrated by the older Men in the tribe (the elders). When a boy's journey to manhood begins, the elders separate him from the company of women. He is initiated into manhood through intense training and many forms of physical—and often painful—acts that require courage, daring, and strength. Videos of many of these ceremonies are available on YouTube; they are not for the faint of heart. These ceremonies and rites require boys to demonstrate mental and physical toughness to be considered Men, and they can only be successfully undertaken after the boy has received years of preparation by the elders.

Introductions to the ways of Men are now largely nonexistent in Western society. Our boys are mostly raised at home by their mothers and are taught at school by mostly female teachers. Even as boys try to find their own way to become Men, their female caregivers discourage them from roughhousing with other boys and step in to resolve interpersonal difficulties before a fight ensues. Schools and parents severely chastise boys who fight at school or home. I am vehemently opposed to bullying in any form, and I am not advocating that boys be encouraged to fight in school, but I am advocating that when boys do fight, the resulting discipline should reflect that boys are living out their biological destiny as a trainee Man. Fighting among boys does not mean they are delinquents. Schools need to maintain discipline without emasculating their boys.

The remains of the rites of passage for a boy in the Western world are mere fragments of what came before. Instead, a boy is often pushed into sports and team membership, as if the sports will make him a Man. Apart from associating with other boys, it's not clear that any sport has much value as a rite of passage. The reality is that while sports *may* help a boy on his journey to becoming a Man, team sports probably damage more boys than they help. While boys may receive more masculine guidance from their team coach than their own fathers, the coach's main interest is in winning games, not helping boys become Men. In fairness, many coaches do model some masculine behavior pride in performance, teamwork, self-discipline, resilience, commitment, focus, and so on—but many coaches (especially the younger ones) are struggling to be Men themselves because they suffer from the very problems I highlight in this book.

When boys become adult males without proper training in the ways of Men, the result is a store of undisciplined energy. This lack of training is a major source of the confusion from which young (and not so young) adult males suffer. Young boys are taught little about what it means to be a Man or how to live as a Man. Sex education in schools is sanitized because of religious, political, and parental pressure. As a result, it mainly deals with unwanted pregnancy and sexually transmitted diseases. These classes often use pictures of hideously disfigured genitalia, specifically designed to crush a child's developing sexuality, as if when they become adults they can simply forget the horrors they were taught in school. In a truly remarkable example of the law of unintended consequences, the reduction in quality of school sex-ed classes resulted in a surge in the incidence of anal sex, presumably so a girl could engage sexually and claim she was still a virgin with the added benefit that she would not get pregnant.

I could find nothing in the current sex-ed curriculum about how a boy/man should behave on an emotional level with a female partner, or how to treat her body with respect and her heart with tenderness, or even how to ask permission before touching her. Instead, boys have to figure this out by watching TV and movies (including, no doubt, pornography), talking with their friends, or experimenting with equally undereducated girls. These are all poor sources of information for young men who are struggling to find someone to have sex with and figure out what to actually do when they find a willing partner.

Many young men are not even sure how to behave with other men. While many twentysomethings realize that their lives are not going as well as they had hoped when they were teenagers, they have no idea how to correct what is going wrong because they have no idea what *is* wrong. Although the situation is dire, an even greater tragedy will surely follow. Unless our young men learn how to become Men (and somebody will have to show them how), they may be forever unable to embody what it means to be a Man. The tragedy will unfold further because there will soon be no Men to pass on their knowledge to the next generation of boys. Without a return to balance in the roles of men and women, it's conceivable that the art of being a Man will be lost forever in the developed Western world.

My Rites of Passage

Although I did not endure ritual scarring or death-defying ceremonies, I was fortunate to undergo many rites of passage and receive excellent preparation for adulthood from my family, friends, and coworkers. I was not unique back then; my friends had their rites of passage too.

I was born in the industrial heartland of northern England in 1950. Post-war Britain was not an easy place to live. Work was often scarce and much of the housing stock had been destroyed by enemy bombs. As a result, when my parents married, they lived in a room rented from an older couple who evicted them when my mother became pregnant (with me). Forced out, they had no option but to move in with my grandparents and my father's five siblings. That meant ten of us in a four-hundred-square-foot house with gas lighting, a single outdoor toilet, and only cold running water. My parents and I lived in one downstairs room that measured about twelve feet by twelve feet. The house had only a small gas water heater that could heat a gallon of water in about an hour.

While my housing was adequate and quite normal for Britain in that era, the neighborhood was a *perfect* place to grow up. By my third birthday, I was playing in the streets with the other children with virtually no adult supervision. Such supervision as there was came from the older children, who were probably only a few years older than me. It was easy to grow up fast because I simply watched what they did and copied them. We played in the cobbled streets and around the nearby factories. We played soccer with a tin can because nobody had a ball. The older boys played rugby and soccer on a cinder "field" (it did not have a single blade of grass) because there was nowhere else to play. A favorite pastime of mine when I was five years old was pushing a car tire, almost has big as me, around the streets with my bare hand as I ran alongside it. If I was lucky, I found a stick to push the tire. If I had a good-looking stick and a tire with some tread left on it, I felt special. It seems such a small thing now, but little things count when you are five years old, especially when you are trying to hold your own in a posse of little boys. We engaged in many dangerous activities. For example, we would climb anything, run and hide anywhere, and play tricks on unsuspecting adults. In a not-so-shining example of boys being boys, when I was about five years old, an older boy hit me in the face then ran inside his house and taunted me through the window. I picked up a large rock and threw it through the windowpane at him. He was not hurt but he never came near me again. My father had to repair the window but he never punished me. I think he was proud that I stood up for myself against a much bigger boy.

At three years old, my grandmother took me to preschool. I distinctly recall the first day with all the other children crying and clutching their moms' apron strings. When Grandma left me, I was completely unfazed by her departure. I was independent because of how I had grown up. At the age of five, I walked a mile to the grade school with my uncle Colin, who was just a few years older than me. He was worldly and independent, and I loved and admired him. Colin commanded the respect of his peers. Nobody messed with Colin. I wanted to be just like him when I grew up. He was my first role model.

A particularly damaging outcome of pervasive adult supervision for modern children is that the children never learn how to resolve differences by themselves. The idea of fighting among children is anathema to modern parents, but being able to fight is a good skill for a male to have, and it's a skill best learned while young. A significant benefit of knowing how to fight is that a boy learns that he can stand up to injustice when he sees it.

My father may never have heard of a rite of passage, but whether he knew it intellectually or not, he instinctively gave me many rites of passage by which to grow. In 1959, in an effort to expand his business, my father bid on his first major contract; it was hundreds of times bigger than anything he had done before. His job was to clean a large new building before the owners moved in. Unfortunately, he underestimated how long the job would take and his winning bid was far too low. To meet the deadline, he had to press into service everyone he could find—his brothers, his friends, and me. At just nine years old, I was included in the gang of helpers who rode in to rescue his fledgling company. I remember it being backbreaking work. I used a razor blade to scrape away dried concrete and paint from the windows and floors, cutting and blistering my hands and wearing down my fingernails. Such treatment of a nine-year old these days would be considered child abuse.

This work led to my first rite of passage. On a cold and very dark Friday night, I was at work alongside my father late into the evening, just the two of us in this immense new building. He was so busy that he could not afford the time to take me home, so he patted me on the head, gave me some words of "manly" encouragement, and sent me home alone. Before I could even exit the building, I had to walk down a one hundred-yard unlit corridor, with the building creaking and groaning all around me as the new construction settled. I was terrified. When I found the door, I was so happy to have made it out alive that I almost burst into song. I then set off on the one-mile trek home. Snow was falling as I trudged down the muddy road; there was no moon, no street lighting, and no sidewalk. I was not even sure I could find my house, but I was determined not to let my father down. When I arrived in the general area of my house in the inky blackness, a layer of snow covered me from head to foot. The snow and darkness made all the houses look the same. I picked what I thought was my house and knocked on the door. My mother opened it, and I heaved a huge sigh of relief; I had guessed right. Mom's first words came out in a horrified screech. "Where's your father?" She was aghast that I was alone.

To this day, when I see how fragile a nine-year-old boy appears to be, I find it interesting that my father sent me home alone, late at night, down a snowy, unlit road. Even then, I *knew* it was a big deal. I felt pride for my courage, my independence, and my sense of direction. It was a seminal moment in the development of a little boy. My father, my hero, had believed in me enough to have me work alongside him doing adult work *and* find my way home alone. I did it all again the next day too, although my mother walked me home. Puberty was still several years in the future, but I had passed my first rite of passage, the first of many such rites for me.

By the time I was eleven years old, I frequently worked with my father. I was good at the job, and he paid me handsomely. I paid my own way on a school-sponsored trip to Belgium, which was my first trip outside the country. Traveling to a foreign country as a pre-teen without my parents was a minor rite of passage. During my teenage years, I worked every school vacation day from eight to five with my father. I also worked with him most Saturdays from eight in the morning to noon. It was tough manual labor, but I was spending time with the Men who worked for my father, and I learned a lot about being a Man from them. They had little formal education, and they could be crude, but they were rock-solid Men. They took delight in sharing secrets about their lives, including their many sexual exploits and adventures. If my father was aware of this aspect of my education, he never commented on it. I think he was happy to let the Men teach me about sex so he didn't have to do it.

My work with these Men, often in miserable conditions, was a major step on my journey to becoming a Man. Working with them in the cold and wet British winters was brutally hard, and hot summer days with high humidity were little better. Learning to just "get on with it" without complaint made me mentally and physically strong.

By the time I was fourteen, my father felt confident enough to leave me in charge of up to a dozen of his workers. He would drive us to a job and come back at the end of the day to take us home. In his absence, I was in charge. It was my first management experience, and my first "adult" rite of passage. Telling these Men, who had so recently been my protectors, what to do was an object lesson in diplomacy. I had to cope with the fact that I, a young teen on school break, was issuing orders to Men who did this work every day and were decades older than me. Bringing them back to redo their work when it was not good enough gave me the confidence to step into a leadership role in all my future endeavors.

I also learned that before I asked these Men to do something, I needed to be able to do it better than they could.

By the age of seventeen (the legal driving age in Britain), I was in total control of many aspects of the business—moving staff around, monitoring their work, and recruiting people to work in the business. I also identified new work, for which my father paid me a finder's fee (my first foray into *sales*). This phase heralded a quantum leap in my development. I was operating as an adult male while still technically a child. I was running large portions of a significant business, and overseeing the work of many adult workers (both male and female). The things I learned doing this work in the company of solid Men were the foundation upon which I built my life. There is no doubt that the responsibilities heaped on me as I grew up did not break me; they *made* me.

Although I could have stayed in my small hometown and succeeded my father in his thriving business, I had different ambitions. I knew I had to leave if I was to develop on my own path. I had no idea what I wanted to be; I just needed space to expand so at the age of 19, I joined the Royal Air Force as a pilot and, at the same time, began a degree at Manchester University in England. Three months after I joined the RAF, the squadron commander ("Boss") put me in charge of all the other students during an extended training period. Many of the other officers were RAF veterans, but the Boss chose me for this leadership role because I had years of leadership experience, and it showed. This new rite of passage quickly faded into the rearview mirror as I managed this group of feisty young officers. Although some of the veterans tried to destabilize me, I simply ignored their attempts to rock my boat. They were still children in the ways of leadership and command.

Now that I have told you about my rites of passage, please take the time to consider what your rites of passage were. When you recall one, write down the details. It will help you identify other rites of passage.

7

SET YOUR INNER MAN FREE

IT'S NOT EASY TO BECOME a Man these days. To do so, you have to be in touch with your inner femininity *without* actually being feminine, dress well but still look Manly, and, of course, be confident and deliver the goods while under assault from an apparently insatiable woman. I assure you it's much easier than it looks. You just have to be yourself, and to do that, you only have to set your inner Man free. Let's unshackle him and open his cell door together.

Put Your Burden Down

Forgiveness is giving up the hope that the
past could have been any different.
Oprah Winfrey

The effect of what happened to you in your past may last forever, but only if you let it. You don't have to forget your past, but you do have to shake off its effect on your present. Do any of these stories sound familiar?

- I can't trust people because of what my mother (father, lover) did to me.
- I am not going to open my heart because when I do, someone always breaks it.
- I want to dance, but I don't because I am a lousy dancer.

- My mother (sister, girlfriend) was mean to me. I never trust women now.
- My father beat me when I was a child. Men are cruel.
- At school, my friends called me Dopey. I hated that name.

If you have similar words rattling around in your head, you are not alone. I am shocked at how many people I know were molested as children and how many males report having received severe beatings from "friends" or family when they were young. If you were called "Dopey" and still carry the scars, it will affect your entire life unless you can shed the pain. There seem to be no end to the variety of foul acts people have suffered in their lives. I don't minimize the devastating effects these acts had on you at the time, but to have a good life, you have to eliminate the effects of such acts on your present and your future.

Boys tend to suffer physical or emotional abuse, rather than sexual abuse, although the Catholic Church (among others) looked the other way while their employees preyed on vulnerable boys and young men. Too many of the males (and females) I have spoken to about this subject seem to carry some burden of traumatic childhood events. The effects of these events linger decades later. Emotional abuse is just as traumatic as physical abuse, and its effects seem to last much longer. I suffered no abuse from anyone in my family, but from the earliest age, my schoolteachers and my *friends* visited numerous beatings upon me, and some of those beatings were severe, with broken bones, broken teeth, bruises, and lots of blood. In addition, English schools harbored teachers who got their kicks by caning, or otherwise brutalizing, the boys in their care. I recall more than one of my sadistic teachers telling me that the caning I was about to receive was for my own good and that it would hurt him more than it would hurt me; if you believe that, I have a nice tower in Paris I would like to sell you! In addition to caning (on the palm of my hand and on my buttocks), I suffered teacher-inflicted hair pulling, painful cheek pinching, and other acts of sanctioned brutality. Such acts were commonplace for British boys (at least through the 1970s), and though they have largely been eliminated from government-run schools, they probably continue in the exclusive private schools throughout the country.

When I was ten years old, I was standing in line to go into lunch at my school. I whispered something to my friend, even though talking in line was not allowed. The duty teacher, Mr. Green, saw the whisper, and even though he had not actually heard anything, he called out, "That boy—come and see me after lunch." After eating a miserable lunch in dread of what was to come, I went to Green's room. There, I was told to bend over while Green whacked me three times on my butt with a cricket bat that was almost as big as me. My pain and bruising were awful, and my humiliation complete.

This story has an interesting follow-up. Nine years later, when I was a muscular and wild nineteen-year-old, I played in a rugby match and Green was on the opposing team. When I brought him to the ground in a tackle, I punched him in the face multiple times and then asked him, "Do you know why I did that?" His one-word reply, "Yes," was satisfaction enough.

Fighting among groups of young males is common on both sides of the Atlantic. Therefore, many (most?) growing boys will be involved in some kind of physical trauma during their young lives. If you are weighed down by trauma-related baggage, it will be difficult to live a full life. If your past is clawing at your present, fear not. I'm going to show you how to drop that miserable load and regain your authentic self.

I never think about those awful times, unless they become relevant to a conversation, or a book. I live my life in the present, and you will be happier if you can live in the present too. Try this: Stop *thinking* about your past even while you remember it. Thinking about your past will cause you to churn it around in your head, where its importance will grow. When you think about your past, you are inviting it into your present, where it will hurt you again and again.

In addition to the pain you feel for what people did to you, you also may be wracked by guilt, shame, or embarrassment for things you did to others. These thoughts about your actions in the past are all just baggage too. The good news is that you can jettison your baggage. When you are no longer burdened, you will be able to face your future without dragging such a heavy load behind you. Carrying baggage from your past will grind you down and wear you out. Do what you do when the airline loses your suitcase—give away all attachment to your baggage. Once you dump your baggage, even if it takes a landfill to accommodate it, your past will no longer contaminate your present.

Forgive Yourself

Shame is like everything else; live with it for long enough, and it becomes part of the furniture.

Salman Rushdie

For deep-seated pain, whether guilt, shame, or embarrassment, you may need help from a trained professional to guide you through the process of letting go. Seek professional help if you need it.

Three definitions: Shame is what you feel when you breach societal customs. Guilt is what you feel when you breach your own standards of behavior. Embarrassment is what you feel when you do something to humiliate yourself. Embarrassment is short-lived; in a day or two, you will have forgotten all about it. Shame and guilt, on the other hand, are time bombs in your brain that will detonate when the right trigger comes along.

Here are some examples of what might have caused you to feel shame or guilt, but please make your own list:

- Imposing physical, emotional, spiritual, and financial abuse on others.
- Aggressive or mean-spirited behavior toward others.
- Using others for your own gain.
- Criminal acts.
- Lack of self-care and lack of care for others.
- Broken promises.
- Breaches of trust.
- Cheating your partners, your friends, or your family.

Now I am going to describe how you can take all the shame, guilt, blame, anger, and their attendant mental clutter and let it go. You may find that focusing on letting it go as I describe below works for you. If so, fine. If not, you may need the help of others (a trusted friend, a professional therapist, or a spiritual workshop) to identify and release the shame, guilt, blame and anger that you feel.

The first step to letting all this baggage go is to create a ceremonial space in a way that works for you (a clearing in the woods, a mountain peak, a blanket on the floor of your home). If appropriate, burn some incense, light candles, and add other special lighting. Your ceremonial space should connect you with your deepest being. With this process, you can let go of all the hurts of the past. Only you can do it, but you don't have to do it alone. If you know people you trust enough to see your most basic self (they need to be as developed as you are), consider asking them to join you in your ceremony. You can even create the ceremonial space together. If they do join you, you will each take a turn letting go of your shame, guilt, blame, and anger. Joining a group of like-minded people in this manner will enhance the power of your ceremony because you will be sharing a deeply meaningful time together. There is strength in that sharing, so don't fear it.

There are other ceremonial ways to let go of big stuff but for now, see if this works for you.

Pick one instance of shame or guilt you are carrying around. Focus on it. Recall all of its elements: who said what; who did what; what else happened; how you felt; and what you know about how others felt at the time. Write down everything you recall. It may take a while to write this down, but do it anyway. You can also add, delete, or amend anything you feel needs correcting after you write it down.

Then, go to your ceremonial space and speak out loud all the details you wrote down. At a minimum, say.

- The names of the people involved.
- What was said and by whom.
- What your role was in the event (innocent victim; partially to blame, all your fault).
- How you felt at the time this event unfolded.
- How you feel about this event now.

You may feel odd as you speak like this. Be brave. It's important to voice these names and actions. You can even shout what you wrote to make yourself heard above the noise in your head; and feel free to shout with your friends there too. It is most important for you to say aloud what your role was in these events.

When you have said everything there is to say about the first event, look down at the ground and imagine a drain hole about a foot in front of you. See the drain. Look down into the drain, and while you are looking, pour all of the shame or guilt you wrote about down the drain. Watch it go down the drain, swirling around the edges and making a stink. As you watch the swirling shame and guilt disappear down the drain, say, shout, or scream, "I let go of [this episode, this event, this person, this story, whatever it is]," and ... *Whoosh!* just like that, the shame or guilt you have been carrying regarding this event washes down the drain, and you are free of it.

Repeat this as many times as you need to let go of all of the shame and guilt associated with past events that you wrote about. If you later remember something else, just repeat the process for that too.

If you have to give something away more than once, that's not a problem. Just do it until you have watched all of the shame or guilt associated with that event go down the drain. From now on, you will remember what happened, but you will feel dispassionate about it because the shame and guilt will no longer affect your present.

That wasn't too hard, was it? You are a valuable human being. It's vital for you to let go of the shame and guilt you feel, and forgive yourself for what you did. Once you have forgiven yourself, learn from your history, and resolve to do better in the future so you don't repeat the actions that caused your shame or guilt. You are no longer the person you used to be. Whatever question you have about letting this stuff go, the answer is always the same: Let it go until your history is no longer a burden. You can practice letting go of something small first. If you want to start with something big, go ahead—whatever feels right for you.

Forgive Others

I wondered if that was how forgiveness budded;
not with the fanfare of epiphany,
but with pain gathering its things,
packing up, and slipping away
unannounced in the middle of the night.
The Kite Runner
Khaled Hosseini

Hanging on to the pain others inflicted on you will keep hurting you if you let it. The way to make it stop is to forgive the people who hurt you. The beneficiary of your forgiveness will be ... *you*. So let's get started.

Make a list of all the hurts you suffered at the hands of others. When you recall a person or event, write down what happened. If you were partially responsible, write down your role too. Be complete but brief—the notes are just to keep you on track for your ceremony. For example, think of these things, and add more to the list if you can.

- Physical, emotional, spiritual, and financial traumas and abuse.
- Humiliation.
- Unjust punishment (especially from teachers and bosses).
- Rejection by your family, friends, or lovers.
- People who fired you, shunted you off into a backwater, or froze you out.
- People who betrayed you, abandoned you, or let you down.
- People who trampled on you to get where they wanted to go.
- Former spouse(s), for whatever you think she (they) did.
- People who abused you in other ways, no matter how they did it.

Forgive your parents, family, teachers, church, friends, and lovers. Forgive your bosses, your colleagues, your team members. Forgive your enemies too. That should cover just about everyone. The older you are, the more likely it is that many of the people you need to forgive are already gone from your life. Even if they have passed away or moved, you still must forgive them. Think of them, and then forgive them. It's that simple. Whether you forgive the people who hurt you makes no difference to *them*, but it will make a big difference to you.

Dig deep. You probably have a lot of this stuff. Dig it all out, and name each person and each event so you can forgive everyone. On your first attempt, you won't get close to a complete list of people to forgive because there are so many. Don't worry if you miss a few. You may already have forgiven the ones you have forgotten. Realize that forgetting an event and blocking it from your memory are not the same. Please be especially aware of any abuse or trauma that you have buried deep inside. Find all such buried memories (with professional help, if necessary). By identifying these people and events, you can let go of the pain they caused you and forgive those responsible.

When you are ready to eliminate the effects these people and events had on your life, create your ceremonial place as you did before. Again, if you have friends you trust, ask them to join you in your ceremony. They should participate in the ceremony, just as you are, by forgiving the people who hurt them.

Speak your intention to let go of your pain by saying something like this (it does not have to be word-perfect):

"I let go of all attachment to the pain you [name the person; if you can't remember a name, say something appropriate, like "monster"] caused me when you [describe what happened]. My hatred/dislike of you is going down this drain right now, and what you did to me has no hold on me any longer. I forgive you." As you speak, picture the people and the circumstances of what happened and speak, shout, or scream at the top of your lungs to that mental picture. If you begin to cry, let your tears flow. That is the power of ceremony. Just feel your attachment to these people and events slip through your fingers and slither down the drain you saw earlier.

When you have released all of your attachment to the first event and forgiven the people involved, go on to the next event on your list, and repeat the process. You may have many items on your list and may not be able to do all of them at one sitting. That's not a problem; come back as many times as you need.

Revisit your role in these events, and forgive yourself for what *you* did too.

Your first unburdening will probably be the most powerful, and may be all you need. Some people find it difficult to forgive all the people who caused them pain, and they have to go through the process more than once. If you need a trained therapist, perhaps because your past hurts are hidden by a thick defensive wall, please find someone qualified to help you. If other hurts bubble up into your consciousness later, you can use the process I just described to let them go too. Whatever you let go of will probably never trouble you again, but if it does, just give it away again until it's gone forever.

Once you have given away the pain you felt and have watched the pain flow down the drain, you are no longer attached to these people or events. You have given everyone who hurt you a full pardon and given yourself one too. You can tell your ego that henceforth, it can rest a lot easier. You no longer need so much protection because you have no fear of your past, present, or future so you can lower your protective wall. You are now free to grow and become who you really are. You will like who you are about to become. Believe it or not, you are about to become a real, authentic, amazing Man; *YOU*!

Take Control

Control your destiny, or somebody else will.
Jack Welsh

To be a Man, you must feel, at the very core of your being, that you are living *your* life. If something is necessary for you to achieve your goals (e.g., a job), you accept that necessity. It's almost impossible to achieve any significant goals without a job or help from others, and there is no disgrace in accepting direction from a supervisor while holding down a job. Accepting help from others is no betrayal of your freewill principles either. Try not become like Marty …

Marty the Marionette is clever and witty. Audiences laugh at his jokes and his crooked smile. Marty has a nice friend, Vic the Ventriloquist. Marty and Vic have a great time together. Marty thinks he knows who he is.

Of course, Marty's life is an illusion. He doesn't even know he is made of wood. If you are like Marty, dancing to someone else's tune, regain control of your life by severing your connection to the people pulling your strings. It may seem scary to cut the strings someone else has pulled for so long, but do it anyway. Don't *ever* let others make decisions for you. Remarkably, when you allow others to rule your life, they won't thank you or even respect you. They are only happy with you when you do what they tell you to do.

Remember that you are an adult, and you have choice. Whatever you do, *you* are responsible for your actions. Your boss or supervisor may be able to direct you to write a report, move that truck, or dig a bigger hole, but you must decide whether to comply. Don't allow anyone to control you. If your boss asks you to do something illegal, it's easy to say no. It's harder to decide in the gray areas, where the boss asks you to do something legal but that does not feel right to you. These are harder choices to make, especially when you have a family to feed or a mortgage payment to make. The price you have to pay to retain control of your life may seem onerous. Nevertheless, you must pay that price. Many things are worth dying for, as we have discussed; retaining control of your life is one of them. I can't put this more bluntly: A Man does not allow *anyone* to control his life, no matter what price he must pay.

The corollary is that other people deserve to be free too, which means that you never control someone else. For example, you may think you have subdued a lover by controlling her. Even if she does as you say for a time, eventually you will lose control of her. To see what can happen when your partner retakes control of her life, Google "Lorena Bobbitt."

In your effort to control your own life, be careful that you don't try to take over someone else's life. Do not become a Lester!

Lester "shoulds" people to pressure them into doing what he thinks they should do. Lester knows just what your next step *should* be and is not at all shy about telling you what it is.

I recently witnessed a conversation between Lester and Marcus. Marcus is a streetwise fifty-year-old Man with a PhD. During the twelve-minute conversation, Lester said *should* seven times (I know I am a sad creature, but it has become normal to count how many times Lester says that awful word). Seven times in twelve minutes is too many, you might think, but the reality is worse. Lester has mastered the art of using other word forms that mean the same thing as "should." As a result, many of Lester's *shoulds* come out sounding like:

- Don't you think it would be better to …
- Have you thought of …
- Maybe you might …
- Couldn't you …

There were six more of the disguised *shoulds* in the twelve-minute conversation, more than one *should* per minute. Although it was not a pleasant conversation to hear, it yielded a valuable insight. Marcus knows that the Lesters of the world are not worth fighting. He did not respond to any of Lester's shoulds (literal or figurative); he simply ignored them … and so can you.

Of course, the implication was that Marcus *needed* advice. Lester showed no respect for Marcus while attempting to manipulate him. I have seen Lester grow angry if his advice is ignored. You may safely decide to cut off a Lester because the energy you waste deflecting his advice is more than his friendship is worth. If the person won't stop telling you what to do, you have no choice but to say good-bye. Constantly having to deal with the negativity of ignoring a Lester will wear you down. Just live your life, and you will feel so much better. Let others live their lives too.

If you are a Lester, please stop telling people what to do. Let them live their lives without your advice. Oh man! Everyone will feel so much better now, including you Lester!

Trust People

People have grown more suspicious of others in the last fifty years, even though the crime rate declined dramatically over the same period. Parents accompany their children everywhere. People stay close to home and avoid certain neighborhoods. Schools teach "stranger danger" to children, effectively making them fearful of others from an early age. As a grown Man, you don't live your life as if everyone is out to hurt you. Such a caustic thought will slowly eat away your humanity and cut you off from connecting with other people.

Trust is a necessary condition for a successful relationship. When you trust someone, it's easier to open your heart and for that person to open their heart to you. Trust feeds on itself. If you trust others, they will usually reciprocate, and you will grow closer. There is strength in that closeness. Make your default position that you trust other people until they give you a reason to distrust them. Even then, you may give them several chances because everyone screws up from time to time.

Open Your Heart

The other side of your trust of others is being open enough to let other people know they can trust you. As an authentic Man, you have nothing to fear so you can be open with your heart, and open with your love. That is what makes you so attractive to others, especially a woman. If you and a woman are both open books, vulnerable, and deliciously available as friends or lovers, you can develop a deep connection that will make your life together more rewarding until you overflow with pleasure. The only time to close yourself is when you are in emotional or physical danger, and that rarely happens to a Man.

Resolve Conflicts

A woman can be ferocious with her anger, and her ferocity may make you angry and tempt you to fight back. You may raise your voice (and the tension) as you tell her why you are right and let her know why she is wrong. As a Man, however, you know how to push your anger back down where it came from and how to remain calm. The best course of action is to do very little. The less you do, the better. You stay centered and simply absorb her onslaught. Don't fight back. Don't defend yourself. Don't tell her she is wrong, even if you think she is. Remain centered and calm when she chums the water. If you chase the chum like a big dumb shark, you may find yourself on the end of her hook! Stay engaged but don't walk away, turn away, or fight back. Maintain soft (non-threatening) eye contact with her, remain passive and ignore the chum. Simply allow her anger to wash over you. Don't uproot yourself or explode; just be a rock, and her ferocity will dissipate.

Being a rock while your woman melts down does not mean you conceded or lost anything. If you think, *I will just agree with her; anything for a quiet life*, think again; that is a false concession and a badge of man behavior. As a Man, you are steadfast against verbal assaults by anyone, including by your woman, but being steadfast does not mean becoming angry, aggressive, or defensive.

At the Men's Workshop, with Helen my co-teacher, I demonstrate two ways to respond to a woman's outburst. Helen explodes at Steve for coming home late from work. In Scenario One, pay particular attention to the words in *italics*. Both Helen and Steve use these words to increase the intensity of their fight. Like all partners in a long-term relationship, Helen knows exactly where to toss the chum to elicit the response she seeks in Steve and he, like that dumb shark goes right for it. Notice too, how Helen's incendiary language ratchets up the energy of the argument, and how Steve eventually does the same thing. Steve wisely ignores the chum in the second scenario.

Scenario One

Steve walks through the door and calls out, "Hi, darling. I'm home!"

Helen curls her lips into a snarl as she looks at him. "Don't you *'darling'* me. I worked *for hours* to make a nice dinner for you. That *thing* you can smell *burning* is your dinner. The other thing you can smell *burning is my heart.*"

Steve replies calmly, "I am so sorry, love. I was in a meeting, and I couldn't call you."

Helen icily replies, "You couldn't excuse yourself for *a moment* to call *or even* text me? Are you so *damn* important that you can't step out of a meeting for a minute?"

Steve's reply is louder and less calm. "Well, actually, *yes, I am.*"

Helen says, "*Bullshit!* If you were as important *as you say you are*, you could do what you want. I think you are just a *little cog* in a big machine. I don't think you are *important at all*. You *never* listen to me."

Helen's anger causes Steve to lose his center and he torches Helen right back. "*Me, listen to you*? That's *a laugh*. Did your *silly little head* forget that I told you I would be late tonight? It's not my fault *you burned* the dinner. It's you who *never* listens to what I say. You *always* make a scene like this for no reason. It's *stupid*. You need to *grow up*."

Helen *stamps her foot* and *storms off*.

In his anger, Steve shouts after Helen, "*Go back to fucking China*."

Helen screams back at him, *"Asshole. I'm not Chinese; I'm from Taiwan."*

Steve drops his briefcase on the floor and pours himself a large Scotch. He is fuming, and it takes him an hour to calm down. By then, his speech is slurred as he finishes his third Scotch.

In ***Scenario Two***, Steve refuses to be drawn and the conversation goes much better.

"Hi, darling. I'm home!"

His wife, Helen, curls her lips into a snarl. "Don't you *'darling'* me. I *worked my ass off* to make a nice dinner for you. That *thing* you can smell *burning* is your dinner. The other thing you can smell *burning* is my *heart*."

Steve replies calmly, "I am so sorry, love. I was in a meeting, and I couldn't get out to call you."

Helen icily says, "You couldn't excuse yourself for *a moment* to call *or even* text me? Are you so *damn* important that you can't step out of a meeting for a minute?

At this point the scenario changes:

Steve replies, "Sweetheart, I am sorry. I can tell you're upset. Let's sit down and talk this over."

Helen responds, "*No!* You *always* do this. This time I don't want you to talk me down. You are a *thoughtless prick.*"

Steve ignores Helen's epithet and hangs in there. "I know you're angry, but let's sit down and talk about it. We won't solve anything by shouting at each other. Come on. Just sit with me, and let's talk." Steve reaches out his hand to her.

Helen looks at Steve's outstretched hand but does not take it. She says, "Forget it! I *know* how that will go. You'll talk me down by telling me some *bullshit* story."

Steve ignores Helen's refusal to discuss the situation. He lowers his voice even further. "You know we can't resolve anything in this way. Let me tell you exactly what happened."

Steve reaches out to Helen and slowly and carefully takes her hand. He puts his other arm around Helen's back and leads her gently to the sofa. They sit. They talk. Helen's anger subsides.

In Scenario One, Steve blew up, and both he and Helen were losers. In Scenario Two, Steve was a rock. He did not *win*, but better yet, neither he nor Helen lost. You don't lose anything by being the steadfast rock as your woman vents her fury. You know that raising the temperature of the argument will make everything worse. While the scenario may seem simplistic, the approach Steve is demonstrating works to calm things down and allows time and space for a reasonable conversation to occur. It's clear that Scenario Two is far better than the unresolved anger that follows a fight between couples. It doesn't matter if Helen's energy hits Steve like a tsunami. When Steve doesn't over-react, Helen's tsunami dissipates and tranquility returns. If Steve joins Helen in battle, the situation will deteriorate, as it did in Scenario One.

I know it's difficult to be the rock when your woman attacks you for some real or imagined transgression. Your natural tendency is to defend yourself. Refrain from doing that, and you will be fine. Actually, this is a good way to respond to a verbal assault at any time; it has wide application to the world at large, not just when you are responding to your woman. When you behave in a calm, centered manner, it's easy to see what works and what does not. If you lose your center, the argument will spin out of control, something I have allowed to happen too often in my life. I learned the better approach I describe here after many years of practical experience. It may seem weak to stand there and let your woman pour an ocean of vomit on you. You may be thinking, *there is no way I am going to allow a woman to do this to me*. You are not the first man to think this way, but as a Man you let your woman vent her feelings because you know they are just feelings. Even if you have done nothing to deserve her wrath, she feels the way she feels, and it would be futile for you to tell her that she should feel any different. You will both feel better about yourselves and about each other if you are the calm, resolute rock.

You can repair the rift in your relationship after an occasional fight, but if these fights happen frequently (and they do happen frequently in many relationships), they will destroy the relationship. Similarly, if you resort to epithets (she calls you a *shithead*; you call her a *bitch*), the end of the relationship is close at hand. If you want to preserve your relationship, don't be insulting. If you insult your partner, it is like spraying battery acid into her brain (and vice versa, of course).

One way to respond to an angry person is to adopt a *dead-face* which has no smile; no tension; and no eye contact. Instead of eye contact, which can seem like an aggressive move, a dead-face looks at the middle of the other person's forehead or chin. Don't look away either. You want to be aware of what the other person is doing, especially if the other person is an aggressive male. With your dead-face leading the way, you will be impervious to the other person's efforts to beat you in a verbal altercation. When you are a disengaged, soulless death mask, you won't seem like a living person, and your antagonist will have no idea what to do next. If you resist the temptation to be drawn into a fight, the fight will evaporate. Resist the temptation to scream at your tormentor. If you do scream, you are playing your tormentor's game. In an encounter like this, if you feel the need to say anything, try this: "I'm sorry you feel that way." There is no need to say anything else.

Know Yourself

Although you may have thought your beliefs are the very essence of who you are, your beliefs, however strongly held, are not you. The totality of who you are is far greater than the sum of your beliefs. Your beliefs can change, but you still have to be *you*, and you can't become you until you know everything about yourself. Sure, you already know yourself, right? Sadly, unless you have been doing the necessary work, you probably only know yourself at a superficial level. There are many layers of you, and someone else plastered most of those layers right over the top of your natural self (your inner Man). You can't become you until you separate the parts of yourself that are *actually* you from the parts of you that others put there. To figure out which is which, you must trust your body and leave your mind out of it. Your mind will get in the way of discovering yourself by saying things like, "I know who I am. I don't need to figure myself out." Let's try a little exercise. Suppose…

- A woman waving a gun ran into your office. Would you run and hide? Call 911? Hustle your colleagues to safety?
- Someone offered you a chance to earn a 37 percent return on a real estate deal within six months. Would you go to the bank and withdraw all your money to get in on the

deal? Sell everything you have and make a killing? Walk (or run) away?

- You learned you had incurable cancer and only six months to live. Would you go on a world cruise? Take yourself to Geneva for an assisted suicide? Make sure you had your affairs in order, speak to your loved ones about your wishes, and write your own obituary?

If you don't know the answer to these questions (and many others just like them) without having to think about them for days, you have some discovery to do to find out who you are—the person you are when stripped down to your most basic self. While the above scenarios are intentionally extreme, as you learn about who you are, you will learn about yourself in the context of less challenging scenarios. You will never know everything about yourself, but you can learn something new about yourself every day, provided you keep challenging yourself to know more. Therefore, take the deep dive into yourself, and seek out your true nature. Challenging yourself in new ways will help. Workshops, expeditions, meditation, group and solo retreats, soul searching on a mountaintop (my personal favorite), and many other avenues to discovery are available to you. Take advantage of them, and keep discovering more and more about who you really are. You may be surprised by what you find.

Another aspect of yourself to consider is your belief system. I make no judgments about your beliefs, but if you don't do the work, consider this: The beliefs instilled in you from childhood represent a layer of you that may not actually be what you would believe now, if you took the time to reconsider. In particular, reconsider beliefs that have been with you so long that you can't recall where they came from or who gave them to you. Whether they are right or wrong for you *now* is what matters, and you can't know that without questioning them and feeling, in your body, whether they are right for you. Many beliefs accompany you on your journey through life. We have already covered several of them (e.g. I masturbated, which is a sin, so I am going to hell). Here are some other examples:

- Being wealthier will make you happier (a belief to question).
- Do what the boss tells you to do (another belief to question).
- You need a woman to make you a Man (a belief you can safely reject).
- I cannot leave my wife no matter what she does. I made a vow to stay until 'til death us do part' (It is your life. If the relationship is dead or your partner is abusing you, you owe it to yourself to leave).

Questioning your beliefs does not make them wrong, but if you simply accept what someone told you, especially someone who had authority over you at the time, you have subordinated your natural self to someone else's notion of who you *should* be. Subordinating your own thinking to that of others allows those people to control you, even if you never consciously accepted their ideas and even if they told you what to believe decades ago. Subordinating your thinking to what others told you, was the primary means by which those people (e.g., parents, teachers, clergy) forced your inner Man into his prison cell.

What can you do about this now? Identify every belief you hold and consider them from every angle. Once you have a good handle on what your beliefs are, then accept, modify, or reject each one as you see fit. Doing so is your call. Make it, and move on. If you are unsure what to believe, challenge each of your beliefs by spending time alone. For example, try camping in the woods while you think things through. Or, consider your beliefs while walking fifty miles alone in silence. Or, meditate on each belief until what you actually believe becomes clear. In other words, do whatever will allow you to question each belief, then determine whether that belief still works for you. When you reach a conclusion, do what your body tells you is right for your inner Man.

There came a time when I questioned everything; absolutely everything. I did this by sitting alone on a mountaintop for several days. I was moved by the beauty of the valley below me and asked myself questions about my religion, my life, my value system, and what it all meant for how I should live my life in the future. I considered what love meant to me. I questioned everything about myself and, as a result, changed almost all of what I had thought was true. I saw things with a clarity I previously had not experienced. I threw out many long-held beliefs, and I adopted many new ones. I also gained respect for, and gratitude toward, the people who made me who I am.

You may come to realize who you are by deep reflection or meditation over the course of years. You may need help from a teacher, guru, or therapist to help you develop your understanding of yourself. You may find out who you are in a blinding flash of insight, when, for the first time, you shake free of the external pressure to be the person someone else wants you to be. When you see yourself as you really are for the first time, relish the moment, and introduce yourself to your inner Man; he is your true self. Open his prison door and let him out!

If you need more help to discover your true nature, countless workshops and books are available, (see Resources for a few of them). I believe that workshops are necessary to discover who you really are because they are the only way to calibrate yourself against other people. You can reach out to the Men in your life, and ask them to help you. Some of what you learn will cause you to rethink parts of your character that you have taken for granted. "That's just who I am" is the first belief to reject, because it is a silly notion that suggests you are happy with every aspect of yourself and that you can't grow, improve, or change. If you feel that way, you need to reconsider whether you are as perfect as you believe. A

Man knows he is not perfect and that he has faults like any other human being. Being a Man is not about being perfect. It's not about being smart, or witty, or intellectual. It's not about being tall or having a great body. It's about being yourself without shame or guilt, and about working to be a better Man every day of your life.

Claim Your Power

You must claim your power because nobody else will give it to you. This is one way I staked my claim to my power as a young man:

I learned early in life that it was not possible to argue with my father. Arguments with him never went well. Nevertheless, as I grew up, I resisted his efforts with all the means at my disposal. My go-to defense mechanism was detachment.

The last major battle to establish my identity occurred when I was 17 and was over the use of my car. I had bought the car with the money I had earned helping him run his business. I bought the gas and did my own repairs. My father even borrowed my car for use in his work. One summer evening, I took some friends out for a drive to the beach, and although we were home at a reasonable hour, a confrontation ensued. My father forbade me to go to the beach in my car. I immediately stopped cooperating on *all* family matters. I ignored my parents for days. If they spoke to me, I grunted some monosyllabic non-reply and walked away. They were furious but had no response to my silence.

Days later, my father needed to borrow my car, but I had the keys. He came to me and calmly asked, "Do you think you have been unfairly treated?" I said, "Yes. That car is mine, even though I allow you to use it for your work. How can you restrict what I use it for?" My father replied, "I regret the events of the last few days, and while I hope you won't abuse the privilege, from now on you can go wherever you want in your car." I gave him the keys.

Victory! I had stood up to an injustice, maintained my center, and refused to be cowed into accepting an inappropriate restriction on my movements. It had been an excruciating few days, but it was worth it. Neither of my parents ever again questioned where I went or with whom, and I never abused their trust.

On this occasion, I had held my ground and stood up for myself by marking the boundary that separated me from my father. This event caused a major shift in my relationship with him. He started to treat me as an equal and never again lapsed into his old father/child manner with me.

Unfortunately, there was a flaw in my approach. Although it had worked for me in this instance, I have long had misgivings about a passive-aggressive approach to solving a relationship problem. When you are in a relationship, becoming silent and withdrawn will make matters worse because the silence creates distance between you and your partner. Instead, deal with interpersonal issues in an adult manner, head-on, calmly, quietly, and preferably in a special or ceremonial space. Once you know how to resolve issues in this way, you will find that your life with others becomes much better. I describe this process in greater detail in Chapter 7.

Does standing in your power mean you are always right? That you are above criticism? That you get to tell everyone else what they are doing wrong? The answers are no, No, and HELL NO! When someone criticizes you, listen carefully to what they say. Look upon the criticism as a chance to learn something about yourself. If the criticism is warranted, accept it. If you reject the criticism at the time, you may be surprised how often you later realize that not only was the criticism well meant, it was valid.

Control

In a relationship, each partner may be trying to control the other, and both may be doing so at the same time. If you feel the control beginning, stand in your power and simply refuse to play the game. Here is just a small example of controlling behavior:

Benny wants to watch *Monday Night Football.* Paula wants to watch *American Idol.* The shows overlap, so Benny strikes first. "I really want to see *Monday Night Football* tonight, Paula. Everyone will be talking about the game at work tomorrow." Paula says, "Oh, Benny, I have to see *American Idol* tonight. It's the first in the new series."

As happens many times in a relationship, it's difficult (or impossible) to satisfy both partners' desires at the same time. As a result, manipulation, the lubricant of control, soon flows.

After a brief skirmish, Benny sullenly yields. While Paula settles down to watch *Idol,* Benny exits the room in a rage, slamming the door and shouting, "Well, watch your damn show. It's always the same. A bunch of lousy singers." He calls a friend and talks loudly on his phone to annoy Paula. After several minutes, she asks him to tone it down, so he speaks even louder.

Does any of this sound familiar?

When *Idol* ends, Benny watches the nightly news, turning up the volume to annoy Paula, who has gone to bed. Paula angrily expresses her disgust with Benny's behavior and screams at him from the bedroom.

Benny feels like he would have lost something (his manhood?) if he had conceded control of the TV without a fight. He rationalizes his behavior as a point of principle, but the reality is that his ego could not bear to lose to his wife. Of course, by making it a point of principle, he guarantees that he will lose in the end. There are few points of principle in a relationship, and which TV show to watch is definitcly not one of them. Benny's churlish behavior does not win him any points with Paula, who recognizes that he is being childish again.

This scenario is classic control behavior and it is pathetic. The reality is that relationships founder because one partner tries to control the other over issues as silly as a TV show. When control first begins, a *controller* (the person doing the controlling) will test the *controlee* (the target of the control) to see how much control they can exert. As a trial, the controller will pick something small to fight about. If the control works, the controller's position solidifies. Over time, the controlee gives away more and more of their power, and the controller's screws grow ever tighter. Even if the relationship survives such controlling behavior, it ultimately will become unsatisfying and either fail or become a so-so relationship.

If we turn the scenario around and allow Benny to behave as a Man, he does not let Paula control him but he does offer a solution that is workable for him:

Benny says, "OK, Paula. I'll record the game on the DVR and watch it later. You can watch *Idol*. Will that work for you?"

In this example, it was Benny conceding the point and putting himself out for Paula's benefit. But Paula could have compromised too by recording her show. Benny's compromise allows both partners to be reasonably happy. Benny does not behave like an oaf, and peace reigns everywhere. They worked it out like adults because Benny was a Man. Imagine that!

You have all the tools to behave in this way when you realize that concessions freely given don't represent (or even feel like) losses. Finally—and this is critical—when you are a Man, you don't even want a woman you can control. Treat your woman as your equal partner, and you will grow as a Man in the process, and you will be stronger as a couple. Success all around.

No Self-Inflicted Injuries

Consider the following illustrations of two apparently happy and financially secure couples:

Janice and Jim have been married for eleven years. Jim is a stay-at-home dad, and Janice is the sole breadwinner in the family. One night, Janice tells Jim that she has been seeing *Larry* for over a year and that she wants a divorce.

Jim is distraught. His wife's affair blows his self-esteem out the window. He has no income of his own and a large mortgage to pay off. And he dreads losing contact with his two children. He lashes out at Janice in a fit of unfettered rage, bruising her face, forcing her into the street at midnight, breaking up some furniture, and smashing windows in the house.

Janice calls the police, and they arrest Jim. A judge later sentences him to twelve months in prison for assault. When he is released, it's impossible for him to find a job suitable for his degree in social work. Janice is granted a court order that allows Jim, the stay at home dad, only supervised visits with the children he has raised from birth. He loses his friends because they are no longer certain who he is. Jim is alone, and his anger feeds upon itself as his thoughts oscillate between suicide and murder.

Jim is horrified that he reacted the way he did and can't believe he would do such a thing. Unfortunately, when he heard of Janice's betrayal, his emotions spun out of control, and he destroyed himself.

On the other hand…

Mandy and Mike have been married for eleven years too. Like Janice, Mandy is having an affair. As the stay-at-home father, Mike had also lost his client base when he gave up his practice. When Mike hears Mandy's news, he is devastated, but Mike stands in his power as a Man and does not allow Mandy's betrayal to diminish his self-esteem. He accepts that has no choice but to let Mandy go, and over the course of a few weeks he meets with Mandy to discuss how to manage their permanent separation.

Mike has no income, but he will receive child support and alimony (from Mandy's successful practice), which gives him time to restructure his life. Mike realizes he can no longer afford their house and moves into something smaller. His friends rally around him and often cook dinner for him and his two sons. They also look after the boys when he needs help. While he is sad about what he will lose in the divorce, he accepts that it's better than living a lie, which is what his marriage had become.

Within a year, Mike has rebuilt his practice, and the children are doing well in school. He uses the child support to cover day care for the children when he is working. Mike soon finds a new love interest with whom he and the children are happy. Mandy has moved in with her new lover and his three daughters, and they are happy too.

What a difference between Jim and Mike. Jim lost his center, and what followed was a catastrophe that destroyed several lives. Mike maintained his center and pushed his anger and fear back down where they belong. Standing in his power, he controlled himself and dealt with the understandable pain of Mandy's betrayal. While being rejected and cheated on made him feel terrible, Mike acknowledged the pain, and then let it go. He controlled his emotions rather than letting them control him.

Of course, there are other challenges that can knock you so far off your center that you end up hurting yourself. For example, a good friend betrays a confidence he had promised to keep; a woman you have faithfully supported for years cuts you off without explanation; you lose your job and your house in an economic crisis; your boss berates you in front of colleagues. You can no doubt think of many more challenges that might cause you to lose your center. The solution to all of these challenges is to:

- Push the adrenaline back down into your lower abdomen.
- Back away from the problem.
- Carefully weigh your options.
- Retain control of your emotions. If you lose control of your emotions, you will lose control of yourself and you will live to regret it.

Jealousy

Do you recall the feelings you had when you first fell in love; that first flush of love; that warm glow of deep affection mingling with the volcanic heat of lust and passion; the desire that blots out everything else because your new lover inhabits your every thought. There is nothing to compare with it. Remember that feeling.

The dark side of being in love is the fear of losing your lover. An accident or sudden illness may make you sad, but if you are a man, losing your woman to another male will probably make you *jealous*, which is one of the most corrosive forces in human nature. Jealousy can hurt you for a very long time. Why? Because you *know*, deep in your lizard brain, that the pain of losing your woman to another male would be the worst feeling you could ever experience. As a result, you go to great lengths to prevent that from happening. You might stop her from freely meeting other people. You might spy on her emails to see what she says, and to whom. You might even put an electronic tracker on her car. There really is no limit to what you might do to keep track of your woman because if she left you for another male, you would surely go *mad*!

If this behavior describes you, you have forgotten your woman is a human being with free will. Make no mistake; you are not doing this to protect her. You are doing it to protect yourself because this is all about ownership, which is the very opposite of love. Jealousy is your ego at work, and it corrodes everything it touches; most of all, it corrodes you. If you think losing your woman will diminish you, you are not yet a Man. Remember, if you are a Man with a train, your woman is probably not going anywhere, and if she does decide to leave you, let her live her life while you go on living yours. You don't need her to complete you; you are already complete. Let her go if that is what she wants.

So how do you navigate the troubled waters of jealousy? Right at the beginning of the relationship, you remind yourself that your woman is not *yours*. You both have free will, and you are both free to leave at any time. You have no right to a future with her, or she with you. If she leaves you, ask her why. If she tells you, even if her answer hurts, you may learn something about yourself. If you decide to leave her, you can do so in a rage, or you can do so calmly. I know which I would choose, and if you are a Man, so do you.

8

FEMINISM AND THE MCP

Women are the only oppressed group in our society
that lives in intimate association with their oppressors.
Evelyn Cunningham

As you read this section, do not blame the women you know for your confusion.

Powerful Women

The world has had powerful queens and imperially minded women for thousands of years, but in the last thousand years at least, Western cultures adopted laws that favored men and oppressed women. For centuries, wives were considered chattel, which means a wife was on par with a horse or a cart. For a century or two, under a US legal doctrine called *coverture*, a woman had no separate identity from her husband, and any property she owned before she married became her husband's property when she said "I do." A woman's rights upon divorce were almost non-existent, as she could be dispossessed of *everything* in the marital estate, even those assets she brought into the marriage. It was only in the twentieth century that women gained the right to vote in elections in the United States and throughout the Western world. The idea that women were incapable of making a wise choice at the ballot box may seem laughable now, but it was not laughable until the Nineteenth Amendment to the US Constitution gave women the right to vote in 1920 (it was 1928 in Britain). In addition to the vote, women had valid social, marital, and cultural concerns that society needed to address.

Women made significant gains during the two world wars as they demonstrated that they could perform many tasks previously thought to be beyond them. The push for change became an imperative as women gained freedom through education and paid employment outside the home. After the Second World War, the fight for equal rights gained momentum. In the 1960s, the momentum increased again, as the contraceptive pill gave women control over their reproductive life, and the media gave them a platform for their collective voice. Women eventually won the fight for legal equality in employment and politics. Equality in remuneration is a work in progress. Now, women enjoy essentially equal rights under the law, and in certain areas, the law is weighted in their favor. (If you want to know more about this, start by watching the documentary *The Red Pill* which, at the time of writing, is available free with Amazon Prime).

**Feminism may have slain all the fire-
breathing masculine dragons
but now women are complaining…
there is nobody to light a fire!**

As revolutions tend to do, the feminist revolution had unintended consequences. In this case, the revolution led to the deconstruction of masculinity throughout the industrialized Western world, as the fight for equal rights for women underwent a metamorphosis and became a crusade against all things masculine. Feminists vilified any male who resisted the crusade, and over the last 50 years, the cacophony of female and, incredibly, *male* voices decrying masculinity has grown exponentially worse.

In the 1960s, women began using a particularly nasty phrase, *male chauvinist pig or MCP*, to describe all males. It was the start of the degradation of Men, who were castigated for all manner of "crimes" against women, when all Men were doing was being Men. Some males may have been chauvinists, and perhaps all males have been chauvinistic at times, but the term is a disgraceful epithet when applied to male behavior across the board. Women did not seem to realize (or care) that they were shaming males for doing what males had been doing for eons—providing for and protecting their families. It was as if a male's protections and provisions had no value any longer. At the same time, most women were doing what women had historically done. Both sexes had onerous responsibilities, and both sexes had privileges the other sex did not enjoy. Oppression (i.e., a deliberate act of subjugation) was not part of the calculus for the vast majority of males.

The damage did not end with name calling. Feminists wanted to fundamentally *fix* males (even though they were not actually broken) and abandon a hundred thousand years of biology and culture. The result was the demolition of masculinity, and millions of males who became less and less masculine. If you think this campaign against males sounds like emasculation, you are right. For five decades, women pushed their husbands, sons, and male friends to become more feminine.

All over the Western world, males by the millions obliged by complying with the feminist demands, ignoring the fact that being more feminine went against their masculine biology. When some males failed to comply, women tore them apart, claiming they were out of touch with their feelings and their women. Popular culture now portrays all males as unfeeling brutes who use women to satisfy their carnal desires and give nothing in return. In my own hearing, women have labeled males (including me) as misogynists, Neanderthals, pigs, bullies, social morons, and worse.

Most women did not set out to emasculate males. They wanted equality, not eunuchs, and they wanted men to stop treating them as second-class citizens. While many such changes were long overdue, once feminism gained momentum, it became a tidal wave that was impossible to control. A male could not respond or even discuss the issues women raised without being labeled a chauvinist pig. Thus, the fight for equal rights (which were attained by the 1980s) became a crusade to change the fundamental nature of males at their most basic level. As the war on masculinity progressed, men lost their masculine footing. The absence of rites of passage and the lack of masculine leadership from a dying breed of Men exacerbated the situation. As confusion spread like a blight across the industrialized Western world, it left hundreds of millions of confused men in its wake.

A perfect example of the effects of fifty years of feminist acculturation occurred at the Battle of the Sexes Salon, which I chaired in the spring of 2016. To begin the Salon, I asked the attendees (a mixed-age group of both sexes) whether the sexes were actually fighting a battle and, if so, what the fight was about. It did not surprise me that most of the women were immediately able to answer that question by saying (I quote):

Men need to:

- Be more in touch with their hearts.
- Be more open.
- Feel their emotions more.
- Understand women better.
- Know how to behave with women.
- Be kinder, more gentle, more understanding, less aggressive.

There were many more comments along similar lines, but they all boiled down to one thing: Men need to become more feminine. I was shocked to hear some of the male attendees agree with the women.

Feminism's devaluation of masculinity not only changed the relationship between males and women but between males and other males, as some clung to their masculinity while others crumbled before the feminist onslaught. The result was that males could no longer trust other males. Here is a perfect example of what is going wrong: On Facebook (that cauldron of every personal thought), there was a site called the New Masculine Community. I joined the group because I thought it might be helping men regain some of their masculinity, and I wanted to see how they did that. Sadly, what I found was that feminine thought dominated the New Masculine Community. Postings were often by women, but even those proffered by men were riddled with feminist thought. It was clear that a cadre of feminist women and feminized men pushed the conversation in a feminine direction and punished any male who expressed views outside their ideal. There was no place in the New Masculine Community for Men who know how to stand in their masculine power. Nobody to help men become more masculine. No forum for men to push back against feminism without an immediate and severe backlash. All dissent was immediately quashed. Members of the group were expelled for expressing non-feminist (i.e., masculine) thought. The New Masculine Community is a prime example of the wreckage that is twenty-first-century manhood. Thankfully, the New Masculine Community did not last long.

Here is another example, posted September 4, 2017, on an allegedly "masculine" Facebook page. The stated focus of the page is males, but like other supposedly masculine Facebook pages, this one's female members drive the discussion. This is an exact quotation of an item submitted to the page by a writer who claimed to be male:

"It's time to trust the wisdom of women, for men are turning toward and into the feminine, and who would be better guides?"

Who, indeed? So here is a male, posting on a supposedly masculine site that males need women to help us be more feminine. *More* feminine? The problem is that most men are already out of balance because they are too feminine. Unless we reverse the tide, the damage to Western life, as we know it, will be catastrophic.

Women complain about the men in their lives, claiming the men are unsure of themselves and lack direction (i.e., they have no train). Although women would find all the traits they desire—and more—in a Man, few women can find a Man. Women got what they asked for, but they are paying a terrible price for their victory because a Man has become almost impossible to find. How could it be otherwise? For half a century, women attacked males for behaving in accordance with their biology and demanded that they become more feminine. The result is millions of men, and millions of women who want a Man but can't find one.

Too Much Woman

Nothing is slower than the true birth of a Man.
Marguerite Yourcenar

A mother's role in the development of her son requires patience and understanding, and a few goddess qualities would not hurt a bit! For example, a mother must often let her son go in harm's way without saving him, or he will never learn to stand in his own power—a lack that will haunt him all his life. Mothers often push their sons to be kind and gentle and caring, which are predominately feminine characteristics. There is nothing wrong with these characteristics. They are essential qualities in a Man's overall makeup. The problem for mother-centric boys is that they grow up lacking the counterbalancing characteristics of strength of character, prowess, confidence, and the ability to fight. If a boy accepts his mother's domination, he may be sensitive and caring, but he will disappoint women all of his life by being too *soft and squishy*. A Man has nothing in common with a cuddly toy.

Potential problems between mother and son begin at puberty, when the boy first feels the rush of hormones that will make him an adult male. The struggle reaches its zenith when the boy is between 15 and 18 years of age. By then, he is a young man who needs to be making his own decisions without being dominated by his mother. Long before his 18th birthday, a boy should be choosing what to wear, where to go, and who to spend time with, both in and out of school. Inevitably, he will make some bad decisions; that is what growing up is all about—even more reason to let him practice being an adult while there is still supervision around. If he does not have enough rope to hang himself, he will never learn how to assess risk, or how to balance the potential risks and rewards that flow from making a decision. As a result, he will struggle all his life to become a Man.

Unfortunately, a female-dominated childhood is the norm for boys these days. Surrounded by women, boys rarely see what Man behavior looks like. When a boy grows up to be a man, he will fight with the women in his life to prove to them that *he* controls his life, not them. In effect, he will be fighting his mother throughout his life.

9

THE BATTLE OF THE SEXES

Our duty, as men and women, is to proceed
as if limits to our ability did not exist.
We are collaborators in creation.
Pierre Teilhard de Chardin

What Women Want

Women tire of men because men cannot excite them in the way they desire or because they become disappointed in their masculine performance (domestic, emotional, sexual, financial, or otherwise). As I sought to understand the dynamics driving the divide between men and women, I asked women what they liked about the men in their lives (with acknowledgement to Alison Armstrong; see Resources). Although what follows is not a complete list of what they said, the selections are quoted verbatim and in the order they were given:

Women like a male's: *cock* (really; this was first thing they said); ability and willingness to be providers; daring; confidence; protection; sensitivity; sense of humor; heart-to-heart connection; passion; stability; kindness; strength; love of life; knowledge of tools; adventurous spirit.

Women did not like that males: are too competitive; discourage them from connecting to their (i.e., the female's) inner masculinity; fail to recognize their biological differences; pretend to listen but don't; expect women to be responsible for all the domestic duties; take more than they give.

Although some of the items the women *liked* about males were predominately feminine traits (sensitivity and heart to heart communication), a woman is more likely to find that only another woman possesses the qualities on list 1 without the more masculine qualities on list 2. Of course, a male is a package deal which, unlike your cable bill, can't be unbundled. Happily, the list of characteristics women found attractive in males include many of the qualities that a Man exhibits: tenacity, power, strength, desire, a willingness to protect and provide, and more. A Man provides such qualities naturally, so it was wonderful to learn that these are qualities women actually admit to desiring.

Even if you are a Man, a woman may pressure you to change to fit *her* idea of a perfect male. Of course, if you are a Man, you will not change until *you* decide to change. You also know that your woman cannot tell you how to be a Man. Remember, even if you make every change your woman demands, she won't be happy with you and will later reject you.

The women I know who have a Man as a husband or lover are happy for him to be who he is. Even the women who are with a *man,* will give him the benefit of the doubt and be patient as long as he is making progress toward becoming a Man. Once a woman notices that her man has stopped trying to find his train or to grow in other ways, she is likely to leave him, which will make him more confused than ever. Even if she does not leave him because of the big mortgage, the children etc.), their relationship is doomed to become a miserable experience.

What Men Want

At the same Salon, I asked the male attendees what they like about women (again, this is not a complete list, but the selections are quoted in the correct sequence and verbatim).

Men like a woman's: submissiveness; vulnerability; beauty; sexuality; caring; emotional support; *pussy* (literally what they said); sex; flirtatiousness; playfulness; passion; nurturing; femininity.

This list shows that males have a good understanding of what women have to offer their partners. By the time the Salon was winding down, even the most critical women (those who earlier had poured their scorn on adult males generally) realized that what they wanted was not a squishy, feminine, pushover man that they could wrap around a finger. What they wanted was a Man. My work in the Salons is a small step in redressing the balance between the sexes.

Women Are Told What to Want

If you are a woman reading this, you know the sigh well.
It's the sigh that whispers, "I just want him to
care enough to really see who I am."
It's the primal need to be known, to be
valued, to be accepted just as you are.
What Women Want Men to Know.
Dr. Beverly DeAngelis, PhD

Of course, women want to be seen and known and valued and accepted just as they are. Women have sent out this message for decades, but have you heard *anybody* suggest that a male wants to be seen, known, valued, and accepted for who *he* is? No? Thought not! The one-sided demand is preposterous in light of the barrage of criticism feminists have heaped upon men over the last fifty years. The feminist efforts to feminize you (and all the other males) is the opposite of women accepting you "...just as you are."

Presumably, Dr. DeAngelis and many other women believe that men are failing their female companions, and I could not agree more. Sadly, Doctor DeAngelis is on the wrong track if she thinks that making males more feminine is the answer to every woman's dream. The underlying cause of these failures is the unrelenting tide of feminism that has been systematically destroying the foundation upon which masculine behavior is built. Males have been vilified for decades. The feminists demand that males conform to some mythological *ideal* they themselves dreamed up, and damn to hell 100,000 years of masculine biology. You have no doubt heard cries like the following leveled at you, or at males in general, from more than one woman:

- When will you grow up?
- You only want one thing!
- You are so stupid!
- You just don't get it!
- You never listen to me!
- You don't do enough to help me!
- I do way more than my fair share in this family!
- All you do is watch TV and play video games!

I have heard words like these too many times to count. It's only a short leap from one of these starting points to a woman deciding, "Dammit, you [boyfriend, husband, or lover] are not giving me what I want." In a heartbeat, you become (take a deep breath) … a *project.*

Being a Project

Be not angry that you can't make others as you wish them to be, since you can't make yourself as *you* wish to be.

Thomas à Kempis (emphasis added)

If you become a woman's project, she will try to *fix* you. In the process, she will feminize you by pushing you to behave like her girlfriend, which will kill *any* chance you have of remaining (or becoming) a Man. A woman can no more tell you how to be a Man than you can tell her cat how to be a cat.

So how does a woman go about fixing you when you become her project? She begins by feminizing your expression (the way you speak, especially to her), your manner (the way you move and react to whatever happens, especially to her), and your naturalness (masculine behavior is bad; feminine behavior is better). If you accept her control, the capital M in your Man status will start to shrink (and your M will not be the only thing that shrinks). If you allow her to make you kinder, gentler, softer, you will soon become unmoored from your masculinity. Even if you were a Man when she began to fix you, if you yield to her efforts, your capital 'M' will shrink and you will become a confused man once more. But worse is to come—even if you do *exactly* as she asks, she will become more and more disappointed in you because she was asking for the wrong thing. If you are lucky, she will leave you. If the relationship continues, you will both end up miserable. Trust me, she will never be happy with you in the long term unless you are a Man and no woman can teach how to be a Man.

Does this mean you can learn nothing from your woman? Of course not! I hope your woman can teach you a great deal. The difference between being a woman's project and being a Man is that *you* decide when and what to change. If a woman tries to "should" you into changing, she is not interested in you. She is interested in her misbegotten ideal of who she thinks she would like you to be. If you accept her direction, you will become more and more feminine, and then she will reject you. If this progression feels like someone dumped fifty pounds of frozen fish down your pants, you are right. That is what being a project feels like. Don't allow yourself to become a project. If your woman insists on treating you as a project, walk away. Some suggestions for my female readers:

- If you are fixing a male stop. You have no idea how to fix him. You would have more luck fixing Middle East politics.
- If you think your male needs fixing, walk away. Find a Man; he does not need to be fixed.
- Even if your male gives you exactly what you ask for, when your male-fix fails, you will judge it to be *his* failure. Why? Because you asked for the wrong things and pushed him in the wrong direction. You don't want a project male, so don't make your male into one.
- If you find a man with every quality you think you want and none of the qualities you don't want, walk away; he is too feminine and totally confused. (Tip: get yourself a girlfriend because she will better meet your specifications).
- After you spend years trying to fix him, your man will be a proto-man. He will be a half-constructed project that you will abandon. In the process of "fixing" him, you will have destroyed whatever masculine qualities he once had. His recovery from the damage you did to him will be a slow process.
- Be aware that if you are able to fix a man to your satisfaction, you will have become his mother and, henceforth, he will treat you as his mother. His mother prevented him from becoming a Man, and you have too.
- If your man is heart-centered and emotional, be aware that he may already be too feminine, and you will soon tire of him.
- For your man to match your specifications as a male, you will have to castrate him. If that is what you want, you deserve all you get.

If you are a feminist who has tried to fix the men in your life, ask yourself how it went. Poorly? Yes, I bet it did. The only way to help your man to be more like the Man you would like him to be is to become more feminine yourself. That means you stop fixing him, stop telling him what to do and how to behave, and focus on being the best and most feminine woman you can be. If you have to be masculine to survive at your work, learn how to drop that mantle and be feminine when you go home each night. You will not be happy with a man who lets you dominate him, and a Man won't tolerate your attempts to change or control him.

10

THE PENDULUM SWINGS

Self-doubt is a persuasive mistress;
careful not to shag her or you'll never get your balls back.
Simon Hunt
English Rugby Union star player

The Pendulum

You go through many different stages in your life, and each stage has its own stresses, burdens, and responsibilities. Because we no longer have rites of passage in the Western world, advancing from one stage to another often goes unnoticed and unheralded. You don't become a Man at any set age. Some teenagers are already Men. Some adult males will never be Men. You may become a Man at 16 or 66. It's also possible that you were once a Man, but you stumbled and became a man again (this is most likely to happen when you allow a woman to change you). It takes effort to maintain your status as a Man, and if you stop trying, you will lose your capital M.

Interestingly, something just might be happening in the Western world that could start a new balance between the sexes. At a minimum, it appears the pendulum has stopped swinging further against the masculine. What is causing this change? Largely fueled by the blogosphere and the willingness of some Men to push back against feminism, males are starting to claw back some of the masculinity they have lost.

Rollo Tomassi's book, *The Rational Male,* takes the position that men have been gullible dupes for too long; they have certainly allowed women to win the media fight over the last 50 years. *The Rational Male* may seem misogynistic to many readers, and many women will find the intensity of the commentary to be particularly challenging. Nevertheless, the book is worth reading. At a minimum, Tomassi is waking men up to what is going on, and his is one of the most prominent voices leading men back to their natural masculinity. The revival of masculinity may yet save western Manhood from extinction. No matter what you think of the way the message is expressed, both men and women will be better for understanding Tomassi's point of view. It may well be the first step on the road back to Manhood for many men.

Women have outplayed males in the western world for at least the last 50 years. The reawakening of men from their slumber is not yet a counter-revolution because the mainstream media are terrified of saying anything critical of feminism, presumably because they are afraid of losing their female audience. But the emasculation of adult males seems to be slowing, with some men becoming Men again.

Paradoxically, Men who refuse to behave the way women say they want them to behave, are the Men who attract women like bees to a picnic! At the same time, women are beginning to sense that the emasculation of men has not served them well and that the deconstruction of masculinity has gone too far. In addition, men are learning to stand their ground against the subtle power of critical women. In short, they are waking up to the need to become Men. As I mentioned earlier, I suggest a critical look at the documentary *The Red Pill.* I learned a great deal from it, as did the feminist woman who made it. It's essential viewing, in my opinion, even if you don't agree with all you hear.

As the pendulum of power between the sexes begins its swing toward the center, we can expect some chaos as a new relationship between the sexes emerges. It would be best if the pendulum stopped somewhere in the center so we have balance. When this happens, Men will no longer be confused and will be able to once again stand in their power, without shame or guilt. At the same time, women can regain their innate humanity as powerful, feminine women, who no longer have to carry as much of society's burden as they have inflicted upon themselves for the last fifty years.

The Remasculation of Males

A Man never lets a woman put his balls in her pocket.
Luis Sosa

To begin your remasculation[1], you must find your balls, and put them back where they belong. Once your balls are back under your control, you will find it much easier to set your inner Man free. You don't have to be loutish, crass, controlling, or bullying to win your balls back. Just be a Man, without shame or guilt, and be proud of it. A few men have already found the key to their prison cells, cast off their chains, and become Men. To do so, they had to steel themselves against criticism from the feminists who dominate the media. What is so wonderful about the Men who have bravely chosen to do so, is that the women who know them find they love their Men more than ever.

Now it's your turn. You must become your own master and decide where your train is headed and what you want out of your life. This is not about being self-centered, unfeeling, or uncaring. On the contrary, if you are to become a Man, you have to be open to feel; you have to care about others, and you have to care about yourself.

---

1 Remasculation: My word for the process by which an emasculated male puts his balls back where they belong.

Stress

In the last one hundred years—and at an accelerating pace in the last fifty years—women have played an ever greater role in the workplace at all levels. To do so, they had to develop skills and adopt a persona that was different from what made a great woman, wife, or mother, a hundred years ago. Men also had to change in response to these societal upheavals, which dramatically altered both work and home life. The new work/life balance pushes a male to behave in a more feminine way as he tries to respond to the needs of his working wife, while at the same time his wife behaves in a more masculine way as she tries to survive and prosper in the workplace.

The rebalancing of family responsibilities (work, chores, parenting, and so on) that has occurred in the last fifty years has resulted in an imbalance that was bound to strain relationships. To survive, many couples have found that to have a family with two working parents, they must pay for day care, gardeners, and babysitters out of taxed income, which means the family "fun money" is probably less than it was fifty years ago, even though couples are now working harder than ever. The extra load has been too much for many couples, and the result is domestic tension and marital strife. I have recently heard the early rumblings that some people (mostly the millennial generation) are realizing that the society we have created is not serving us as well as we hoped. Could this be the first movement back to a better work/life balance. Only time will tell.

Marriage

Just under half of all marriages end up in divorce. If airplanes crashed at the same rate as marriages fail, we would ban them from ever taking off. While the divorce rate and the infidelity rate have rocketed upward over the last fifty years, the situation is actually much worse. In *Marriage Confidential*, Haag states that most couples are locked in a relationship that is not good enough to make them happy but not bad enough to leave. Haag states that the only glue holding many marriages together is the fear of economic and emotional catastrophe following a divorce. The fear plays a major role in keeping couples yoked together like two oxen dragging their cart through a marital wasteland. We can't know precisely how many couples endure miserable, unsatisfying marriages while they wait for their marriage, or their partner, to die (Haag's book suggests it's a large majority of marriages, which would put it in the tens of millions in the US alone). While these marriages have been dead on a romantic and emotional level for decades, fear trumps all, and the couple stays married because of: the children, mortgage, religion, or inertia. These are not love-relationships, they are business arrangements.

The solution to society's marital woes is not to force women to stay home and look after the house and the children. Neither is it to make men give up their masculinity. The solution lies in making Men, so that women can drop their masculine mantle and be women again. When they are with Men, women naturally become "Women" with a nice big W!

Milestones

In the United States, boys move from grade school to middle school to high school, with graduation ceremonies to mark each occasion. They get a driver's permit and license. They go to their prom and graduate from high school. They get a job or go to college, and before they know it, they are twenty-one. These milestones may seem significant to a boy at the time (who can forget the exhilaration of taking a group of friends out in the car for the first time?), but they are not rites of passage. For example, there is no rite of passage for a boy who turns twenty-one; surviving the alcoholic deluge at his birthday celebration does not count as a rite of passage. Even though there may be pleasure and satisfaction associated with each milestone, these are mere events, and they have nothing to do with becoming a Man.

Historically, a boy would transition from boyhood to Manhood long before his twenty-first birthday. Unfortunately, although boys may always have developed later than the girls of their contemporary eras, in the last fifty years, too many boys have stayed in their childhood far too long. Sadly, if being a child is *too* comfortable, a boy may remain a boy forever. Recall the popular feature films that have had the theme of men who never grow up: *Failure to Launch* (in which a thirty-five-year-old man lives at home and refuses to grow up) is but one example. Stars like Adam Sandler, Owen Wilson, and Vince Vaughn have starred as adult men who are still wearing their metaphorical short pants. These adult characters are funny, but they are not Men. What is sad is that many men watching these movies are able to relate to what they are seeing on the screen because they live a life similar to that portrayed.

While some modern boys grow up to become Men, in the last few generations it has become common for adult males to remain boys for decades. Gone are the days when I cycled to school in the sleet or steamy heat. For the past forty years (or more), boys have been bussed or chaperoned to all their activities (at least until they could drive). Parents structure their son's time from wake-up to lights out. Boys rarely play in an unstructured environment without adult supervision. Their school day is also highly structured, with no time for rough-and-tumble play and little time to *hang out* with other children. Recently, some schools have cut recess time and instituted a shorter lunch break, which are disasters for school-age boys because it leaves them no time to bond with their peers.

As a result of such changes, a boy growing up now lacks many of the basic life-skills that boys learned by playing with other boys fifty years ago. Time spent playing is not just *playing* for a developing boy. Think of all the things a boy loses when he spends no time with other boys in unstructured play:

- Resiliency: This is necessary after a fall or a failure such as those life doles out.
- Independence: Lack of independence means he doesn't learn to figure out for himself what he can do and can't do.
- Leadership: Being a useful member of a team and learning to lead a team are masculine skills. Leadership is a skill that takes many years to develop because it involves trial and error, with multiple failures and successes.
- Negotiation skills: He never learns to influence a group that he does not control.
- Risk assessment: Without exposure to risk, he never learns to assess his chances of success.
- Dispute resolution: Because adults control most outcomes for a boy they are supervising, he never learns to plan what he wants to do, or even how to resolve disputes by himself.

Exacerbating the difficulties a boy faces today, are the many hours he spends in the company of electronic media. Finally—and most tragic of all—a boy spends little or no time with his father and other Men, learning how Men interact with each other and the world around them. A boy must master these basic skills to become a Man, and a modern boy has few opportunities to do so.

My father was a golf fanatic. He played almost every day, and once the "bug" got him, we did not see much of him at home (I mostly saw him at work). I didn't like to play golf. It was boring and took too long. The fact that I could not hit the ball where I wanted it to go did not help! However, on the many evenings when my father took me to play as a young teen, I really enjoyed spending time in the bar after we had finished our game (being in the bar when I was so young was not illegal in a private British club). There were always other Men in the bar, and I was encouraged to join in their conversation and express my views, which I did on a variety of subjects. My exposure to these accomplished Men (senior corporate executives, successful business owners, a nuclear engineer, and more) helped form my character and informed my thinking. Such social involvement with Men almost never happens for boys in the United States. It is one of the unintended consequences of the puritanical US drinking laws that the social aspects of boys mixing with Men in a bar setting is that it can't legally happen until the boy is twenty-one years old, by which time he has his own group of friends. There is almost no time available for a maturing boy to spend significant time with a group of intergenerational Men.

My heart aches for the boys who are growing up now! The fathers of these boys may themselves be struggling with the confusion this book addresses, which means they will be unable to teach their sons how to be Men.

Stages

Here are the various stages that you, as a developing Man, will go through. Although setbacks can happen at any age, remember that growth and expansion can happen at any age too (often when you least expect it). So keep your mind open, and be willing to receive the growth and expansion messages when they arrive.

In your teens: In your teen years, you may have heard someone say, "These are the best days of your life. Enjoy them while you can." The essence of this message from your family, pastors, and teachers is that life becomes progressively worse. Whoever is mouthing this cliché is usually saying it when you already feel bad about something (bad grade, workplace termination, or a fight with a friend). Therefore, the message is, "I know you think this is bad now, but don't worry, it will soon be worse." What a depressing concept. The idea that childhood is better than adulthood is ridiculous. Life is better when you are an autonomous adult, with free will and a life that you control. If your adult life is actually worse than your childhood, it may be because you are confused, and it is never too late to change that.

In your twenties, you are forward-looking. Your possibilities are endless, and your world is a huge unfinished painting that could become a watercolor, an abstract, or, if you are not careful, *a still life*. At this young age, you are trying to figure out how to relate to your work, parents, siblings, friends, and lovers, all while trying to figure out who you are yourself. You don't spend much time looking backward. Instead, you look to the future. You have dreams, plans, and aspirations (you do, don't you?). The world is yours to conquer even though you know there is much to learn. You probably feel that the adults you know can teach you little. You are also likely to believe that your parents are has-beens whose sex life ended the day they conceived you. The idea of people as old as your parents having sex is unimaginable (and at least mildly nauseating) for young people.

As a teenage boy, you probably assumed that everything would be better once you could make your own decisions (I certainly did). You dreamed of an income, friends, and sex. So what happened? Did your demonic boss stop your career in its tracks? Did your long-term girlfriend walk out on you? Did your friends desert you too? Whatever your personal situation, when the benefits you assumed would accrue as an adult failed to materialize on schedule, you may have felt that all was lost. This is the time when resilience and courage count. Success takes time. Don't quit. Once you fire up your train, and set off down the track, everything will get better.

You may not have a job, much less a career, and your net worth is almost zero, but the world is at your feet, and you have taken some early steps to adulthood. If something bad happens to disturb this rosy picture, it may cause you to have doubts, especially when you look at *successful* people and realize how hard it will be for you to become as successful as they are. Doubt may also come from a bad boss, a lousy job, or the end of a treasured relationship. Whatever the trigger, when you see no way to navigate the road ahead, the seeds of doubt will start to grow—but only if you let them.

If your lovers and lovemaking turn out to be uninspiring, you will assume that your female partners are to blame. You can reduce the chances of a bad relationship affecting your future relationships by learning about women and how to interact with them. You don't need a woman to complete you, but you must spend time in the company of women because if you ignore them, you will be a poor companion and lover later. To be successful in your relationships, you need to know how to move in the right direction (with masculine power and a deep understanding of yourself and your partner) and at the right tempo. The good news is that if you did not learn about women while you were young, there is time to catch up. There are thousands of workshops and other resources to help you. Once you do the work to become a Man, it will all be much clearer.

Females graduate from high school and college at higher rates than males, and they develop in other areas earlier than males. As a result, when you are a twenty-something male hanging out with a twenty-something woman, you may find that the woman seems wiser, more knowledgeable, and more grounded than you. If thoughts like these have occurred to you, don't worry. They occur to most men, in one form or another. It is true that young women tend to be intellectually and emotionally more mature than males of the same age, but males catch up eventually. You are going to be fine if you are authentic, centered, and growing; in other words, when you have a train and you are going somewhere, you will be more than a match for a woman, however old or advanced she is.

In your thirties, the details may not be clear yet, but if you aren't already a Man, you can make huge leaps forward in your efforts to become one. By now, you have a sense of how your life is going to work out. Your first job has come and gone, and if your train is heading where you want to go, life starts to make more sense, economically and socially. You may suffer some setbacks here and there, especially in the fluid work environment of today, but if you hold on to your status as a Man, life will soon be good again.

If you elect to leave your job to further your goals, you will feel good because you have *chosen* a new destination. Your confidence is intact, and you believe in yourself. You know you will succeed in the end. As a resilient Man, you will overcome the inevitable setbacks as they occur. Even if you change direction, you pursue your new direction with all the energy and means at your disposal. No matter what, you do not quit!

No Idling

"I am confidently expecting something to turn up."
Mr. Micawber in David Copperfield
Charles Dickens

A Man does not wait for "something to turn up" because he, not chance, controls his life. As a developing Man, you know you need much more than a job to be fulfilled. You need to interact with other males. You must seek out solid male friends (including some Men I hope). You also know that you want your life to have a purpose. You know you can't sit back like Mr. Micawber. Good things come to you because you seek them, not because you need them! Your train runs on a fuel called *desire*, and one of your desires must be personal growth. If you keep growing, you will become a better Man than you already are. Another desire is to drive your train down the track to your next destination. Even if you run out of fuel before you arrive at your destination, at least you were busy being born. Keep searching.

I was flying high (literally and figuratively) in my Royal Air Force career, but when an international fuel crisis grounded me, I realized that the Royal Air Force was undervalued by the government. While I sat on the ground for weeks, I spent time pondering my future and scouring the jobs section of the newspaper trying to find a new direction. I wanted a career that was not dependent on the government. When I found one I resigned my commission and went to work as a chartered accountant in London (like a CPA in the United States).

From soaring in the blue sky over the green fields of England to pushing dusty pieces of paper around in an office was, without doubt, going from the sublime to the ridiculous. I loathed my accounting work, and the exams I had to pass were brutally hard. I eventually got a job with a US company and the company moved me to the US in 1980. Subsequently, my career suffered massive swings between success and failure, and from prosperity to penury and back again (creative destruction is truly the American way).

No matter what happened, I always had a train. I never wavered or slowed down in my effort to succeed, and my family provided a supportive environment throughout. I was the exact opposite of Mr. Micawber. I did not wait for something to turn up. Either I went out and found it, or I created it.

Mentors

Mentors can make a huge difference in your life, if you let them. Mentors may simply be role models for you to emulate at work and in life. Other mentors may comment on your behavior or what to do in a particular situation. It's your choice whether to act on what they say. If you are eager to learn from mentors, help them to know you better.

I have benefited from numerous mentors and role models throughout my life, and I treasure their contributions to who I became. I also had wonderful guidance from many in my extended family, and from my friends, both male and female.

The guidance I received often stung at the time I received it, but I always listened and learned. I also benefited from spending time with women at every stage of my life, and I started young. Unlike every other boy I knew, there was never a time when I thought girls had cooties. When I was eight years old, I had two girlfriends at the same time. I took them, together, to meet my mother. So cute! As I grew up, I often spent time with girls and listened to what they had to say because they knew things I didn't know; in fact, they seemed to know a lot of things I didn't know! I didn't know it at the time, but these girls and women were mentoring me. I don't think they knew it either.

In the Resources section at the back of this book, you will find a list of workshops where you may find teachers and mentors who are right for you. You can become a mentor yourself in organizations such as the Civil Air Patrol, Little League, ROTC, Boy Scouts, Boys to Men (boystomen.org), YMCA. As you help these boys and men to develop, you will learn a lot about yourself.

Just Say Yes

Life as a Man is not an event. It's a journey, and saying *yes* more often will help you on your journey. Try to say *yes* to every opportunity that offers you the chance to learn something. Things might not all work out as you'd hoped, but you will learn from the failures too. When you are centered and resilient, nothing will hurt you too badly, so just say *yes* more often. Whatever happens, the sun will still come up in the morning.

Your Opinion Matters

If you are like many thirty-something men, you will find a partner, marry, and start a family. The marriage itself can be daunting. You may first experience a loss of control when your future wife and her mother take over the wedding planning. Because you are male, you are assumed to be clueless about weddings, after all

"This is *her* day?" If you cede control over this important event, it's the beginning of the end of your autonomy. Your wedding is important to you too, so right from the outset, don't accept the tyranny of your future wife and her mother, or you will pay a heavy price down the road. Behave as you mean to live when the wedding is over. If that means calling off the wedding, do it! You are a Man, not a naïve rube.

Support

If you are in your thirties and have a train, having a strong woman on the footplate with you can help keep the fire burning. Her support of your train and direction can make the journey far easier. You don't *need* her all the time but she can provide support and advice on those occasions when you need a friendly nudge. Sometimes, the advice will infuriate you. Whenever anyone calls you out, it never feels good at the time, but it is usually worth listening to what they say. You may be surprised how much you have learned from people who pointed out your shortcomings.

At age forty, you pass what seems like a major milestone—*the Big Four-O*. A Man is careful not to let it become the Big Four-Ugh! Your fortieth birthday is when others make jokes about your sexual prowess (and impending lack thereof). People intend for these jibes to be amusing, but some of them sting because even if they don't apply to you now, you suspect they will soon become a reality. However, as a Man with a solid hold on the attributes we have discussed so far, you deal with life as it comes. Even if your job is consuming you, even if you struggle in your role as a father, and even if you have had a few failures along the way, you keep going. If you have children, the rewards of raising them will come when they are successful adults, but you will probably see them begin their journey when you are in your forties.

Keep Going and Pay It Forward

At forty, you also feel that not only is the first half of your life over, but that it went by in a flash. It may feel like your tenth birthday was just last week. Maintain your focus on living your life as a Man; after all, this life is the only one you can be certain you will ever have. Decide to get the most out of your life, and give back to the world whatever you have to offer. When you are busy being born, you will make mistakes. Don't sweat the mistakes. People who are growing make them all the time. Learn from them and try not to repeat them. Put your head down, and charge forward. Growing older is not for the weak, but the alternative to getting older is bleak indeed.

Complacency? Never!

If you think you have achieved everything you wanted in your life (spouse, children, house, bank balance, and good friends), beware. Forty is too soon to be settling for what you already have. If you become complacent, you'll be busy dying. A lack of growth, dreams, and aspirations means a slow death. Don't stop being born. There are new people to meet, new challenges at work and at play, and never-ending opportunities to learn something new. In short, your life is about to take off from that great foundation you have built. Your train is picking up speed, and you are not going to let anything stop you. Here is a real example of what can happen to you if you let it:

Francis and Alice had been married for 30 years. Alice frequently told Francis, "We are living the perfect life. I don't want to change a thing." When he heard Alice say this, Francis cringed. He still had multiple trains running down various tracks. He had dreams for his future, and he was committed to his personal growth. Complacency was not an option for him. Francis and Alice divorced a few years later. It was the only way Francis could continue his journey.

In your fifties, you can assess where you stand vis-à-vis your goals for family, work, and even yourself. You probably know whether your children will be successful. You will have memories about any woman you left or lost, especially after a long relationship. You will also be able to assess your current relationship, if you have one. You will probably have a good idea whether your retirement will be economically secure or disastrous.

Where Do I Go From Here?

This is a good time to ask yourself, "Am I done? Am I satisfied with my life? Do I just coast along until I die?" These questions come up because your fifties are when you are most likely to enter a midlife crisis—the so-called male menopause. The medical community is divided on whether male menopause is a real medical condition (if it is real, it's usually attributed to declining testosterone levels). Whatever the medical experts say, don't give up at fifty years of age; there is too much life left to live. If you are already a Man, don't stop striving; strive to become a better Man. Give yourself permission to develop new skills, meet new people, and do new things. For example, it's not too late to study masculinity, sexuality, and relationships. If you give up and stop growing, the warehouse of the dying awaits your arrival. Which is it to be—another train to an exciting new destination or a ticket to the warehouse?

Life is a mystery that will unfold over time. If you remain open to something new and actively seek it out, opportunities will pop up out of nowhere, often when you least expect them. New friends will come into your life. Keep growing, learning, and developing—or die; it's your choice!

At sixty years old and older, the temptation is to conclude that your life (or work life, at least) is over and that everything significant in your life has happened already. If you don't recall the

"I'm Not Dead" scene from the film *Monty Python and the Holy Grail* (EMI Films, 1975), watch it on YouTube,

> Dead Collector: Bring out yer dead!
> *[Large man appears with dead man over his shoulder.]*
> Large Man: Here's one.
> Dead Collector: Nine pence.
> Dead Man: I'm not dead.
> Dead Collector: What?
> Large Man: Nothing. There's your nine pence. *[He hands the Dead Collector his money.]*
> Dead Man: I'm not dead!
> Dead Collector: 'Ere, 'e says 'e's not dead.
> Large Man: Yes, he is.
> Dead Man: I'm not.

Don't slip into the trap of assuming your life is over when you turn sixty. You are not dead yet! You are only just beginning to contribute the important stuff to your family and the world. The space to expand is wide open, and the time to accept the challenge is now. Take the time to reflect on opportunities taken and missed. This is the time to try again if it didn't work first time around. You may also reflect on your loves and lovers. Did you choose your lovers well? Did you give your lovers the best you had to offer? Was your marriage a success? Were you there for your children when they needed you? Were you a Man? Are you still a Man?

No Regrets

As you reflect on your life so far, you will know there have been times when you have not behaved well. Whatever you did that fell short of your own standards, give away the associated guilt or shame, as I described in Chapter 7. If you realize you could have achieved more than you have so far, don't give up. Allow yourself to be disappointed that you didn't try harder to succeed, and pledge to try harder in future. There are opportunities in abundance if you will only seek them out. Look forward to the future you plan to enjoy. I know Men in their seventies and eighties who are still growing and learning. Some of them are still working and enjoying an income they never expected. More important, they are still challenging themselves to become better Men. Whatever time you have, spend it wisely by constantly learning and growing, then pass on what you know to someone else.

Life is a Mystery to be Lived, not a Problem to be Solved[2]

Whatever your age, you always have much to learn. Almost nothing that happened to me after I was forty-five was what I expected. In fact, so much has happened in my sixties, it's difficult to contemplate how much my life has changed. Whatever else, it has never been dull, and the pace of change in my life today is greater than ever. As you do the work to become a Man, or become a better Man, your life will be exhilarating. Don't worry if your life becomes messy for a while as you grow; growth and change are often messy. If you are still inauthentic at times or if you are unsure about what you want, you may become frustrated. Fear not. Keep living until you actually need the Dead Collector's services. If you have already quit, get back in the game, or join those miserable men in the warehouse of the dying.

---

2 Often attributed to Adriana Trigiani.

11

STORY

Mother, do you think they'll try to break my balls?
Mother, should I build a wall?
Mother
Pink Floyd

If you believe that you have repressed memories, or you just need help to discover the source of your story, please see a licensed therapist.

What Is a Story?

We make countless mistakes as we go through life. We commit social blunders that make us look naïve or worse. Our partners, lovers, and friends hurt us in many ways, as we hurt them. When we fail, others make us pay for our mistakes, and the pain may seem unbearable. Usually, of course, whatever mistakes we make, we are able to make peace with ourselves and keep going but you are probably still carrying scars on your psyche because of what happened to you or what you did. If so, you may have created a *story*, and your story can ruin your life.

A life may contain many stories. One example is a "Poor Me" story: "It's happened to me before, so it's bound to happen again." Another story might be, "My mother controlled me as a child and is still trying to control me now." Other stories sound something like this:

- I always screw up. I never do anything right. What I do always turns to shit.
- Everyone is mean to me. People pick on me. Nobody wants to be my friend.
- Men are angry and out of control.
- Women are manipulative and controlling.
- Women are stupid.
- Women only want me for my provision and protection.

Whatever it is, your story will ruin your life if you allow it to control your present because your story can taint every aspect of your life.

Interestingly, your story may not have happened the way you remember it. Even if you recall what happened with crystal clarity, you have probably enhanced the facts over the years and made it a *better* story (e.g., you have made everything about your story worse than the reality). Maybe you added some ego-spin on the facts to deflect blame onto someone else (because your story is *almost* never your fault).

- It was not my fault. *She* was angry all the time.
- *Her* constant complaining caused our relationship to fail.
- I didn't do anything wrong. *She* never listened to me.

One Man's Story

Stories are powerful and can hold you in their thrall for decades or forever. How bad can a story be?

Hush now baby, baby don't you cry
Mother's gonna make all of your nightmares come true
Mother
Pink Floyd

Here is Matt's story:

Matt is a manager with a large multinational company. Before he was born, his older sister died. Throughout his childhood, Matt's mother told him, "You will never be as good as your sister." How could he compete with his deceased sister because, of course, she *never* made a mistake or screwed up at school.

Matt is a handsome man with a good sense of humor, but his life was a train wreck because his story affected everything he did. For example, Matt loves to chat, but he found it impossible to initiate a conversation. Left alone, he would stare in a trancelike state for long periods, gazing at some distant vision that betrayed his inner turmoil. He simply could not walk up to someone at a party and just say, "Hi. I'm Matt."

In his early fifties, Matt realized that his story had him in its viselike grip, but he was unable to let it go. He had seen counselors for decades, but none of them was able to help him shed his story. Fortunately, he met Sean and Sandra, two friends who had the spiritual depth and understanding to help him. Sean provided the masculine model for Matt, and Sandra became the silver lining in his large black cloud. She refused to let him lean on his story to explain his quirky behavior. Over time, with some bumps along the way, Sean and Sandra helped Matt shake off his story. Once he was free of his story's death grip, he discovered that many women found him attractive (more than one woman described him to me as a "catch"). Matt set his inner Man free and became the Man he was always meant to be. Although it was brutally hard at the time, when Matt chose to fight for his life and kill his story, he succeeded, even though his story had ruled his life for fifty years. That is a testament to a Man's determination. Go, Matt!

If your story, like Matt's, is real (i.e., something that actually happened to you), it might manifest now in a variety of ways. For example, you might think:

- Women are crazy.

- Women always want to control me.
- The guys at work are stupid.
- I never know what to say when I am with a woman so they reject me.
- I always get hurt in a relationship.

Stop trying to figure out why you think these things. It is time to jettison this baggage (because it *is* just baggage). For example, if your story is that women always try to control you, you will interpret everything your woman does according to that preconceived belief. Women are not all crazy or trying to control you; it's just your story running your life. And women do not try to control Men, because they know it would be futile. Try to figure out where your story came from. If the source of your story is a mystery to you, you may have suppressed the memory or simply forgotten. Happily, you don't have to know the source. You just have to know the essence of your story to let it go. You can't become a Man until you identify your story and give it away. There are ceremonial ways to give away your story, which we will discuss below.

Story as a Crutch

In addition to holding you back, you may lean on your story like a crutch when things are not going well. You may be wondering how a story that is holding you back could also be a crutch that you lean on for support. Here is the reality: When you have a story and things go wrong, it is never *your* fault. You simply blame your story. "It's not me who is hurting you. It's my [lover/mother/father/boss/friend] who did this terrible thing to me years ago."

Giving Your Story Away

You give away your story in the same way you forgave yourself and others in Chapter 7. In other words, you create a ceremonial space. Identify all the players and all the details of your story, then say or shout out the names of the players, and the details of your story as you watch them go down that drain hole. If you are struggling to let your story go, there is help, even if you don't have Sean and Sandra by your side. If you feel you need a group ceremony to give away your story, I urge you to go to a workshop that incorporates such activity and participate fully in the process. Amara Charles does wonderful work in this area. Another great resource is a couple, John Kent and Kristin Viken (for Amara, John and Kristin contact information, see Resources). I can tell you from personal experience that Amara, and John and Kristin really deliver potent practices to lower your defensive walls and eliminate the effects of your story. You may have to give away your story more than once, but for most people, once is enough. If you feel you need a licensed therapist, seek one out.

You don't have to erase your memory of what happened to you to let go of your story. The memory of your story is still there. You simply stop allowing your story to affect your current behavior, throw away your crutch, and become your authentic self instead of dancing to your story's tune. After you shed your story, you will be surprised how much easier your life is. You will be able to live in harmony with the people around you because you will have grown into harmony with yourself. This is such a huge step; feel free to pat yourself on the back and resolve never to let another story into your life.

Who Are You?

Paradoxically, it's difficult to learn who you really are at your core. Some easy questions to ask yourself as a starting point:

- What motivates me?
- Why am I here?
- What do I want?

- Do I have a train?
- Do I know where it's going?
- Did *I* choose where my train is going?
- Do I have more than one train?

Try to determine whether you are hurting from something that happened to you long ago:

- Who hurt me?
    - Parents
    - Other family members
    - Teachers
    - Friends
    - Religious leaders
    - Workplace supervisors
    - Co-workers
    - Enemies (both military and nonmilitary)
    - Lovers (lovers are the source of much pain)
- What effect did the hurt have on me at the time?
- What effect is the hurt having on me now?
- What did I learn from what happened?
- Who is hurting me now, and how are they doing it?
- Why do I still allow people to hurt me?
- What have I done to hurt others in my life?
- Why do I still hurt other people?
- When I hurt other people, why does it always end up hurting me?

While these questions focus on the negative events and pressures you have faced so far, you must recognize and accept all the good things that happened too. There are many other questions to ask yourself, but considering how you were hurt is a good place to start.

Living in the Past

Just sitting back trying to recapture a little of the glory of…
well time slips away
and leaves you with nothing, mister,
but boring stories of Glory Days
Glory Days
Bruce Springsteen

For a musical illustration of a glorious past, study the lyrics of Bruce Springsteen's "Glory Days," and promise yourself you will never become bogged down in "boring stories of Glory Days." And don't fall into the trap of thinking that only bad stories hurt you. Good stories can hurt you too. For example, if you believe that everything used to be better than it is now, you will carry that belief into every connection with another person. If you think everything used to be better, chances are you'll be right because your attachment to your past will dull your present. By all means, remember the past, but don't live there; live in the now. Be present with everything you do and everyone you meet. Don't become distracted by thoughts about another thing or another time. Mastering this one characteristic (being present at all times) will take you a long way down the road to a better life (more about presence later).

Now try these questions:

- What really matters to me now?
- What do I need to do to heal myself?
- What do I need to do to improve myself?
- Who are my friends?
- How do they help me?
- How do I help them?
- Who is precious to me now?
- Do I appreciate my good fortune?
- What do I want in my life?

    - o Partner/lover/wife/child
    - o Friend
    - o Happiness
    - o Satisfaction
    - o Growth
    - o Purpose
- Who might help me find what I want?
    - o Friends
    - o Lovers
    - o Family
    - o Teachers and guides
    - o Counselors
- What have I done right in my life?
- What good fortune have I enjoyed in my life?
- How am I building my life and my future?
- What am I learning about women, Men, spirituality?
- How am I improving my situation?
- What am I doing to enhance my relationship(s)?
- How committed am I to my train(s)?
- What example am I setting for others?
- How will I live, and what will I do in retirement?
- How will I live my life from this day forward?
    - o Be kind.
    - o Give more than I receive.
    - o Shine light wherever I see darkness.
    - o Be a good citizen/father/friend.
    - o Stoke my fire.
    - o Drive my train.

To gain insight into yourself, try the following to see if they work for you:

- Workshops
- Meet-up groups

- Salons (as I describe in this book)
- Martial arts
- Volunteer work
- Blogs, podcasts, and other internet sources

There is an enormous store of information and many tools available for you to use (many of which are inexpensive). Take advantage of these resources to grow. Answer the questions you posed (as listed above or otherwise) after deep reflection; they will help you discover your inner Man, who is, of course, the real *you*. There is always more to know, so keep searching. As you discover more of you, you will become brighter and shinier, and the M in your Man will grow ever bigger.

12

THE BROTHERHOOD OF MEN

A man needs "other men who won't settle for his bullshit."
The Way of the Superior Man
David Deida

AS A MAN, YOU ACCEPT and honor others as flawed human beings, just as you are flawed. They are fellow travelers on their journey, as you are on yours. You choose whether to spend time with them, but you respect them until they reveal that they are not worthy of your respect.

Rarely will a man acknowledge that he is a work in progress, but by now, I hope you are willing to admit that *you* are a work in progress—we are all a work in progress until the Dead Collector comes for us. Does this mean I have written these men off? The answer is a categorical *No*! I have tried to live as an example to them in the same way other Men have been examples to me. I have been determined to never "should" another male, wherever he is on the Man scale. If a male asks for my opinion, I tell him what I think of his situation, but I never tell him what to do (unless he asks me). Even when asked, I try to give a male the information and tools he needs to figure out what to do by himself.

When I pondered who helped me to become a Man, I realized that the list was longer than I thought, and much longer than there is space for here. My family included many remarkable people who were both amazing human beings and wonderful, caring models (grandparents, parents, brother, aunts, uncles, cousins), who helped me on my journey and helped me up when I stumbled. As I described earlier, I learned a lot from my father's employees and his friends, as well as numerous school friends. When I put on my big-boy pants as an RAF officer, I learned how to behave from my senior and junior colleagues. Many wonderful sportsmen that I played with, and against, taught me about manliness and fairness. In addition, throughout my life I constantly learned from my friends. From this vast group of people, I learned how to live as a Man until I eventually became one. I owe them all a king's ransom for their patience and their perseverance. I hope to repay some of their kindness by bringing this book to you, so you can follow your own path and become a Man.

Over the years, I learned what *not* to do by watching confused men act like children—men unable to relate to women; mindless drunks; men addicted to sports, television, or video games; men with no train or purpose; men who lacked intellectual, spiritual, or emotional curiosity; men who lacked the confidence to stand in their power; men who had lost their spark; and men who lacked vigor. These men were all in the warehouse of the dying and seemed to be resigned to their fate. All of them could have fought their way out of that warehouse but all had chosen to stay right where they were, waiting for the Dead Collector to cart them away. This book is an attempt to help these men find their train and get it started down the track.

Alpha Males

I like spending time with alpha males. Doing so has helped me become a better Man. An Alpha Male never forces a solution on anyone, except (perhaps) in a crisis. They are often able to help others solve problems by the strength of their character alone. If you feel that you become somehow *less* when you are with an alpha male, please consider changing your thinking. Seek out alpha males and spend as much time with them as you can. Doing so cannot hurt you, and you are likely to learn a lot from them. A side benefit is that you may make a great new friend. If you shy away from alpha males, you still have a way to go to become a Man.

Models and Commentators

When other people see how you behave and then try to emulate your behavior (i.e., you are not telling them what to do), you are a role model ("model") for those people. Not all model behavior is positive. For example, a model may exhibit a characteristic you wish to avoid, such as a short temper. Whether their influence is positive or negative, if you change your future behavior because of what you observed someone do, that person was a model for you.

On the other hand, a commentator will tell you what they think of your behavior, whether you asked for their opinion or not. For example, a commentator might say, "Stop looking so sad all the time. It scares the women away." When you receive advice from commentators, try not to reject it out of hand; they may be right. However, don't allow a commentator to "should" you out of your authenticity or naturalness. You only change your behavior because *you* choose to change.

It's generally easier to accept what models have to offer because you can come to your own conclusions about your behavior in your own time. A commentator creates pressure to conform, which may cause you to reject some good advice. In this book, when I describe how I behave in my life, I am modeling behavior you might consider emulating. When I suggest you adopt certain behaviors, I do so as a commentator. Both men and boys need to see Man-behavior in order to emulate it. So please step up your game, become a Man, and model Man behavior for the men you know.

Kinship and Friendship

Treat all adult males as brothers, and support them when they need it. Accept their support too. This is how kinship works. If you are open to kinship with your brothers, new friendships will follow. This is what humans (the most social of animals) do in a healthy society; it's a highly desirable process. Your kinship with other males will affect how you feel about *your* place in the world. Obviously, if you want kinship, you have to meet other males and spend time with them so you get to know them on a deeper level. Your workplace may be an easy starting point for meeting male friends (especially if you work for a large company), but clubs (tennis, athletics, golf, hiking, meet-up groups by the score) are also good places to meet fellow travelers.

Praise is a wonderful social lubricant. Giving praise when it is due will help establish friendships you might otherwise miss. Don't hesitate to let a fellow traveler know how much you admired what he did, and watch him grow shinier as he basks in your praise. Praise costs you nothing and may help set someone's inner Man free, or help a Man become a better Man. Just be sincere.

To become a friend to an adult male, you must learn about him in all his complexity. Only then can you decide how he *feels* to you. If you opt not to become his friend, you owe it to yourself to figure out why. Did you judge him for things he can't control, such as how tall he is or the color of his skin, or did you judge him for things he can control, such as his behavior? Whatever your reason, you ought to be aware of it.

As Deida points out, a male needs other males who "...won't settle for his bullshit." Just don't expect thanks when you question someone's bullshit. A male will be embarrassed or even triggered by your observation, but give him a chance, as others have done for you. If you try to help a male several times to no avail, let him continue his journey without your help. You do not want a man to become your project.

As you step into your power as a Man, you will naturally become more interested in other people (and they in you). You may find this difficult at first, second-guessing yourself. "Will she be offended if I talk to her?" or "Will he reject me if I reach out to him?" You will never know where that conversation may have taken you if you never start it. Wherever you are, provided you can do it without being patronizing or creepy, take a chance, and talk to someone. Many people will sense your openness and respond by engaging in conversation because they don't feel threatened by you. You may also be surprised at the coincidences that occur in your life as result of your openness. By taking the chance and speaking to someone, you will grow a little too.

All-In, All the Time

A man is often afraid of trying something new because he fears failure. As a Man, you are all-in, all the time, and that feels good to you. You don't fear failure because failing does not make you less of a Man even if it temporarily derails your train. If you try to do something and it works, congratulate yourself and move on to the next thing. If it doesn't work, try again, or try something else. Here is an example of a young man learning from his father how to be all-in, all the time.

Monty was the center for the high school basketball team. He was an excellent player because of his father's influence (his dad, Kevin, had been a professional coach, and he had taught his son well).

When Monty threw a bad pass in the final seconds of the game, the other team intercepted it, strolled down the court and scored an easy basket to win by a point. Monty felt he had let down both his team and his father. After the game, when he asked his father about the error, his father said, "Monty, you played really well tonight. You were the only player on your team willing to try something. It didn't all work out as you hoped, but that's okay. Many of the boys on your team didn't do anything wrong because they didn't do anything at all. I would be far more critical of your performance if you had been afraid to try."

Monty was shocked that his dad was not angry at his mistake (basketball was his dad's passion). Monty learned a valuable lesson that day: if you don't try, you will never succeed. It was a key learning moment in Monty's development. Learn to make lemonade when life gives you a lemon. Here's the lemon:

In a different game, Monty played a great game. He scored 36 points and starred on defense too. It was the best game he had ever played. As Monty boarded the team bus to head back to his school, this conversation occurred:

The bus driver asked Monty, "Are you Kevin's son?" (Monty looked just like his dad).

Monty nodded. "Yes, sir."

The driver smiled and said, "You played great today, boy. You were easily the best player in the game"—Monty puffed out his chest a little as he listened— the driver continued, "but you'll never be as good as your dad."

Here's the lemonade:

The driver's comment galvanized Monty into action. He did not give up. He rose to the challenge and determined to be better than his father at *everything*. He became the all-in, all the time Man I know today.

As a Man, you are always on a quest for more knowledge, more tools, and a better train. You are constantly learning, growing, and expanding. You have goals, dreams, and aspirations. Even though your love life is beautiful and satisfying, you are always striving to become a better lover. You are always on the lookout for the next thing, but you also can sit quietly, pondering some great principle of life. You have a train, and you are steaming down the track. Put more coal on the fire, open the vents, and melt the rails. Now you are really living!

Routine

And to those who believe that adventures are dangerous
I say try routine, that kills you far more quickly.
Manuscript Found in Accra
Paulo Coelho

Life is a gamble, and if you are going to get much out of your life, you have to take chances. Stop saying something is too hard or that someone stood in your way. If your train is derailed, it's still your train; get back on board and set off again. Success and failure are all on you.

Regrets, I've had a few, but then
again too few to mention.
My Way
Paul Anka

The above lyric from "My Way" is a great line. If you are always trying new things and taking chances, you are bound to suffer some defeats and setbacks. As a Man, you shake off all your defeats because you learned something from every one of them. There is nothing to regret so, in the end, your regrets are "too few to mention." I lived all my life with one abiding idea: I want to die with no regrets. I don't want to regret the things I did, and I don't want to regret not doing the things I didn't do. I'll never stop trying to do something new, and I always strive to do everything better. I agree with Señor Coelho: Routine will kill me! It will kill you too. To see how routine your life is, ask yourself how long it has been since you took a chance and did something you had never done before.

Risk

If you never climb a tree, you will never fall from a tree, but what a pity to miss the delight of standing in the topmost branches, looking down on the people below. Life is a risk but if you live your life avoiding pain (physical, emotional, spiritual) you will be wasting your life. Taking a risk may not work out as you hoped, but you must still strive to climb to the top of your tree.

As a boy, I climbed everything possible. I took extravagant chances that would have been fatal had I fallen on the wrong side of the risk curve. For example, as a ten-year-old I climbed forty-foot trees to the topmost branches. At the same age, I climbed the walls that guarded the disused mine shafts dotted all around my town. The owners of these mine shafts never filled in the holes. They just built eight-foot walls around the shafts. My friends and I hammered large nails into the mortar between the bricks so we could climb the walls and sit with our feet dangling over the edge of the crumbling walls, some of which were hundreds of years old. We would drop rocks into the watery grave at the bottom of the pit and count the seconds before the splash. An older boy did the math for us and calculated that a typical three- to four-second plunge was between one hundred and two hundred feet. We were well aware that a slip or a collapsing wall meant certain death, but we sat on those walls for hours, imagining, accepting the obvious risk, and growing. Even now, almost six decades later, I can still feel the thrill of sitting there with my friends. We were brave and strong, and we knew things other children (and most adults) did not know. We were masters of our universe.

My willingness to take risks continued into adulthood; the alternative was death by boredom. Of course, sometimes things went wrong. My train sometimes jumped the tracks, but playing safe would have meant never striving for what I wanted to create. Risk is the price you must pay to overcome death by routine.

When you take a stand for what you believe is right, you usually risk economic, emotional, or physical harm. As a Man, you trust your body to know what is right, and you ignore all the alarm bells in your head. Whatever the situation, you do the right thing and deal with the consequences later.

If you want a relationship, you have to accept the pain you will feel when it ends—and they all end in separation or death. The better the relationship is while it lasts, the more it hurts when it ends. Don't be like Don.

Don is a successful professional who has always wanted a relationship but has never had one. When I asked him why, he said, "If I am in a relationship, it's my responsibility to look after my woman, and I would not be able to do that if I lost my job." Don, who is now retired, had been with the same company for more than thirty years.

It was heartbreaking to hear that Don had never had a relationship with a woman because he could not accept the risk of failing her, even though he had been with the same firm for decades! He had never asked a woman to join him on his train because he feared a *possibility*. There is hope for Don, but time is running out. If he does not make a change soon, he will be alone for the rest of his life. Don't be like Don. Take a chance. Sit atop your tree, throw rocks into your mine shaft, and invite a woman to join you on your train. You can only avoid pain by ceasing to live. Pain is not the issue. How you handle the pain is what matters.

What a Woman Wants

Despite what she says, a feminine woman wants a masculine Man who will take her places, treat her like a sexy siren, and desire her for her beauty and power. She might never admit it, but she wants a Man who desires her on a primal level. That means he desires her body for steamy, wild, sex. She also wants a Man who will protect and provide for her (although these days, *what* he provides for her may not be an income).

She will recognize his masculinity as an asset in the relationship, rather than a threat to her safety or autonomy. If your woman can't accept your masculinity, your relationship can go no further.

A powerful woman wants a Man who is strong enough to express his emotions clearly and without shame because doing so makes him accessible. She also knows that a Man is aware of the people and events around him, so he always knows how she is feeling. She likes a Man because he takes her to emotional and spiritual places she did not even know existed.

A woman wants a Man who is:

- On his train and knows where it's going.
- Masculine but does not use his masculinity as a weapon against her.
- Standing in his power because he knows who he is.
- Strong enough to resist her attempts to control him and test him.
- Growing.
- Admirable.
- Happy for her to be feminine and to stand in her feminine power.

If you ask a woman what she wants from you in a relationship, she may not voice any of the above. Women are both complex and "elastic" in their tastes. Women don't operate in only one direction, and it's fair to say that what she wants *all depends*.

> I want a Man who knows how to keep
> me safe but who excites me,
> and even feels a little *dangerous* (emphasis
> spoken in the original).
>
> *A woman speaking at The Man Salon*

For example:

Jillian wants a peaceful home life in the suburbs with two kids, a golden retriever, a Volvo hatchback, and a white picket fence around a pretty house. She likes her life to be a predictable round of wake up, look after the family, watch TV, and go to bed with her husband, *William*. Sex is always the same and happens in bed, once a week, on Sunday morning, at nine o'clock.

Jill is quite happy living with *Bill* in their modest apartment in the center of town. She likes the local nightlife and has joined a spiritual meet-up group. Bill works hard as a sales representative and makes enough money for them to vacation around the world. He likes to join Jill at the meet-ups, where they have met most of their circle of friends. Although they have no children yet, they plan to have a family once they have finished exploring the world. Jill and Bill are exploring their sexuality and have attended a variety of workshops. They love to share their desires and concerns with each other.

Jilly is happy to live and love on the edge with *Billy*. She likes that every day is a mystery tour and that life often comes at her out of the corners of dimly lit bars. Jilly loves to be on the back of Billy's 1200 cc Harley in her T-shirt and cut-offs. Although she has never studied sex, Jilly loves that sex with Billy is so unpredictable. They recently rolled around naked in a hay-strewn barn and made passionate love, then curled up in each other's arms and slept for two hours.

Jillian, Jill, and Jilly are different aspects of the same woman. It may seem odd that one woman could be happy with any of these situations (and many more) because what she wants *all depends* on who she is with at the time. Admittedly, from a white picket fence to a hay-strewn barn may seem like a stretch for some women, but it is not too far-fetched. In spite of what she might say, however, a woman will only be happy over the long haul with a Man who can hold his center with her, no matter how she expresses herself. I have learned that many women keep themselves on a short leash because they believe (heck, they *know* from experience) that the men in their lives are incapable of withstanding the full expression of their feminine sexual power. A Man standing in his power, on the other hand, can match any woman's power, sexual or otherwise.

A Man does not try to change a woman. He does not want a project woman any more than he wants to be a woman's project man. He lets her be herself to give her a chance to love the Man he is.

Polarity

Throughout the universe, magnetic fields abound. In a magnetic field, there are two opposite poles; a north pole and a south pole. In a strong relationship, there must also be two opposite energies: masculine and feminine. Sadly, what most women ask for these days is a *gentle soul.* A gentle soul is not gay or effeminate. It does not mean he is physically weak. It means that he is kind, gentle, understanding, and helpful. It means he *gets* a woman, *sees* her, and *understands* her. He is also in touch with his feelings, and open to sharing them with anyone, but he especially likes to share his feelings with a woman. He is heart centered.

Unfortunately, the polarity of a gentle soul is so close to a woman's polarity that their initial attraction for each other often (and sometimes, quickly) breaks down. Once that happens, their attraction is too weak to keep them happy, and they drift apart. Even if a gentle soul gives his woman everything she asks for, it's never enough without the polarity she needs to thrive, sexually and emotionally. He has surrendered too much of his masculinity and is more like a girlfriend than a Man who can keep her satisfied over the long haul.

Perhaps pressure from feminism caused the *gentle soul* to surrender so much of his masculinity. Perhaps a woman sought the qualities of a *gentle soul* assuming such a man would make her happy. However the relationship came about, a woman will not be happy in a relationship with a gentle soul for long; at best (for her anyway) she will keep him as a friend after she gives him the *Let's just be friends* speech!

The best chance a heterosexual couple has for a life together is a male with balanced masculinity (i.e., a Man) and a female with balanced femininity. A Man allows a woman the space she needs to be feminine, and most women will step right into the space he provides. Unfortunately, in the 21st Century, many women must accentuate their masculinity to survive in the workplace and are unable to take off that mask when they go home at night. If a woman can't be feminine when she is with her Man, he will probably be unhappy, and eventually leave her. If the relationship continues, the couple is doomed to the so-so relationship Ms. Haag describes in *Marriage Confidential.*

Both Men and women want to be recognized for the contribution they make to family life, no matter how large or small the family. Sadly, if they even notice what the other does for the family, they rarely say thank you for the effort. At a Salon, I led a ceremony in which each Man thanked his woman for what she does for the family:

I first asked the attendees to make male/female pairs (none of these 'pairs' was a *couple* outside the Salon). In order to take them out of their normal place and time, I created a *scene* taking them back to a pre-historic village, where there were powerful ties between Men (true, battle-tested, tribal Men) and equally powerful women. I asked the pairs to stand about 12 inches apart and place their left hands on their partner's right hip; the male to place his right hand in the small of the woman's back, and the woman to put her right hand on the male's left shoulder. I asked that the pairs look into each other's eyes then to start breathing in unison. Their posture and stance made it easy for them to feel a physical, emotional and spiritual connection with each other as I slowly led them into the ceremony.

I asked that both partners allow themselves to be completely open and become present in their ancient village. Then, one item at a time, I led the Men through the ceremony to thank their women for:

- Taking care of our hearth and home.
- Caring for our children while I am away hunting or fighting.
- Making good food to keep us healthy and make us strong.
- Leading the other women of the tribe to become stronger together.
- Tending to our animals.
- Tending to the family's wounds when we are injured.
- Learning about medicine plants to help us when we are sick.
- Teaching our children how to be useful members of the tribe.
- Standing by me through thick and thin.
- Satisfying me sexually.

This was a powerful exercise in which we recreated the prehistoric village in all of its simplicity and all of its complexity. We went back to the basics of what makes a relationship valuable and desirable. Many tears were shed during and after the ceremony, and everyone spoke of how meaningful each other's words had been, which was all the more remarkable as none of these people were in relationship with each other.

All you can do is be the best Man you can be, and then hold the space for your woman to be the best woman she can be. These goals are best accomplished by a proper recognition of what each partner contributes to the other.

What a Man Wants

A Man wants a woman who:

- Admires him.
- Supports him on his journey.
- Is feminine when she is with him (e.g., when she is not at work).
- Likes him to be masculine when he is with her.
- Is powerful in her own right.
- Above all, does not make him a project.

A Man does not want a woman he can control or who tries to control him. Given this list of ideal qualities, let's consider whether it's possible to find a woman with whom you want to bond, as well as to protect, and to cherish.

Have many of the women you had a relationship with tried to control you? You may be surprised to learn that of all the women I know who are in relationship with a Man (and I know a lot), not one is controlling. This is because they don't *need* to be controlling, and they know it does not work when they try. On the other hand, women who are in relationships with men frequently seem to be controlling and demanding. If you feel that your woman is controlling or demanding, look to your own behavior to figure out why.

More times than I can count, I have heard a woman say some variation of… *men have no idea how to treat a woman—they just want to drink beer, watch TV, and have sex—and do it in that order too.* Women know that what they are saying is not entirely true, but there is some truth in it. Many of the men I know watch a lot of TV and drink beer. Oh, and they like sex! These are natural male tendencies. Males need time to do masculine stuff, including sports, working out, and spending time with other males. As for the accusation that males don't know how to treat a woman, that is only true for men. A Man knows how to treat a woman and is always looking for better ways to do so.

Many men say they want no-strings sex with a great-looking, willing woman. This is not what a Man wants. I have posed the question in multiple ways to many Men, and the surprising answer has nearly always been, "I want a family. I want to be in a relationship. I want to love someone. I want to be loved. Above all, I want to be admired for what I do and who I am." Unfortunately, it's now rare for a woman to thank her man/Man for what he does (or even *notice* what he does). She is far more likely to focus on what he is not doing. If you believe your woman is not noticing what you do, it is time to talk about that and ask her how she feels about your efforts. At the same time, don't forget to notice what *she* does and thank her for that.

A Special Ceremonial 'Thank You' to Men

Sadly, many Men returning from battle (or the daily struggle at work) find it difficult to ease back into a home life. Over the last fifty years, hundreds of thousands of military personnel have returned home after fighting in foreign lands, so the problems associated with readjusting to civilian life have been common. Not surprisingly, coming down from the "battle high" and adjusting to a home life again has been difficult for many and impossible for some (e.g., the suicide rate in the ranks of our returning military personnel is a national tragedy). As a society, we need to reassess how we thank our returning military for their efforts and how we go about helping them to reintegrate into civil society. Perhaps a ceremony like this might become part of a whole new way of welcoming our military people back home.

This ceremony took place in Prague, Czech Republic. It was by far the most powerful ceremony I have ever done; it shook me to my core but in an uplifting and affirming way. The ceremony was created to allow women to honor their Men for what they do. To set up the ceremonial scenario, assume these Men have been away fighting to protect their families and their homeland. As you read, notice how often what I write about is how I *feel*. My amazing teacher, Amara Charles led the ceremony and orchestrated each step. Throughout, Amara's soft incantations enhanced the solemnity of the ceremony. My ceremony partner was Maxine; we had never met or spoken to each other before we came together for the ceremony.

To begin, I stood facing outwards, shoulder to shoulder in a circle with other Men. As a former Royal Air Force pilot, I felt a strong bond with these Men and what we were about to do. Maxine came to stand in front of me, a few feet away. Other women stood in front of 'their' ceremonial partner. When I looked into Maxine's eyes, I saw genuine compassion as we quickly created a powerful bond with each other. I felt her gaze penetrate every crevice of my being with an intensity I had never felt before. It was as if she was seeing right into me. As Amara spoke a few feet away, I felt myself melt into Maxine's body and just knew she was an intimate part of my life (such is the alchemy of ceremony). Even though we were several feet apart, I could feel Maxine's heart beating in her chest while my heart was pounding in mine. I felt her healing energy envelop my body in a warm and loving glow. When my legs began to buckle from the powerful emotions flowing through my body, the sheer force of Maxine's feminine power helped me regain my equilibrium. After several minutes, Maxine started to sway to a silent rhythm, offering me a dance of welcome for my return.

After a few minutes more, which could have been a hundred years, Maxine dropped to her knees at my feet and looked up into my face. In this new posture, I could see even deeper into her. I began to shake, alternating between unbearable sadness for my time away and unbridled joy at my return. These feelings were incredibly powerful and felt absolutely real (more alchemy).

Maxine told me how she had missed me and how she had longed for my return. As our eyes looked deep inside each other, we were drawn further and further into the ceremonial and spiritual realm. Everything I said and felt was vivid and as real as anything I had ever felt. Maxine became a divine goddess in my eyes as I became her fearless warrior. After a few minutes, I slowly sank to my knees so I could face her, and told her through my tears what it meant for me to be safe at home with her, and with our children once again. I told her how much I had ached for her touch and how I had missed our children as they grew. Although I had never expected to see my family again, I said nothing about that to her, knowing that this might not be the last time I must fight to protect them and our way of life.

That Maxine and I were long-term lovers with a family did not feel like make-believe. Neither did it feel like a contrivance for the purpose of a ceremony. I *had* fought for their survival, and they *had* waited in daily fear of losing me. Even though we were two feet apart, Maxine and I became one being as the strength of our connection grew. An even greater revelation was to come.

While I was still in the ceremony, I felt a sudden and powerful shift in time and place. This shift transported me to my old RAF flight crew quarters, wearing my flight gear and helmet. It was 50 years ago and I was once again a young RAF officer, training to defend my country against Soviet aggression. I might have been only nineteen years old and still a raw trainee pilot, but I was full of piss and vinegar and prepared to drop bombs on the enemy or shoot down their aircraft.

Maxine is from the Czech Republic, which was formerly in the Communist Bloc, my sworn enemy 50 years ago. Given Maxine's age, if the Cold War had become a hot war, one of the men I would have been fighting was her father. Like a bomb going off in my brain, I realized that if I had killed her father in battle, she—this beautiful woman who was kneeling right in front of me—would never have been born. I was overwhelmed at the realization and began to sob uncontrollably. I have still not shaken off the dread I felt about the possible intersection of our joint destinies (Maxine's, her father's, and mine) and how those destinies might have been changed by war.

No man ever received a more beautiful welcome and thanks upon returning home from a fight than I received from Maxine. Her pure grace, her abundant feminine power, and her beautiful heart allowed me to see how much masculine warriors need to be admired and welcomed home after their fight is over. I believe this is true even if the male's fight is only another day grinding away at work to support his family. A woman standing in her power needs to give her warrior the admiration and thanks he deserves and needs to thrive. Her feminine energy can repair his broken body and mend his fractured spirit.

This ceremony showed me that inside his strong masculine body, a Man's greatest fear is not that he will be killed or maimed in battle; they are mere trifles to a Man. His greatest fear is that he will fail when it really matters: fail by making the wrong decision; fail by not being strong enough; or worst of all, fail by being a coward and running away. A Man knows that any of these failures could mean disaster for his woman, his child, and his tribe. For a Man, such a failure would be a fate far worse than dying for his cause.

Attraction

Larry desires a committed monogamous relationship with Lexi. Larry wants a family (a basic biological drive). Lexi wants Larry to provide for her, and protect her. Larry is attracted to Lexi's beauty and voracious sexual appetite. Lexi loves Larry's stability, strength, and ability to hang in with her during hard times and difficult conversations.

Larry and Lexi's mutual desires are the basis of human attraction. Women have evolved to attract into their lives adult males with strong masculine genes and to keep them around until their children mature. Evolution provides women with an array of gifts to help them do so. One example is a woman's ability and willingness to engage in sex 24/7, which is a highly attractive lure for a male, especially if together they can maintain the sexual energy they shared when their relationship began. A woman's highly developed breasts are an obvious attraction and the source of endless pleasure for males, young and old. Hollywood and Madison Avenue, purveyors of breasts on a commercial scale, have defined "perfect" breasts as perky, medium-sized, with slightly upturned nipples, and aureoles that are darker than the surrounding skin but not too dark. While a male may like Madison Avenue's idea of a perfect breast in a magazine or a movie, once he is dealing with a woman *in the flesh*, a male is happy with large, medium, or small breasts, perky or saggy breasts, nipples of any size or shape, and aureoles of any color. In other words, Men (and most men too) like the breasts their women have to offer, no matter what they are like.

Although I discuss female genital anatomy in greater detail later, for the purposes of attraction, there are many elements of a woman's anatomy that are attractive to a male. Let's begin with the Labia (vaginal lips). If you are a male who got his education of female anatomy from pornography, you may think all labia look alike—smooth, hairless, with few folds, and little color variation. In fact, labia come in a wide variety of colors, textures, shapes, and sizes. They may be small or large or somewhere in between. They may be slightly or highly convoluted, or they may be smooth. They may be folded in or out or hardly folded at all. They may be brown, pink, or multicolored.

While they are the most obvious (visible) part of the female genitalia, labia of themselves are not generally thought of as being the primary focus of a male. Rather, the labia represent the first sight of, and entrance to, what for most males is a woman's primary attraction, the ultimate prize… her vagina. I am fairly sure most males assume that once they can see and touch a woman's labia, access to her vagina is only a matter of time. Do not be ashamed of feeling that a woman's vagina is her primary attraction. That focus is built into your biology.

Once an attentive male begins to explore his partner's labia, he will appreciate the complexity of their shape, texture, and color. More about how to pleasure the labia later. Whatever they look like, no male has ever told me that he does not like the look of a woman's labia.

In the Resources section, I reference an online documentary called *The Pussy Talks*. I recommend this documentary for anyone who wants to know more about female genital anatomy. If you have open-minded friends, you can organize a film night and watch it together. This is an explicit presentation of female genital anatomy that is not at all pornographic. These are ordinary women (not actresses) who are actually quite *extraordinary* as they share with the viewer the relationship they have with their genital anatomy. None of what you hear or see on The Pussy Talks video was scripted or directed; the camera just rolled. The women simply say what they were feeling in that moment. The Pussy Talks is an incredible addition to the lexicon of female genital anatomy, sexuality, and thought, as well as a woman's relationship to her own genital anatomy. Enjoy.

13

RELATIONSHIPS

Love and Commitment

Some years ago, I heard a song that shook me and, in a way, changed the way I live my life.

I will face the world around me
Knowing that I am strong enough to let you go
And I will fall in love again
Because I can.
One Way Ticket (Because I Can)
Judy Rodman and Keith Hinton

The lyrics say that the female singer is strong enough to let her lover go. I asked myself whether I was that strong. Should I not try to keep my woman? If she left me, what would happen to me? As I pondered these questions, a picture popped into my mind. The picture was of an exquisite songbird that was sitting in the palm of my hand. The bird was so beautiful that I fell in love with it and wanted to keep it so I could hear it sing for the rest of my life. All I had to do was close my grip and the bird would be mine. Then the realization hit me. The only way to keep this beautiful creature was to crush it to death. Of course I decided that if the bird chose to fly away, I must let it go.

It was obvious to me that the bird represented my lover, Karen. She is exquisite and beautiful too. The only way I could be sure she stayed with me would be to constrain her. But by constraining her, I would destroy what made her so attractive to me. My insight made me realize that I can't own anyone, least of all the woman I love. I don't own a second of her time or a hair on her head. Loving her means I want the best for her on *her* journey through life. I am just happy that she is choosing to share some of her journey with me. I accept that if she decides to leave me, I must step out of her way and let her go with good grace. I know that if Karen ever decides to leave me, it will hurt, but I will help her leave and wish her the best as she goes (and I will mean it). I will recover after she is gone. The moral… if you truly love your woman, you must let her fly away, like the little songbird, if that is what she wants. Karen holds me in the same way, with an open palm.

The Price of Admission

When I ask men what they are willing to do to get the kind of relationship they want, many say the price is too high. If you want a relationship, you have to be *in* a relationship that functions *as* a relationship. If your idea of a relationship is behaving like a single man, a relationship won't give you what you want; namely, your woman's admiration, companionship, love, and, possibly, a family. Your woman deserves all of you, the Man you really are, not a cardboard cutout that only looks like you. Giving your woman anything less than your full self is not fair to her or to you, and will inevitably lead to failure. Realize that failures of this kind can hurt you for a long time because you will know that you sabotaged the relationship (which is a form of manipulation).

You may have to compromise as you go through life, but you must still be yourself. Of course, once the relationship begins, a woman may pressure you to change, but if you change just to please her, you will no longer be authentic, and your capital M will begin to shrink. Of course, you may change because of your natural development or because you have been doing the work to grow. Such changes don't affect your authenticity because you are still authentically yourself when it's *your* decision to change.

Paradoxically, if you change and become the person your woman demands, she will doubt your authenticity because she will know your character is not stable. Once that happens, you can flush the relationship down the toilet. But wait, there's more and it's worse - if you *do* change to please her, she will try to change you even more. At that point, whether you leave or stay, the end of the relationship is just a matter of time. You must maintain your integrity, your standards, and your self-respect. You must act the way you do because you believe it to be right. Helping with the laundry, dressing the children, or watching this movie instead of that movie does not mean you lost your identity, nor does it mean you became any less of a Man. Compromising costs little and can lead to places you may never have found on your own. There is pleasure and satisfaction in a relationship, and while it requires some effort from you, if you are still yourself, the price you must pay is not too high.

The Competition of Generosities

The competition of generosities (thank you singing star, Madonna for this gem) works when both partners in a relationship are striving to give each other, and the relationship, everything they have to offer. It means you don't keep score. It means you never count the cost. You can't love someone on the condition that they love you back or that they take out the garbage. Love is unconditional, or it's not love. Love is caring for your lover, sharing with your lover, and looking out for her mental, emotional, and physical safety, as well as your own. It means stepping up and taking care of business instead of leaving it for her (you know, emptying the dishwasher, fixing the leaky faucet, or playing with the children). If you can't enter into the "competition of generosities" with your lover, you have a business relationship and a balance sheet, but you don't have a love-relationship.

Engaging in your own competition of generosities is a wonderful way to maintain the juice in your relationship. Delicious connected love is best when both partners are competing to be generous to the other and nobody is keeping score.

Biology

In spite of what many women claim, Men are not all the same, and they want more from their women than sex without strings attached. In addition, Men know that women are not too complicated to understand and that women want a relationship with something more than a checkbook. Of course, it's also true that a Man *does* want sex (along with everything else), and a woman wants a Man who will protect and provide for her and their family (remembering that what a Man provides these days may not be money). These things are not weird demands your partner made up to screw with your head. These thoughts, observations, and complaints—and many more like them—arise from the reality of the human condition. These demands are biological, and they won't change until our biology changes, which is a maddeningly slow process. While these issues are complex, one significant contributor to their complexity is that feminism has blurred many of the essential differences between males and females—so much so that many men and women no longer know how to behave in their naturalness. By understanding what it takes to be a Man, I hope you are able to regain a more appropriate balance of your masculine and feminine essences. You must have that balance in your makeup to live as a Man. Here are some aspects of masculine essence:

- Single-focused
- Curious
- Goal-oriented and active

- Creative
- Resilient
- Team-oriented and independent (these are not a paradox)
- Determined, resolute
- Aggressive (when necessary)
- Honorable
- Dependable
- Centered
- Courageous
- Capable
- Steadfast

Some aspects of feminine essence:

- Diffuse focus
- Multitasking
- Caring, tender, gentle
- Empathic and sympathetic
- Heart-centered
- Intuitive
- Emotional
- Emotionally available
- Receptive
- Unpredictable

For any individual, the balance between masculine and feminine characteristics is rarely an even (50:50) split. In fact, the balance is in a constant state of flux depending on the task at hand. A woman may exhibit all of the masculine traits in certain situations (the workplace being the obvious one for many women), and a male may exhibit all of the feminine traits at various times (looking after a baby, for example, or caring for a sick lover). However, as males navigate their way through life, they tend to exhibit masculine characteristics to a greater degree than women, and women tend to exhibit feminine characteristics to a greater degree than males. Be an appropriately balanced masculine Man so the woman in your life can be an appropriately balanced feminine woman. Once you are a Man, a woman will no longer want (or be able) to emasculate you, so your balls are safe. Oh Yes. That feels a whole lot better!

Women Being Used

It may happen on a first date or after many months of "courting" behavior, but if you and your woman are going to have a relationship, you will eventually have sex. If the relationship founders after the relationship becomes sexual, a woman may claim (and believe) that you *used* her, because she gave you everything (i.e., sex), and you gave her nothing. Abandoned women feeling used by males is a theme that often crops up in movies, books, and TV shows. While these concepts may accurately describe how a woman feels, the feeling is not an appropriate response to what actually happened. Consensual sex means both parties had sex of their own freewill. In the 21st Century, sex is not something a woman *gives* to a male on condition he stay with her, or that he *takes* from her. Neither is sex the price a woman has to pay to buy herself a male partner. If a woman engages in sex with the expectation of receiving something in return (other than sex with a male), she is entering into a business arrangement, and good luck with that!

One way to be clear in a sexual interaction is to require *informed consent.* Informed consent means you and your partner talk honestly and with full disclosure about your intentions before engaging in any sexual activity. A critical element of informed consent is the exchange of a sexually transmitted disease history (with documentation showing recent testing for STD's, positive or negative). Informed consent means that you both agree to have intercourse within stated boundaries, such as, for example, condoms are required; there will be no anal play; and stop means stop. If the interaction occurs within the boundaries agreed at the outset, then even if the sex was not a memorable experience or the budding relationship later founders, nobody was used. The final element of informed consent is an agreement that at any time in the interaction one or both partners may revoke the consent they have already given. When consent is revoked, the interaction stops immediately. No matter how awkward or embarrassing it may seem at the time, you STOP! If a male continues after permission has been revoked, he is at least guilty of lying (because he breached the agreement he made) but if he uses any physical pressure to keep the interaction going, he is likely to be accused of (and guilty of) rape. It is that serious! Remember, revocation of permission means you stop the interaction. You can discuss the reasons for the revocation when you have both taken a break and calmed down.

A related concept to informed consent is Affirmative Permission (*AP*). AP means that before you touch each other in a sexual way, you seek permission to do so. For example, you might say,

- I want to kiss you. Would you like me to do that?
- May I massage your breasts?
- I would like to take off your underwear. Is that OK with you?

It is reasonable that a woman asks that you adopt AP as a practice. AP is not a reflection of what she thinks of you, so do not take this personally. The practice is normal among people who engage in conscious sex. It is also appropriate for a woman to ask a male for permission before she touches him in a sexual manner. You can kill two birds with one stone by granting permission for certain actions during the informed consent discussion.

Once you are comfortable with each other, either of you may respond to a permission request with, "You have my blanket *Yes* to remove my clothing and touch me wherever you would like." If you adopt informed consent and affirmative permission, it's less likely that a woman will feel 'used' even if your relationship ultimately does not work out. Approaching sex in this upfront, open and conscious manner is a great way to eliminate much of the angst that arises before, during and after a sexual interaction, especially if a relationship is not yet firmly established. An added benefit is that as you discuss what the boundaries are, the conversation can be incredibly erotic.

Taking Your Time

Waiting before engaging in a sexual interaction with a woman will allow you to feel more connected to her or to learn something about her that makes you walk away. Waiting may also come with the added benefit of increasing her desire for you until she is not just willing to engage in sex but is silently or actually begging for your sexual touch. A Man who waits, who can say *later* when the woman he is with says, *Now!* will be highly attractive to the woman. Keeping her waiting, won't hurt a bit.

14

DATING 101

Oh, help!" said Pooh. I'd better go back.
Oh, bother!" said Pooh. I shall have to go on.
I can't do either! said Pooh. "Oh, help and bother!
Winnie-the-Pooh
A. A. Milne

Asking For a Date

The first step to a date is to ask a woman to meet you. It will be a June day in May before a woman asks *you* out. Although men know it's their job to invite a woman out, I have observed many men, perfectly competent in other areas, who don't have a clue about how to ask a woman for a date or what to do when she says yes. Even after a date, especially after a first date, many men second-guess themselves:

- When should I call her? In a few days? A week?
- Should I text her or email her?
- What about a handwritten note?
- What should I say?
- Is it too soon to ask for another date?
- Oh dear; I don't know what to do. *Help!*

They wonder:

- Did she like me?
- Would she have preferred a different restaurant?

- Did she hate me for ordering a steak (I think she's vegan)?
- Should I have taken her to the symphony instead?
- Did she like what I was wearing? *Bother!*

Some men downgrade themselves.

- She's too good for me.
- I'm not handsome enough for her.
- I upset her when I held her hand.
- I said the wrong thing. I always do.
- I danced too close to her.
- I blew it ... again! *Help and bother!*

I'm only interested in a Man who
believes he is worth my time.
Karen Lucas Clarke

Here are some thoughts that might help:

On your first date with a new potential partner, be your authentic self without manipulation, games, or pretense. Believe in who you are and be confident in your belief. If you don't rate yourself highly enough, you can't expect her to think much of you. Therefore, even if she looks like a supermodel, you have to feel in your bones that you are worth her time. Actions count way more than words to a woman. She will judge you on what you *do*, not what you *say* you will do. Therefore, as you get to know her, you will need to back up your words with actions that demonstrate that you really are worth her time. If she likes you, great. If not, that's fine too. You can stop wasting your time. Dating is not the time to be tentative or doubtful!

Don't make her guess what you are thinking. If you don't want to see her again, then call, email, or text her to tell her that. A simple "Thanks for meeting with me last night, but I don't think this is going to work out" is all you need say. If you want to see her again, tell her in plain language what you want to do: take her to dinner; take her to a party; meet your parents. She may decline your invitation, but give her the chance to accept! If she declines, let her know that you are disappointed and that you hope you can get together again at another time. If that is not what she wants, she will let you know.

Your role as a creative partner carries with it many advantages. You generally are able to set the tone and pace of a date and choose the location. Being the creative partner also brings the burden of duty, and the duties may seem onerous at times. You have to ask her out. You have to choose a venue. You have to ask her to dance. Generally, you offer to pick her up and take her home (realizing that she may decline your offer of a ride until she knows you better). You may offer to pick up the tab. The woman is the responsive partner. She tells you what she would like to drink, *when you ask*. She chooses whether to dance, *when you ask*. She may agree with your choice of location or suggest a different location *when you ask*.

Don't overthink the date. Where you go is less important than spending time with this amazing woman—if you don't think she is amazing, why are you asking her out? Be aware that she may prefer a different first date from the one you propose. You decide whether to defer to her choice or make another suggestion. Of course, if you expect her to pay her share of the tab, you need to let her know that in advance and understand that she will then have as much say in the choice of location, and what you order, as you do. Therefore, navigate the choice of location with great care. At the end of the evening, she will thank you for a great (wonderful, good, pleasant, or, heaven forbid, *nice*) evening, or she will bid you a swift good-bye. Either way, accept it. A date with a new woman won't always work out.

Both male and female roles have advantages, disadvantages, benefits, and costs, and the blurred gender roles in today's society make each role a little fuzzier than it used to be. When you are a Man, you are more likely to find a woman who is happy to let you create a date that she can simply step into. Sometimes, of course, you have to up your game and be the Man.

When Sonny took Josie out for a first date, he picked a beautiful restaurant at the beach. He had made a reservation, and when he gave his name to the female greeter, she responded with a cheery, "Good evening, Mr. James. Would you like to sit inside or outside on this beautiful evening?" Before Sonny could answer, Josie stepped in and said, "We'd like to sit outside ... at *that* table and move *those* two gas heaters closer to the table."

As the greeter scurried away to rearrange the table and heaters, Sonny turned to Josie and said calmly and quietly, "Josie, don't do that again. *I* made this reservation, and the attendant asked *me* a question. It was inappropriate for you to answer the question. You did not even consult me. We will talk further about this when we are seated." Once seated, Sonny said, "I am perfectly willing to share these decisions with you, but you did not even ask me what my preference might be. If we are to have any chance at a relationship, that will have to change. Do you think you can do that?" Josie nodded. Sonny reports that they enjoyed a delightful dinner and spent the rest of the evening talking about how this new way of behaving would work for her. They agreed it would.

The way Sonny dealt with Josie's masculine rudeness was sharp and immediate. Josie knew from that moment that Sonny was a Man and that she was in good hands. When they went to the restaurant for breakfast in the morning, a different greeter asked, "Where would you like to sit, Mr. James? Inside or outside?" Sonny turned to Josie and asked, "Which would you prefer, darling?" Perfect. Sonny's question was not a tacit agreement to do whatever Josie wanted, but it did allow her to have a voice in the decision.

Asking for a date

- Decide where you want to take her.
- Ask her in person or on the phone (not voice mail or text).
- Tell her what you have in mind: "I want to take you to dinner at "The Palace."
- For the first few dates, suggest a public venue, such as a restaurant, bar, or park.
- If she agrees to join you, discuss more detailed arrangements.
- For subsequent dates, ask her out with full disclosure of your intentions: "I am really attracted to you. I want to pick you up on Friday at 7pm and take you somewhere quiet for dinner. I want to tell you a little more about me and learn more about you."
- Ask with a warm heart, and accept her answer with good grace.
- Forget attachments to any particular outcome.
- Realize that although she did not say *yes*, she did not necessarily mean *no*.
- Ask her whether another time or a different venue would work for her. Just ask her for a date until she accepts your invitation or rejects it.
- Realize that a date early in a relationship is a high-risk proposition for a woman.
- Accept that she may want to drive herself to the date.
- Accept her rejection if it comes.

Don't forget that her *yes* was to go on a date with you, nothing more, and certainly not an agreement to have sex! If you desire her sexually, let her know of your desire when you feel that you are both ready. You never need to rush that fence.

Keep Her Safe

As Alison Armstrong points out in one of her classes, a woman often feels concerned for her physical safety. While a first date presents almost no risk to the male's physical safety, the risk is high for the woman. If you pick her up, she has to get into a car that she can't control, with a driver she doesn't know. She will assume you'll expect an invitation into her house when you drive her home. At her doorstep, if she invites you inside, her risk increases exponentially. Even if you are determined to behave yourself, she does not know that, and she has no idea what might happen once you are inside. You would not be the first male to assume that an invitation into her house after a date means sex is the nightcap.

Therefore, be aware that a woman navigating the tricky waters of early-stage dating faces significant risks. Be aware of her dilemma, and make every accommodation to put her at ease. Put her safety first, knowing that she is probably fearful. Make sure she knows that you will keep her safe. No matter where you are—on the street, in the car, or at home—make sure she is safe, and that includes being safe from you. To show her that you are prepared to protect her, do the following:

- Stand between her and a crowd, especially if the crowd is rowdy.
- Stay close to her but not so close as to be oppressive.
- Don't cut her off from contact with other people.
- Offer to pick her up, but accept her refusal graciously if she declines.
- Protect her from the cold or wind (by putting your arm around her or giving her your jacket).
- Don't drink and drive.
- Don't drive too fast when she is in the car (she won't be impressed).

- See her to her door, if she will allow that (if she declines, accept graciously).
- Don't ask her to invite you in.
- When she says goodnight, leave promptly.
- Respect her space. If you touch her, be respectful.
- Have her back at all times.

As you can see from this short list, your protection is a gentle care, exerted only when the need arises and for a limited time. When properly done, she will conclude that she can trust you. Once trust is established, your lives as a couple will become a lot more comfortable.

Getting to Know Her

A Man with a train is highly attractive to a woman, but don't try to impress her with your train. A woman who is interested in you will want to know whether you have a train and where your train is going, but let that information come out organically. If you boast about your train (or anything else, for that matter), she will see it as a weakness not a strength. She certainly does not want to know about your bank balance or your sexual prowess. Relax. Take a deep breath, and show her that you know who you are and know where you are going. That will be enough. When she senses the heady aroma of Man on you, she will overlook all manner of shortcomings—too much waistline; quirky dress sense; too much talking! These things matter little to a woman when she is with a Man. You don't have to be film-star handsome to woo a woman. You just have to be a Man; no pretense and no games, just straight forward honesty.

If you feel that your relationship has potential, it is time to start learning more about each other. Start the discovery process by telling her about yourself, and let her warm up to the idea of sharing about herself. Your questions should not become an inquisition. Start with soft-balls like these:

- Where did you grow up?
- What do you like to do in your spare time?
- What movies or books have you enjoyed?
- What do you like to do for fun?

If, after exchanging information like this, you are still attracted to each other, you can share more intimate details—what her former relationships were like; how those relationships ended; where she's headed in her life. Eventually, you can talk about your health situation. If she is interested in you, she will reciprocate. If she does not reciprocate, she is probably not interested in developing a deeper connection with you.

When Karen and I first communicated, she lived in Maryland, and I lived in Phoenix (we are an internet couple – so deliciously modern!). A fortuitous business trip brought us physically together a few weeks after we exchanged information through the dating site (it was PerfectMatch.com – sadly, no longer available). As soon as we met, we started to share details about ourselves. Surprisingly, the distance between us made sharing intimate details easier because if it didn't work out we were 2,000 miles apart. Over the course of the next three meetings, which took place over several months, we shared the most basic and intimate details about ourselves; literally everything we could think of. We spent an entire day walking around Washington, DC, sharing intimate details all day and into the wee hours of the morning. Our delicious exploration showed us that we were perfectly compatible. We are not perfect, but we *are* perfect for each other.

It takes courage to open yourself up like this. When you reveal yourself, with your heart wide open and your mind clear, you may feel vulnerable, even judged. Because you are a Man, this exposure does not concern you. She will also have to be open and vulnerable, which requires courage on her part too. Accept your mutual gift of open and vulnerable communication, and see how your exchange develops. Just remember to classify everything she says as *Top Secret* — a Man never betrays a trust.

If your eyes are wide open, and you are both sharing intimate details about yourselves, rest assured that your connection is deepening. That is how a love relationship blossoms. Cool!

The following is an illustration of a common problem (based on what many women have told me).

Be Honest

This is Karl's fifth date with Kristy, and he thinks it's time they had sex. He takes Kristy to a good restaurant, buys a nice bottle of Cabernet, and pays for dinner. He invites her back to his place "for a drink" because he assumes that she would decline if he told her he hoped to have sex with her that night. He further assumed that her acceptance of his invitation was a tacit agreement to have sex (why else would she accept an invitation *to his house*?). After a lot of kissing and petting on the sofa, Karl says, "I think it's time we went upstairs."

Kristy jumps up off the sofa and says, "What kind of girl do you think I am?" She leaves. Karl thinks, *There goes the relationship. I blew it again!*

What went wrong? Karl had tidied up his house, cleaned the kitchen and bathrooms, plumped up the pillows on the sofa, and paid for an expensive dinner. He thought he *deserved* sex tonight because he had done everything right. I hope by now you recognize that Karl's behavior was manipulative and inauthentic. He planned an outcome that was unknown to Kristy and he lied to her (lying by omission is still lying). She trusted him because he had previously behaved appropriately, so she accepted an invitation to have a drink at his house. Even though she became alarmed when the kissing and petting on the sofa went further than she liked, she did not say anything. Like many women, she acquiesced to more than she was comfortable with because she was even more uncomfortable standing up for herself. Many women yield to this kind of pressure because they feel unable to say *No* when they are cornered, especially if the male is in a position of authority or a public figure (recall the discussion of informed consent and affirmative permission in Chapter 13). Karl's suggestion that they go to the bedroom showed her that a nightcap was never his real intention. He put her on the spot, and she did the right thing by blowing him off.

Recognize that it takes a lot of courage for a woman to accept an invitation such as the one Karl made because she has no idea how easy it will be to exit the house once she's inside. In this case, Karl owes Kristy an apology for his lack of integrity. Karl also needs to figure out why he feels he needs to behave in such a manipulative fashion. He hasn't yet realized that being honest with a woman he dates would make him feel better about himself and lead to a stronger connection with her. Remember, once a woman trusts you, look out—*everything* about the relationship is going to get better.

If he had been honest with Kristy, he could have told her about his desire for her while they were in the restaurant. If he had read her feelings reasonably well, he could have said, "Kristy, I find you incredibly attractive and desire you very much. I want to take our relationship to the next level and make love to you tonight. I hope we can go back to my place later, and then, if everything works out and it still feels right for you, we can make love. If you decide the time is not right, that's not a problem. I will drive you home with good grace. No pressure at all." If he had taken this approach, he would have had a much better chance of hearing an enthusiastic *Yes* from her when he made his suggestion. By speaking in this way, Karl let Kristy know that even though she initially agreed to his invitation, she could change her mind later, and the wheels wouldn't fall off his wagon. If she'd said she was not ready to go to his house, they could still have had an enjoyable date, and their relationship would not have been damaged. If Karl had been conscious and paying attention, her *No* would not have been a surprise to him. If Kristy declined his invitation, Karl may not know what her response meant (*not tonight? not ever?*), in which case he is free to ask her what she is thinking about a future together. Everybody gains when partners are up front and act with integrity, even if the relationship ends right there.

An honest conversation about sex with a woman comes with a bonus; it can be incredibly erotic. If your discussion plants the seed of anticipation in her mind and she accepts your invitation, she will be thinking about the sex to come. Never underestimate the power of anticipation for a woman. If she declines your invitation, it's perfectly acceptable to ask her why. Her answer may tell you where your relationship is headed. Honesty comes in different guises.

Ally tells me that she dates many men. They go to a restaurant for dinner or to a bar for drinks. They have a wonderful time. The men are kind and good company. Ally is vivacious and beautiful, and has an easygoing charm. As they say good night, the men invariably ask for her phone number, and they promise to call in a day or so. They rarely call.

I am not going to judge these men for rejecting Ally. That is their choice. She may be doing something to cause these men to reject her—that's not the point. The point is that their behavior is the opposite of Man behavior; it is childish. These men are adult males who have yet to grow up. In this age of instant messaging, email, and constant telephone connection, it's a simple matter to contact Ally and say "Thanks for a fun date, but I don't think we would be right for each other." In addition, a Man who knows there is no future, does not say he will call as he leaves that first date. When a Man *says* he will call, he calls.

A Whole Woman

I used to think that I knew what a woman was like just by looking at her. It felt to me that I was sensing what sort of person she was by her appearance. I just *knew* that a physically attractive woman would be attractive as a person and as a lover. If you think my base instincts were driving my body, you would be right. But, don't be so quick to judge me. Numerous studies have shown that there are mathematical ratios that determine how a male will feel about a woman when he first sees her (there are corresponding ratios for when a woman first sees a man too). These ratios have been known to artists for at least 2,000 years. One ratio is a woman's waist to hip ratio. A woman with a waist measurement that is about 70 percent of her hip measurement, is generally appealing to a male. There are many similar ratios for facial proportions. Therefore, you are not a Neanderthal because you react to the way a woman *looks*. It's a normal biological reaction; enjoy it.

Problems arise if a male allows his biological impulse to rule his actions. He must still respect the woman, no matter how much he is attracted to her. A Man knows how to behave when he approaches a woman he is attracted to. He is restrained, and very much aware how his actions make her feel. He monitors her reaction to his overture, so he can gracefully withdraw if his attention is not wanted. He is never a nuisance to her. In addition to her physical appearance, there are many other aspects of a woman's face and expression that affect how attractive she is to a male. Her smile, her eyes, her general demeanor all play important roles in letting a Man know where she is emotionally and spiritually in addition to her physical appearance.

While you can't escape your biology, try not to let your immediate conclusions about a woman's appearance cloud your judgment. If you do, you may miss many great interactions with wonderful women. I have learned that many of the women I most desired, based on their appearance, were often not so great as people, or as lovers. I also found that many women who did not attract me initially became wonderful friends and lovers. The reality is that I found joy with every woman I ever dated. One important lesson I learned from these women was that I don't make love to a body; I make love to the entire woman. Whether or not you ultimately develop a lifelong relationship with her, treat a woman the way you would like to be treated. She has beauty, complexity, and heart, among myriad other qualities, and there is undoubtedly more to her than you can see. Treat her like you would treat a goddess, and she may become a goddess, no matter her age or appearance. Remember, you need to express your masculinity by your actions (i.e., how you behave), not what you say. When you do, she will respond by becoming more feminine. Revel in her femininity, and you will be delighted when she becomes a true friend, or an inspiring and admiring lover.

Admire Her

Do you find it difficult to compliment a woman? Paying appropriate and sincere compliments seems to be a lost art. If you notice something particularly striking or appealing about a woman, it's okay to tell her what you noticed. You might admire the way she smiled when you met, or how her gaze makes you feel. When you learn to give sincere compliments to a woman, you will see her begin to glow. When you learn to accept her compliments to you with humility and grace, your relationship will grow even stronger.

In your efforts to be complimentary, do not ever say, "You have the *most* amazing [insert a part of her anatomy here] I have ever seen." She will assume you are lying, even if you are not. Saying she has the *most* beautiful or *sexiest* anything will tag you as inarticulate and shallow. For sure, she does not want to feel she is in a competition with all the other women you have ever known. Sincere comments, such as "You are so elegant," or "Your smile makes me feel really happy," or "That dress looks great on you" will be well received, so keep your message simple and sincere. Be aware that most people find it hard to receive a compliment and will try to deflect it by saying, "Oh, I know you don't mean that." You can put a woman at ease by saying sincerely and with an admiring (i.e., not fake) smile, "Oh, but I do mean it." If you receive a compliment, try not to deflect or reject it. Rather, accept it with grace and humility by saying something simple like, "Thank you. That's very kind."

Healthy Communication

You have probably heard the cliché, "The secret of a good relationship is good communication." Unfortunately, the cliché is meaningless. Parties to an argument are usually able to state their cases clearly enough. Unfortunately, clarity alone is insufficient. In the following nasty exchange, there is clarity but no consideration of what the other person is saying.

Rikki and Curtis were having another fight. Rikki was angry and screamed, "You just don't get it, Curtis," to which he responded, "I do, but you never listen to me." Rikki continued her attack, "The problem is that we don't communicate." to which Curtis replied, "I think I communicate perfectly. You just don't like what I have to say."

Unless Rikki and Curtis can find a new way to talk to each other, even if they have periods of temporary peace, they will continue to fight because their arguments are always left unresolved, and unresolved differences will kill a relationship. Here is another example of bad communication:

Sue: Barry, where are we going for dinner? It's getting late, and you need to make a reservation.

Barry (snappishly): I'm busy. You plan it. I'll do whatever you like.

Conversations like this often occur in relationships. Woman wants man to take action; man rejects her request with indifference or petulance. In my example, Sue knows that Barry won't "do whatever" she likes for dinner. Barry's communication shows no respect for Sue, her needs, or their evening together, and another nail goes into the relationship's coffin.

Barry could have said, "No problem, Sue. I know we need to work that out. I'll be done in about twenty minutes. Let's chat then. Is that okay?"

Or this: "Sorry, love, I'm busy right now. I enjoyed that new Peruvian restaurant we went to last month. If that works for you, let's go there. I'd be really grateful if you could make the reservation."

Even if Sue is disappointed by his answer, it was much more helpful. He recognized the validity of what Sue asked and set a time to address it. He also offered an alternative, which demonstrates respect for Sue and a good-faith effort to accommodate her. Of course, Sue was inconsiderate when she interrupted Barry's work. Instead of throwing the task of making a reservation at Barry, she could have suggested a plan:

Sue: Barry, I can see you are busy, so shall I go ahead and make us a reservation at Casa Pisco for eight o'clock?

Barry: Yes. Great! I'll be ready by then.

This example is a good illustration of how minor differences in tone and content can keep a relationship respectful or push it into misery. When you behave as a Man, these communication breakdowns don't often occur, and if they do, the damage is quickly repaired by saying something like, "Darling, you seem upset about something. What's the matter?" The way a couple handles a difference is a bellwether of their relationship's health. New partners never treat each other the way Barry and Sue did.

In the example, Sue disrespects Barry's focus on his task, and Barry signals his disdain for her request by speaking in a way he knows will make her furious. If couples find themselves emulating this pattern and can't figure out how to resolve differences, their relationship is over (all that remains is to give it a decent burial). As I describe below, Barry and Sue could do much better.

A Sacred Space

Create your "sacred space" or whatever you would like to call it, where you can address anything important or challenging. Karen and I call our sacred space *The Yellow Chairs.* Any chairs will work provided they are comfortable. When we have something important to talk about, we turn the chairs so they face each other a few feet apart. I put my feet up on Karen's chair, with one foot on either side of her. In this position, with my legs apart, I am open and vulnerable. Karen puts her feet in my lap, establishing a strong physical connection, which is important to us both. From this position, we look directly into each other's eyes and "speak the unspeakable" and "hear the unhearable." We know that if we hold anything back, our relationship will suffer. There is no place for anger or raised voices. We are there to resolve an issue or to open a dialogue on something important. We can't do that if we are fighting. If Barry and Sue had a sacred space to go to, the conversation would have gone something like this:

Sue: You were curt with me earlier, and I felt disrespected. What you said was hurtful to me, and I don't believe I had done anything to deserve such treatment. I am worried that this type of communication is happening more and more often. Please tell me what is going on.

Barry: I was busy and had no time to make a dinner reservation. I had told you earlier that I would be busy until about 7:30. There is nothing "going on" that is affecting my relationship with you.

Barry's tone and facial expression suggests to Sue that he is not being completely honest, presumably because he thinks Sue could not bear to hear what he needs to say. But Sue is astute enough to recognize his reticence, and she probes further:

Sue: Yes, you did tell me you would be busy, but you didn't mean it when you said you didn't care where we went for dinner. What is important now, though, is that you are not addressing the real issue, which is the way you spoke to me. Please tell me why you were so angry and so rude to me.

Barry gathers up his courage and takes this opportunity to air his grievances:

Barry: Okay. What's bothering me is that you often ask me to do things you are capable of doing yourself. You treat me like your secretary. You also get upset if I don't respond to your requests immediately. I have a busy work schedule, and I am busy keeping the house in good repair. I have become increasingly resentful of you lately because you keep demanding more of me when I am giving everything I've got. You don't help me, even though there are many things you could do to ease my workload.

Sue: I wish you had told me about this sooner. I can do more, and I will, but you have always made the dinner plans, so I have deferred to you. In future, please share these concerns with me. Please don't leave them unresolved. I want to help you in any way I can. When you need help, just ask me—please!

This is a much better exchange in which both Sue and Barry spoke the unspeakable and were prepared to hear the unhearable. As a result, the conversation is more honest and more complete (for example, Barry learned that Sue thought *she had no option* but to defer to him on things like dinner plans). If you are not honest with each other, the acid drip of resentment will devour your relationship. Even if you talk about your issues as a couple, if your communications are less than the whole truth, your relationship is doomed.

If you are thinking, "That's all very well for Clarke to say, but when I'm angry, everything I say sounds like I shot it out of a cannon. I say things I don't even mean and that I instantly regret. I can't help myself. That's just me."

Although we covered this already, I am going to say it again because it is so important. If you are excusing your bad behavior with a phrase like "That's just me," then you are out of control. Unless you have a medical or psychiatric condition that interferes with your self-control mechanisms, you *can* control yourself. Nothing happens because *that's just you*. What you do and what you say are your choices. So own your actions, and always act consciously from this moment forward. Your life will improve the instant you take control of your actions, demeanor and emotions, and accept responsibility for them. The reality is that you can't win anything by browbeating your partner; even an apparent "win" will be short-lived. If you want to quit the relationship, say that is what you want. Don't drag out the end by slowly torturing each other. If you want the relationship to last, find your sacred space and start talking to each other, respectfully, calmly, honestly. In your sacred space, you must both be prepared to speak the unspeakable and hear the unhearable.

Being Open

For the purposes of this book, I am defining openness as a two-way street that lets the real you *out* and lets other people *in* without editorial bias (i.e., lets them know you better and allows you to know them better). When you are open, others can see, hear, and feel you. Being open also means that you accept challenges from others and that you are willing to consider something new, even if it goes against all your prior programming and knowledge. When you are open to whatever comes your way, you will quickly realize that you have much to learn and that you will become stronger and healthier by learning it.

Openness in the context of dating does not mean you have to reveal everything about yourself in a big data dump when you first meet a woman. It does mean that you are willing and eager to:

- Share details about yourself at an appropriate pace.
- Learn about her history and feelings.
- Listen (*really* listen) to what she has to say.
- Accept the risk of being yourself.
- Trust her to match your level of integrity.

When you open yourself to a partner, you take the risk that she might use what she learns against you. It's even possible that she will use your information to hurt you after the relationship is over, as the subjects of many amateur sex videos have found to their dismay. If you feel unable to reveal yourself to a new partner, that means you don't trust her. If that is true, there is little hope for your relationship. Of course, if you never trust people, you minimize your chances of them hurting you, but you are destined to live a lonely life.

There is no formula for opening up to someone new, but it might go something like this:

First Date:

- Where you went to school.
- What you like to do.
- Whether you've been married.
- Whether you have children.
- How you feel about your life, your town/city, your friends.

Second Date (if there is one):

- Your track record (academic, business, personal).
- Where you work
- Where you live.
- How happy you are.

- How you live your life, in general.
- Your views on politics and religion.

When it seems that your relationship is going to become sexual, you must discuss exclusivity. A Man does not have sex with more than one woman without disclosing *to each woman* the non-exclusive nature of his relationship with her. You can pretty much rely on the fact that a woman will assume you are exclusive no later than your second sexual interaction and possibly even before the first.

Beyond:

- Your short- and long-term goals ("I want to settle down"; "I don't want children"; "I want to move to Tahiti").
- What you are looking for in a lover/companion.
- How you feel about long-term relationships.
- How you feel about a long-term relationship with this woman.
- Where your train is headed.
- Your physical and mental health, and especially before your first sexual interaction
    - o whether you have a sexually transmitted disease
    - o whether you have a history of sexual dysfunction

Before too much time passes, you have to be prepared to tell:

- Whether you have been arrested, charged, or convicted of a crime.
- Whether you have a drug or alcohol problem.
- How financially secure you are (details of your finances are not necessary. "I have a job, a house, a car, and a mortgage" should be enough until you are a committed couple).
- Whether you have significant financial commitments (alimony, aging parents, or a child's education).

There is no point dealing with these highly personal issues before you have established mutual trust and interest, but you will eventually have to accept the risk of revelation if you want to forge a strong connection. This is especially important if you have *dark* secrets, such as a conviction or an ongoing bankruptcy. If you ignore these things, she will discover them eventually, and your dishonesty will doom the relationship. Be open physically, emotionally, spiritually, and mentally so she can learn about you without any pretense on your part. Hope that she reciprocates by being open with you.

Intimacy

Intimacy is not only about a sexual interaction, although that is usually what people mean when they use the word. Intimacy means you don't withhold parts of yourself from an intimate partner. You don't blurt out whatever comes into your head, but you do convey personal details in a responsible and timely manner. When you both open yourselves up, you will bond ever more closely together. Of course, intimacy is a two-way process in which you reveal more of your hopes and dreams to each other over time. Intimacy also demands that you let her know when her behavior is not acceptable. For example, suppose your lover has said something inappropriate to you, and you are upset. Intimacy means you can't ignore or brood on what she said. Brooding creates distance, the opposite of intimacy. Tell her how her behavior affected you so that, if she chooses, she can modify her behavior in future. There may be a good explanation for her behavior, in which case your issue may be an invention of your own imagination (i.e., your story). If she triggered your story, you allowed your past into your present, which is always likely to cause a problem because she has no idea what she did wrong. A trigger may go something like this:

Your former lover was angry "all the time," and the woman you are dating became angry when you arrived an hour late to pick her up. You conclude that she, like your former lover, will be angry all the time too.

Projecting your story onto someone else is inappropriate. Jettison your story so it does not affect your present or your future. Reread Chapter 11 on "Story" if necessary. Work to replace your old story with a new one, such as,

I am a masculine Man. I am proud to be a Man. I am going to behave as a Man. Women are not all the same. Women don't only want provision and protection. Women are not angry all the time. Henceforth, I am going to live in the present. I won't allow my past to affect me, my relationship, or my work.

To deepen intimacy with your lover, show her that you are able to:

- Stand in your power as a Man.
- Be active, thoughtful, interested, curious, capable, and open.
- Discuss any topic with her.
- Remain flexible.
- Amend your behavior when appropriate.
- See a project through to the end.
- Defend her against the world.
- Take care of yourself.
- Remain calm under pressure.

True intimacy is a beautiful place to be. It allows you to access parts of another person that few people ever see and find parts of yourself you did not know existed. Once you live your life open and vulnerable, you will be free to become truly intimate with your lover (and others too).

15

FEMALE GENITAL ANATOMY

As I mentioned earlier, *The Pussy Talks* video shows a wide variety of vulvas (which *may* have one thing in common with snowflakes; they are all different). According to *The Vagina Monologues*, a show written by, and starring, Eve Ensler, some women have never seen their own vulvas, which is a sad reflection on how we, as a society, treat sexuality. When you come to know your lover well, ask her if she has ever seen her vulva and other parts of her genital anatomy. If she says *no*, see if she is open to you helping her discover this amazing part of her body.

If your lover will model for you as you explore female anatomy, that will really help. If you don't have a lover, try to find a woman to be your model as you make the exploration that follows. Whoever helps you make this exploration, treat her with enormous respect and dignity. She is being incredibly brave to do this for you. Realize that many women would find being viewed in this manner significantly more stressful than having intercourse with you. Whoever models for you, you will have to explain to her exactly what you want her to do, so there is no misunderstanding on your part about what is acceptable to her. You must go over the informed consent and affirmative permission protocol with her as I described earlier. If she revokes permission at any time you stop. Your exploration is over for the time being at least. Even if your model is your lover, treat her with greater reverence than you usually do.

Let's begin by establishing a starting position, Position A:

The woman is lying on her back, nude from the waist down. Her legs are bent, with her knees up and her feet flat on the surface of the floor or bed. Her feet should be between two and three feet apart. You are lying between her legs on your belly, looking directly at her genital area (i.e., her vulva). If you want to use a massage table, the woman will lie on it in Position A, while you sit on a chair at the foot of the table. All references to up, down, upper, lower and so on in the descriptions that follow, are in relation to where you are looking when you and your partner are in Position A. Therefore, a reference to *up or upper* means toward the ceiling; *down or lower* means toward the floor; *back or rear* means toward her head; *front* means toward her feet; *and left or right* mean to *your* left and right.

Internal Genital Structure (side view)

The image shows a cross-sectional view of a female's internal anatomy. Keep this image in mind as you read about female anatomy in the next few pages.

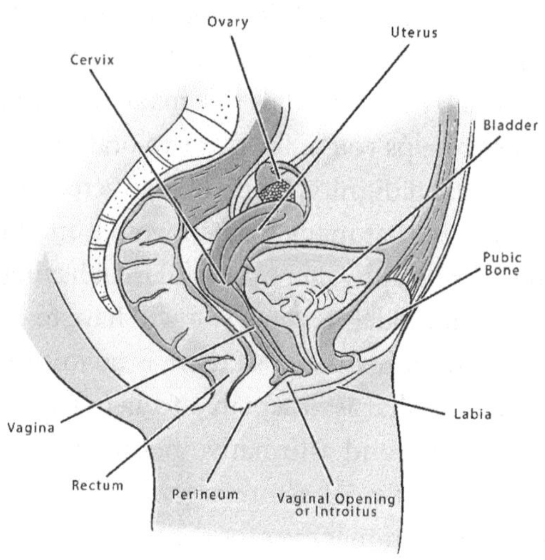

Ovaries

A woman has two ovaries that store her eggs until they are released during her monthly cycle. There is one ovary on each side (left and right) of her body. The ovaries are about an inch or two toward the mid-line from her hip bones, and an inch or two above her pubic bone. Ask her to show you where her ovaries are.

Uterus

The uterus is a muscular structure (think of it as a container) where a fertilized egg develops into a baby. DO NOT try to gain access to the uterus through the cervix unless you are medically trained and know what you are doing.

Cervix

The cervix is the pathway from the uterus to the vaginal canal, through which a baby passes at birth. The cervix is located toward the rear of the vagina, so you may have to use your extended fingers to reach it (the depth of the vagina can vary considerably). It will feel like a raised projection on the upper-rear surface of the vagina. You may also be able to feel a slight depression in the middle of the raised structure. Again, DO NOT try to gain access to the uterus through the cervix unless you are medically trained and know what you are doing.

Perineum

What most people are referring to when they say *perineum* is the one or two square inches between the anus and where the labia minora meet below the introitus. The medical definition of the perineum is somewhat different, and includes far more genital, urinary, and bowel structures which do not concern us here.

Vulva

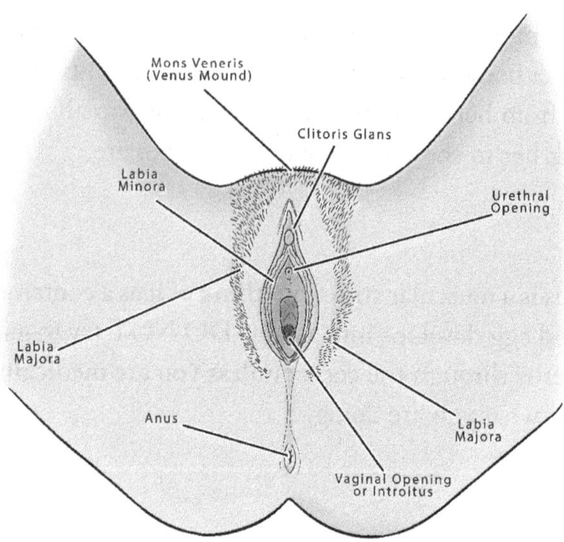

The vulva is the external structure of a woman's genital anatomy. The vulva includes: the vulval vestibule, the mons veneris, (also called the Venus Mount or mons pubis), the labia majora and labia minora, the vaginal entrance or introitus, the clitoris glans, and the perineum. Also included in the vulva are the vestibular bulbs (not labelled), which are adjacent to the introitus to the left and right of the labia minora.

Mons Veneris

The mons veneris is formed by the outward bulge of the pubic bone, which is a significantly larger in a woman than a man because her pelvis has to be large enough to let a baby pass through during birth (a woman has broader hips than a man for the same reason). The pubic bone is covered with a layer of sub-cutaneous fat, skin and pubic hair (unless shaved).

Labia Majora

The labia majora (Latin for larger lips; sometimes called the outer lips), encircle the vulva. They begin at the mons pubis and curve downward to end where the left and right labia join at the perineum. When they engorge with blood as a woman becomes aroused, they may become more pronounced and easier to identify. The labia majora may appear to be inaptly named because, although they cover a large area of the vulva, in many women the labia minora are much more visually prominent. The size of the labia majora is not important for this exploration.

Labia Minora

The labia minora (Latin for smaller lips; sometimes called the inner lips), come in a wide variety of textures, shapes and sizes, and often have many folds, creases, and whorls of fleshy tissue. Alternatively, in some women they are quite small with only a little fleshy tissue visible. There seems to be no limit to the variety of labia minora. Therefore, you can anticipate a high degree of variety in the external appearance of your lovers' genital anatomy. Whatever their shape and size, the labia minora cover the vulval vestibule, so if you want to see the vulval vestibule, you will have to use your fingers to open up the labia minora and push aside any pubic hair.

Clitoris Glans

What most people are referencing when they talk about the clitoris is actually the glans of the clitoris, often referred to simply as the glans. To find the glans, follow her labia minora upward until they meet; the glans is right there but it may not be immediately visible because it is usually covered by a clitoral hood. To see the glans, gently push the hood back toward her navel and you should see the glans as a small protruding organ. If she has a large clitoral hood, you may have to push the hood back several inches to expose the glans. In a minority of women, the glans is always hooded, so you won't be able to see it at all. If you cannot see the glans, don't worry; it is not important that you see it. As long as you know where it is, you will still be able to pleasure it. If you cannot find the glans, ask her to show it to you.

Urethral Opening

The urethra is the tube from the bladder through which women (and men) evacuate urine. A woman's urethral opening is located on the upper surface of the vulval vestibule. It will probably be a slightly different color from the surrounding pink tissue. You may also see two additional marks close to the urethral opening. These are the Skene's gland openings, which are not important for this discussion (if you want to know more about any of these body parts or functions, I suggest discussing your questions with a physician, preferably an OB/GYN, or searching on Wikipedia).

A Closer Look at the Vulva

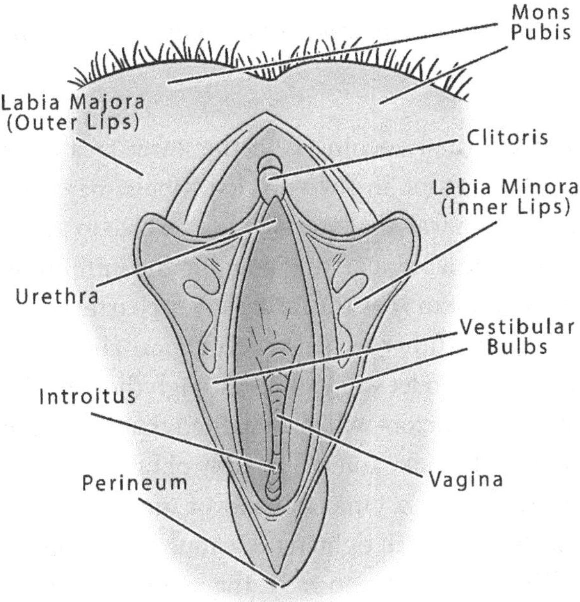

This drawing shows a close up of the main elements of the vulval vestibule. The vulval vestibule is usually covered by the labia minora, which are depicted spread apart so you can see the vaginal opening more clearly. Although the vestibular bulbs are labelled, the open labia minora are obscuring them in this image. The labia would not be so open in a woman who is not aroused.

The vulva may be covered in pubic hair which may be thick, bushy, long, short, or non-existent. The pubic hair could also be blond, black, red or grey. Because many women shave or trim their pubic hair, you may never know what it looks like.

Vagina

The vagina offers a vast array of shapes and internal structures, so do not be concerned if your woman has a different structure from the following description.

The introitus/vaginal opening is in the lower area of the vulval vestibule. Other tissue in the vulval vestibule may press on the introitus in such a way that you will not be able to see it without gently pulling the labia apart and opening the introitus with your fingers. If you want to view the inside of your partner's vagina, you will have to go with her to her gynecological check-up, and ask her and her doctor to let you look in through the speculum. Most women and their doctors will be delighted that you are interested enough to want to look, and will readily oblige.

The introitus has a circular band of muscle around it, and many (most?) women can tighten these muscles to grip your finger or penis. The interior structure of the vagina is a muscle-lined irregular shaped closed *tube* (i.e., the sides are not parallel), which tends to be narrow at the introitus, then widens out toward the cervix. The vaginal walls are highly elastic and expand to allow a baby to pass through at birth. They also exude a fluid that keeps the vagina lubricated.

Clitoris

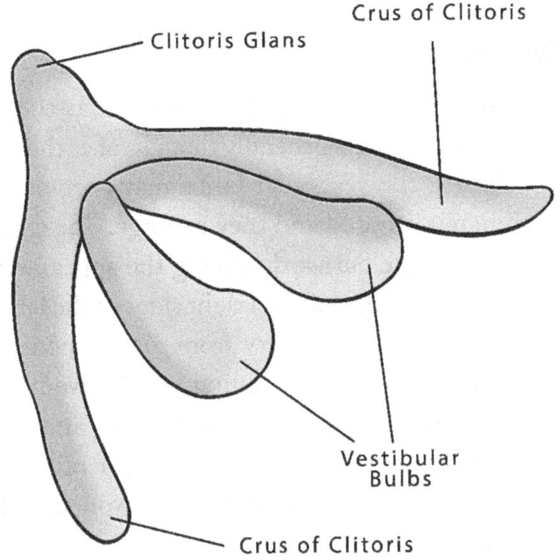

As you can see from the image above, the clitoris has five branches. At the tip of the central branch is the glans. The glans is very small compared to the rest of the clitoris and, while it is the most sensitive area of the clitoris, it is by no means the only sensitive part. In most women, it is possible to see the glans, although (as previously stated) you may have to push back the clitoral hood to see it.

Clitoral Crura

The clitoral crura are the two outer legs of the clitoris (crura is Latin for legs; crus is Latin for a leg). The ends of the clitoral crura are close to a woman's anus (within an inch or two). Although a woman cannot (generally) feel the clitoral crura as specific structures (just as you can't feel your heart beat when you are resting), she does feel sensations in the neighborhood of the crura when she is aroused (just as you can feel your heart beat when you are strenuously working out).

Vestibular Bulbs

The middle two legs of the clitoris are known as the vestibular bulbs. Although the glans is generally thought of as the only visible part of the clitoris, the vestibular bulbs may become noticeable when the woman is aroused and they engorge. The engorgement pushes the skin surface outwards, giving the appearance of subcutaneous swellings on the left and right sides of the labia minora. The size of the swellings can vary from almost non-existent to bigger than a large thumb depending on the woman's genital anatomy, how much subcutaneous fat she has, and her level of arousal. As a result, the vestibular bulbs are generally easy to find and may be a new source of pleasure for your woman as I describe in the next chapter.

Pubic Hair

If you have ever wondered why you have pubic hair, wonder no more. Your pubic hair serves two purposes.

The first purpose is that the hair acts as a lubricant. I know that sounds unlikely but here's how it works and why. Without pubic hair, your bare skin would rub on your partner's bare skin during a sexual interaction. Such rubbing can cause discomfort from chaffing and even cause abrasions. Nature wants you and your partner to be ready for sex at all times, so discomfort from chaffing and abrasions is not good biology. Therefore, you have sweaty pubic hair to cushion the skin and reduce the friction (your sweat is a great lubricant), which means chaffing and abrasions are a non-issue. You have hair on your scrotum and in your armpits for the same reason.

The second purpose of pubic hair is to act as a distribution mechanism for the alluring compounds (pheromones) a human body produces. You and your partner both secrete a variety of pheromones when you are interacting sexually. The pheromone molecules stick to sweaty pubic hair (as well as under-arm hair) and enter the body through the nose or mouth. As you might imagine, your nose and mouth frequently come in close proximity to your partner's pubic hair during an interaction, but you do not even need to be particularly close to the pubic hair for the pheromones to do their job.

The pheromones profoundly affect how you feel and what you do, without any conscious action on your part. For these reasons, I suggest that neither you nor your partner shave off *all* of your pubic hair; leave some of it in place to work its magic. Try living without deodorant as well. Once your body adjusts to a non-deodorant hygiene regime, you will have a better chance of attracting a partner. I know, it's weird but it's true.

So here is a Man tip. Bathe properly every day (sorry but you have to get in there and clean all your dirty, smelly bits) with good quality soap (not highly perfumed) and you will be fine. You will gain the added benefit that your shirts will no longer have an ugly black ring around the color. This tip alone will save you ten times the price of this book *every year* because you will no longer need to buy after-shave or deodorant. You are now free to just smell good... naturally!

G-Spot (not shown)

The G-Spot (named after the German gynecologist Ernst Graffenburg, and more clinically known as the urethral sponge) is located on the upper surface of the vagina. It is not actually a *spot* but we will continue to call it the G-Spot because that's what everyone calls it. The G-Spot is more appropriately described as an *area* of erectile tissue between one square inch and four square inches. In some women, the G-Spot is only an inch or so inside the vaginal opening, while in other women, it might be several inches further inside. It all depends on their genital geometry. Don't worry; it's all good.

You will need short, clean fingernails for this part of the exploration, and be sure to remove any hangnails you might have. To find the G-spot, ask her permission then, with your hand palm up, gently slide your lubricated middle finger into her vagina about an inch or two. If you feel a ridged surface with the pad of your fingertip, you have found her G-Spot. If you don't feel a ridged surface that may be because her G-Spot is deeper in her vagina, so use your extended finger to feel for it. Because the G-Spot has erectile tissue, it becomes more prominent as a woman becomes aroused. If you don't feel the ridged area, and it is OK with her, stimulate her by adding a little upward pressure and moving the pad of your fingertip around in a circular motion. You can also bend your finger toward you, as if you are motioning for someone to *come here*! Add a second finger, with permission, if needed. Your stimulating touch will usually make her G-Spot more obvious as it engorges with blood.

16

PLEASURING A WOMAN

OF COURSE, IF YOU AND your lover engage in good (or even reasonably good) sexual intercourse, she will experience an avalanche of stimulation in many parts of her body. All the body parts that I am discussing in this section will be stimulated and will release a range of hormones, pleasurable sensations, lubrication, and overall flow of sexual energy in her body: emotional, physical, mental, and (hopefully) spiritual. Realize that vaginal stimulation is just one form of stimulation and that for her, it may be impossible to separate one individual stimulus from another as they all become part of her entire experience. Much of her stimulation is mental and emotional rather than physical, so be aware that the pure, raw, physicality you enjoy as a male will probably be quite different from how she experiences a sexual interaction. Don't worry about it. It's all good. Now we have identified some parts of a woman's anatomy, let's consider how you might pleasure her.

Clitoris Glans

The glans has thousands of nerve endings, which make it acutely sensitive. Most men are unaware of how sensitive a woman's glans is. I don't have one either, so we will have to take their word for it—the glans is *super-sensitive*. When you touch it, be gentle and slow. This is true whether you are using your finger, your tongue, or a toy to pleasure her. Resist the temptation to *rub* the glans. The glans can make your wishes come true but, unlike Aladdin's lamp, you don't have to rub it to make it work. The clitoral shaft (i.e., the structure behind the glans that connects the glans to the rest of the clitoris) is easier to find when a woman is aroused.

If you have ever wondered where to touch a woman's glans to give her maximum pleasure, wonder no more. For most women, concentrate on the northeast quadrant of the glans. Where is that? In position A, the northeast quadrant is between the hands of a clock showing three o'clock. The big hand is pointing up (at the ceiling), and the little hand is pointing to your right. When you touch the glans, apply the lightest pressure, and follow her lead for her preferred degree of pressure and speed of motion. If she is not accustomed to taking the lead in communicating what feels good and what doesn't, just ask her to tell you (or listen carefully; her sounds are a good guide). You can enhance your gentle touch by wearing an examination glove. They are available at any drugstore, and they will make your touch ultra-smooth, especially if you add a little lube to the finger of the glove. If she is allergic to latex, there are non-latex gloves. Try the glove, and see if you both like it. Warning: Snapping the glove onto your hand is a cop-movie cliché and a major buzz-killer!

NOTE: A woman will not find it pleasurable if you over-simulate this sensitive spot (it has been described to me as maddeningly unpleasant; like being tickled to death).

During sexual intercourse, the male's movement exerts stimulating pressure on the clitoris and the vestibular bulbs, while the shaft and head of the penis create similar sensations on the G-spot and cervical area. In other words, during sex you are affecting a wide area of your woman's genital anatomy. You may be surprised to learn that some women do not feel much (or any?) clitoral stimulation during intercourse because of their genital geometry.

This means that if your partner needs clitoral stimulation in order to orgasm, intercourse alone will not do it for her. Don't be upset about this aspect of her beauty; it is not your fault you cannot lead her to orgasm during intercourse, and it's not her fault either. If you want to help her with clitoral stimulation to bring on an orgasm, ask her what she would like you to do. Once you know she needs special attention to her clitoris, you can pleasure her before or after intercourse using your fingers, tongue, or toys. If she suggests that she will pleasure herself to orgasm before or after intercourse (ie., without your physical involvement), try to watch what she does and learn to do that for her. Practice will be fun and interesting, and may lead you to new discoveries.

Here are some ways to stimulate your lover's clitoris (if you are already doing this, congratulations):

1. Start in position A and locate the clitoral shaft, which is usually between one and four inches long. Put your index finger and thumb on either side of the shaft, and slide them back and forth along the shaft, as if you were pleasuring a small erect penis. Begin gently and slowly. Don't use lube because it will make your fingers too slippery. Ask her whether she likes the pressure and speed you are using. Remember that the clitoral shaft engorges and becomes much easier to find as she becomes more aroused.
2. With your finger and thumb on either side of her clitoral shaft, gently but sharply snap your fingers to send a delicious shock wave through her body. Start off easy and add pressure as she suggests.
3. Pull back the skin (toward her navel) around the head of her clitoris to reveal the glans, and then circle the glans with your lubed finger or your pointed tongue. Be super-uber-gentle, and focus on the northeast quadrant, as I described above, until she tells you otherwise. I repeat, be girl-gentle, not lumberjack-gentle.
4. With the clitoral hood pulled back (it matters not whether you do it or she does), flatten your tongue and slowly slide your tongue over and around the glans.

5. Stroke her labia minora with really light pressure from the perineum to the glans with your flat tongue or your fingertips. Those tiny bumps on your tongue and finger will give her great pleasure. You can add lube or not; that's your (joint) choice; food grade coconut oil is an excellent lube because it does not dry out and become sticky, which is what many sex-shop lubes do. As I mentioned earlier, some women are allergic to silicone lube, so take care when choosing lube. It is probably best to stick with coconut oil or Sylk (see Resources) until you know the woman better and can choose lube together. Many women have a super-sensitive spot on their perineum. Again, be ultra-light with your touch here. Just wet your fingertip and touch around the area lightly, or use your tongue. If she likes it, you will know.

If you have done all of the above actions before, just use your imagination and try something new. Your lover will appreciate your efforts and enjoy the change.

Urethral Opening

A woman likely will enjoy your tender touch on and around her urethral opening. Not many lovers will have touched her there, so when you do, she will know you are a knowledgeable lover. To pleasure her urethral opening, use a *super-gentle* circular touch around the opening with your fingertip. Vary your touch based on what she tells you. Add lube or wet your fingertip with saliva as needed to make your touch smooth. If she has not been touched like this before, you will be taking her on her first journey to a new pleasure zone. How cool is that? Try the lubed examination glove for this purpose too.

Cervix

Many women find a degree of pressure around the cervix to be stimulating and some women experience a cervical orgasm if stimulated in that area. What is appropriate for your woman, and what feels best to her, will be the subject of a wonderful exploration for you both.

Labia

In addition to her clitoris and urethral opening, a woman's fleshy labia are a major source of pleasure that men often ignore. To pleasure her labia, gently stroke them with your finger or thumb, or whisper-touch them with your fingertips or tongue. You can add more vigorous touch later if she likes it (if you cannot tell whether she likes it, just ask her). Take your time. Experiment with squeezing, pinching, or pulling on her labia with your finger and thumb. Ask her to tell you if the pressure is right for her. Labia are meant to be played with, and some women like to play hard. It is all good if she likes it. If you ever wondered why you have opposable thumbs, now you know!

If your woman's labia are too tiny to get hold of, you may not be able to pull or tug on them. This is not a problem. You can still stroke their edges with your fingers, your tongue, or a toy.

G-Spot

Stimulation of the G-spot is highly pleasurable for most women, and they often will ask you to apply more pressure eventually. As she becomes more aroused, she may want you to use two fingers or a toy.

In the Resources section, I suggest a G-spot video that has excellent information on G-spot stimulation and ejaculation. (*Warning:* the video is pornographic in parts. While some participants appear to be ordinary people, others seem to be professional actors.) The video has some useful information, and the G-spot stimulation presentation is … well, let's say … spirited. Decide for yourself whether to watch this video (maybe watch it alone first) and discuss with your partner whether she would like to watch it.

VestibularBulbs

Before you begin to explore and pleasure your woman's vestibular bulbs (or any other part of her genital anatomy), make sure to cut your fingernails short (no sharp edges or hangnails), or wear an examination glove.

To pleasure the vestibular bulbs, massage the exterior surface of them in position A. Begin with gentle touch, but realize that she may want more pressure as she becomes more aroused. When she is ready (you will probably know, but ask her anyway), gently push your finger or thumb into one of the bulbs at ninety degrees to her skin surface. Then change your focus, and do the same to the other vestibular bulb. It's best to use no lubricant because it will make your fingers too slippery. Stay on the *exterior* surface of her skin so you don't enter her vagina. Your fingers will probably be able to press into the vestibular bulbs quite easily, and in some women, you may be able to push your fingers or thumbs in as much as two inches without entering her vagina. If your woman has a small pelvis or small labia, there may not be enough space in her pelvic structure to insert your finger into the vestibular bulbs very far, or at all. It's all okay. Simply use light touch to pleasure the skin over the external surface of her vestibular bulbs. If pressing on her vestibular bulbs is not pleasant for her leave them alone and pleasure somewhere else.

Once you are exploring the vestibular bulbs with your fingers, you can move your fingers around, pushing left, right, up, down. Your fingers may even be able to reach the back of her pubic bone, which is another pleasure spot for some women. In this position, your fingers are deep inside the vestibular bulbs, but they are still on the outer surface of her skin, and although you have not entered her vagina, it may feel to her that you have. One of the women in The Pussy Talks shows where her vestibular bulbs are located and describes how to pleasure them.

Vagina

If you are like most males, a woman's vagina is the pinnacle of her female genital anatomy. So, how do you pleasure her vagina?

Be Gentle

Overly aggressive stimulation is a common mistake that most males manage to make. Resist the urge to be vigorous until she wants more vigor. Her vagina does not need painting, so don't sandpaper it. Thrusting your fingers in and out of her three times a second might seem like a good idea to you, but take it from me, most women find this action unpleasant even though they may not tell you they don't like it because they worry it will upset you. You may also add a second finger (the combination of your middle finger and index finger is best), but be sure to ask her how the extra finger feels. At the risk of being repetitive, no woman will mark you down for going too slowly—I promise! If she wants you to go faster or more vigorously, she will let you know.

When you are physically connected, maintain your awareness of the tactile pleasure of her lubricated vagina and pay particular attention if you sense any tendency for her vaginal lubrication to diminish. If that happens, you may sense that she is drying up, so make sure she is alright and add lube as needed. Everything about this exploration of your woman's magical body is unadulterated magic. Don't rush it. Savor it.

I cannot stress enough that when stimulating a woman, until she tells you any different: softer is better than harder, and slower is better than faster. Take your time and enjoy the delicacy of her genital structure. Try to pleasure her mind and stimulate her emotions before, during and after you have pleasured her physical body (more about how to pleasure her mentally and emotionally in the next section).

Be Diffuse

Do not become too focused on any single part of her anatomy. You want to pleasure her entire body before you pleasure her vagina. If you can do so sincerely, begin by pleasuring her mentally with words of love. Be sincere or you will sound like a fake, and that will be the last you ever see of this woman. Tell her what you find so attractive about her. Tell her how she makes you feel. Let her know how much she means to you. You may feel strange saying these things, but if you are sincere, you will be fine. If you cannot be sincere, you should probably stop your interaction and figure out why. If you continue with the interaction when you cannot think of anything complimentary to say to your partner, you are engaged in an empty sex encounter. Why would you do this to her or to yourself? A Man would never do such a thing.

While you are speaking to her, use your fingers, tongue, and lips to pleasure her mouth, ears, neck, arms, and the back of her knees. Suck on her toes, and play with her hair. Do all of this before you touch her breasts. When you have spent 20 minutes holding, kissing, stroking and holding eye contact with your woman, then you massaged, stroked, and kneaded her breasts for another 20 minutes, and you pleasured her clitoris and labia for an additional 20 minutes (at least), she will be highly aroused and balancing on a perfect edge of desire and pure animal lust, just waiting to take the plunge with you.

When you can sense that she is ready, ask her to let you into her vagina. ("May I enter you with my fingers). If she agrees that you may enter her, gently move your middle finger inside her vagina up to your first knuckle; use lube if she needs it. Keep your hand and fingers relaxed and the palm of your hand facing up. Move your fingers slowly in and out, and side to side, pressing a little more firmly on the upper surface of the inside of her vagina from time to time. After at least five minutes of stimulation at the one-inch depth, start to move your finger in a little further. Resist the urge to move your fingers all the way inside right away. Take your time to get that far. Eventually, explore the entire depth of her vagina, including the area around her cervix, massaging it gently with your extended finger(s).

Just Ask and Be Conscious

When you think she is ready for your penis to be in her vagina, ask her. She will let you know if she is ready. If she wants more stimulation, or she wants you to back off, or she even wants to stop, simply accept her decision with good grace. It's what a Man does. Make no mistake, if you pressure her at this point with your words, you are browbeating her. If you pressure her with promises (of a gift, or money or a promotion) you are following in the footsteps of many dishonorable, weak men; and you don't want to do that do you? Finally, if you pressure her with *physical force*, you are raping her and deserve all the punishment you get.

17

SEX AND ROMANCE

Even when it's not about sex, it's *all* about sex.

SEX IS EXCELLENT EXERCISE THAT requires thought in the planning, development, and execution. Your brain spends a lot of its precious energy thinking about sex in one form or another—who you want to do it with, how to attract her, and what to do if she accepts your invitation. As a result, sex stimulates all kinds of good responses in your body—physical, mental, emotional, and spiritual. Sex is not just a natural gift. It is the fuel in your tank and the fire in your belly. In spite of its importance, however, many males find it difficult to be natural in their sexuality, probably because nobody taught them how to be appropriately sexual. If you are afraid of women and sex, it's a sign that your inner Man is still incarcerated. Set your inner Man free, take some classes, read every book you can find, and you will learn how to be natural in your sexuality. Now that we have covered some of the basics, and you know to take your time and be gentle (at least at first), let's get started on how to be with a woman, in integrity, with respect, with care and, above all, with passion.

What a Mess!

There was a time, not so long ago, when the topic of sex was taboo for almost everyone in the developed Western world, especially in "polite" society. Even in our permissive society, it's still difficult to talk about sex in most situations (wrong time, wrong place, wrong audience). For many people, it's impossible at any time. It's just not a subject we are comfortable discussing. On National Public Radio's *Diane Rehm Show* (August 23, 2016), I heard a medical research expert declare, "The [US] government can't talk about sex." People still talk about sex in the abstract or in euphemism. Talking openly about sex is likely to bring much criticism your way (up to and including being shunned by people in your community). What follows is not a how-to manual about sex, nor is it a critique of your sexual technique or prowess, and it's definitely not a criticism of how you express yourself sexually. These are just some insights you might not have heard, even if you are an avid reader of sexy magazines. If you have heard all this stuff before, congratulations, you are way ahead of your competition.

You might think you know about sex from watching actors in feature films or pornographic videos. If so, you probably think that sex should look like what you see on the screen. These are terrible ways to learn how to have sex with a real woman, especially a woman you are interested in. Remember that the screenwriter tells the performers what to say, and the director tells them what to do. Magically, sex looks easy, cool (or *hot*), and it only has a downside if that is what the story calls for. Fortunately, you will have sex without a scriptwriter or director, and with a real woman instead of a movie character. There are no shortcuts to becoming a great lover; it takes time, but the journey is magical. What your high school friends told you about sex was, at best, incomplete and probably wrong. The chance that anyone taught you about *love* and its role in a relationship is virtually zero. Few people even understand what love is, and many people confuse love with ownership and control. If you have not learned much about sex since fumbling your way to "first base" in your teens, and even if you have had a lot of sexual interactions in your life, begin by learning all you can about yourself and about women. This book is a start but the sexual content is at best an overview. There are thousands of books about sex and some of them are excellent. I have listed a few in the Resources section.

If your sexual technique contains a few *plays*, congratulations; you are ahead of a lot of men. But you won't improve by doing the same thing over and over, even if it feels good. Whatever age you are, it's not too late to start learning. Sex is fun, and it can be funny at times, so a good sense of humor won't hurt a bit during a sexual interaction. To get started, read all you can about sex (reading David Deida's books on sexuality is a good place to begin). Talk to people who know about sex. Go to sex workshops, especially those that include a degree of spirituality. Don't be afraid of spirituality. It can lead to wonderful sexual experiences. Spirituality, in the context of sex, is not about recruiting you or converting you to a particular religion or cult. It's about becoming more conscious and aware as a lover. Being conscious during sex and in your life, will help you connect with yourself and with others.

Practice what you learn in this book with experienced women, if you can. If you have a lover already, practice with her (it's okay for her to read this book too). Whatever you do, keep learning; the journey matters. I hope that what follows gives you more options to try. If what you are doing in your sex life now is working for you and your partner, then keep rocking and rolling. Just try to keep it fresh by learning more and more. Remember, if you ever stop learning and expanding your sexual repertoire, that rumbling sound you hear is the Dead Collector's cart coming down the street, and he is coming for *you*.

Healthy Sexuality

Healthy sexuality means the following:

- Open communication (speaking the unspeakable and hearing the unhearable).

- A healthy balance between your work life, social life, and sex life.
- Understanding intimacy and healthy sexuality.
- Attracting a partner who understands intimacy and healthy sexuality.
- Sex with presence, dignity, and integrity (as opposed to routine, check-a-box sex).
- Trying a variety of sexual activities to see what works for you, and your partner.
- Honoring your partner before, during and after a sexual interaction.
- Avoiding unintended pregnancy and the spread of infection.
- Knowing how to excite your partner with slow, wild, or experimental sex.
- Welcoming your partner to bring her unbridled feminine ferocity to you without fear.
- Trying something new, frequently.

Healthy sexuality may include relationships that are not traditional, heterosexual, or monogamous. Possibilities include nonexclusive dating ("spinning plates," with apologies to Mr. Tomassi), polyamory and other multiple-partner relationships (three or more people in the relationship), committed open relationships (a primary and non-primary partners), serial monogamy (being monogamous with a partner and then moving on to another monogamous partnership, then another, and another etc.), celibacy (choosing to be sexual only with yourself for some time or for life), and other sexual arrangements too numerous to mention. Not only is there great variety in relationship choices, there is an enormous range of sexual activity too. For example, three categories of sexual activity are kink, bondage, and fetish, but each of those broad categories has myriad sub-categories too numerous to mention. Suffice to say, there are many ways to express your sexuality and to engage in sexual activity.

No matter what your sexual desires may be, a healthy approach to sex means that you do everything in the open; deceit has no place in a healthy sex life. If you want to spend time with a different partner, or do something else you consider to be *far out* tell your partner of that desire. She may walk away from you, but be upfront about it anyway. If you aren't, you will never know what might have happened. If your dating is nonexclusive (i.e., you are "spinning plates"), you must tell your partners what you are doing. Don't tell a woman you are exclusive with her while seeing (or even seeking) other women. If your date is expecting a heterosexual male, but you identify or express yourself differently, tell her before you show up. It is interesting (to me at least) that the areas of sexuality in which mutual respect, care for a partner, and consciousness are most highly practiced and prized, are the non-mainstream areas such as BDSM (bondage, dominance and submission, sadism, and masochism), fetish, and non-monogamous relationships.

One woman's response to how you engage with her sexually (your gaze, touch, sound, taste, smell) may vary greatly from that of another woman. Where your sexual actions may evoke ecstasy in one woman, those same actions may result in discomfort or even physical pain in another woman. So, don't assume that what worked with your last partner will work with the next one. It's up to you to discover each other as you explore the full expression of your sexuality and to keep discovering more about each other as time goes by (and how much fun is that journey going to be?). Whatever you do, keep your relationship juicy, fulfilling, and growing.

Presence

It's vital to be present during a sexual interaction; that means 100% present. Your presence is far more important than any sexual technique you read about in *Cosmopolitan* or *Penthouse.* Learning how to be present during a sexual interaction will also help you be more present in everything else you do. Being present at work might not be enough to get you the corner office, but you will never get the corner office without being present. When you are present, your fun will be more fun, and your life will be more alive. Try it, and see what happens. If you are not present with the woman you are having sex with, your sexual interaction will seem perfunctory, more like checking a box:

> Diary entry for Tuesday, May 7, 2049
> *Cooked dinner at 6:00 p.m. Watched the Dallas Cowboys on TV. Had sex with Katerina.*

In addition to keeping the sexual energy flowing, being present increases the bonding experience and heightens the emotional and physical pleasure you and your partner feel. Be present and committed to your interaction with *this* woman right now, and forget everybody, and everything, else. Being conscious of your woman means you are not thinking about your technique or what someone wrote in a book. What you are concerned about is how she is feeling and responding to you. Forget how you think she *should* be feeling and responding. How she is feeling and responding might be very different from the way she felt and responded last week or even the way she felt and responded ten minutes ago. You will know how she is responding if you are present with her. If you lose presence:

- Re-establish powerful eye contact. If her eyes are closed, just say, "Open your eyes. Look at me." It's okay for this to sound commanding. Your connection will soon be restored.

- Focus on how she smells and tastes—behind her ear, on her neck, and in the pit of her arm (you'll be surprised how interesting that aroma can be). Taste the skin around her toes and in the nooks and folds of her vulva. Try not to seem like a bloodhound searching for Jack the Ripper when you are savoring the delicate aromas your woman's body has to offer. If you do it well, she won't even notice you doing it; she will just admire your amazing presence.
- Consciously decide where and how to touch her (that means no mindless groping, prodding, or fiddling); sense her reaction to every touch. If a touch elicits a negative reaction, ask, "Was that uncomfortable for you?" And if it was, say, "I'm sorry. I won't touch you like that again." Then don't touch her that way in future. It is good to discuss these minor issues with her once the interaction ends. You want to learn from her what happened and what you can change in the future. The best way to do that is ask her what she felt.
- Do what your body is telling you is right in the moment, and notice her reaction to it all.
- Feel every sensation your lover is feeling. You will be able to do so easily once you are a conscious lover.
- Notice the effect your voice has on her.
- Notice every sensation *you* are feeling, no matter how tiny the sensation might be.

It's impossible for your mind to wander if you focus on what you and your lover are feeling. What felt like a trickle of sensation at first can become a torrent of pleasure when you become present again. When you are present, your connection will expand and you can fan the sensations you feel until they become a raging fire coursing through your body. She will be aware of what is happening to you.

Missionary and Other Sex

In the missionary position, the woman is in position A. The male is on top of her facing her (bellies are touching). The male's legs are more or less together. One advantage of missionary sex for males, is that in his position on top of the woman, he can be more *active* as he guides the interaction. Although the woman's movements may be energetic and vigorous, in this position, her role tends to be more *reactive* to whatever her lover does.

Missionary position allows you to maintain eye contact throughout the interaction. It is hard to be anything less than present when you are looking into each other's eyes. Such connection increases the hormone-driven bonding between you and your partner, and an orgasm leads to even more bonding.

For many people, missionary sex, (*vanilla* or *straight* sex in the vernacular) is the only way to have sex. In what is probably the most famous report on the subject of sex, Kinsey found that 9 percent of married women used the missionary position exclusively, and 91 percent of married women used the position most of the time (if you think that adds up to 100% of married women, you'd be right!). Of course, the data are somewhat dated, but it is likely that the majority of couples have missionary sex some or all of the time for religious, cultural, or other reasons.

Although missionary sex allows some variety, it is easy to slip into a pattern in which most (or all) of your interactions are the same. This is *pattern sex* which can kill sexual tension (and therefore passion) fast. If you have ever thought, "*I know what works, so I do it that way to make sure we both orgasm*" you are engaging in pattern sex, and if you aren't bored yet, you soon will be. I hope you are now emboldened to try something different even if it doesn't work every time.

I am not going to describe in detail any of the other possible sexual interactions—the variety is far too great—but other interactions may involve vastly different foreplay activities, starting positions, and changes of position. Participants may also use a wide array of toys (e.g., vibrators, plugs, ropes, clamps, swings, etc.) during their interactions. There appears to be no limit to the intensity and variety of activities that might occur during a sexual interaction, or even the number of participants.

Great Sex

The most important ingredient lacking in empty sex is a connection with your partner in which she *matters* to you. If you have no feelings for your partner, she may as well be a blow-up rubber doll; and you know how sex with that doll would feel don't you? Empty? Yes, of course!

So what is *great sex*? Is it giving your woman multiple orgasms? Is it climaxing together? What about wild, wanton, sweat-inducing lustiness? Is that what makes sex great? Is it sado-masochism, submission and bondage, threesomes or "moresomes"? Is it vacation sex, sex in public places, or mile-high sex? Is it unusual positions, erotic stories, pornographic films, toys, lingerie, or leather? Is it all of the above? Well, the fact is that great sex might include none of these things or all of them at different times, but they are not enough to create *great sex*. Being good at intercourse is little more than technique, and technique is easy to learn. To be *great sex*, there is one ingredient that is critical. It may sound quaint but the ingredient you need for great sex is—drum roll, please—*love*!

Yes, that's it! Love is the key ingredient for sex to be great. A powerful loving connection with your partner will elevate proficient or even really good sex into great sex. A sexual interaction may be a mind-blowing, gymnastic, marathon-length orgy of the senses, but without love, it won't be great sex. For cosmos-shaking, earth-shaking, body-rejuvenating sex, you need to feel a powerful loving bond between you and your partner, whether you are life partners or not. Love makes it easy to flow into, around, and through a sexual interaction, whatever form it takes. Love and sex cause your body and brain to flood with chemicals which generate powerful feelings for each other as you make love (and I don't just mean have sex, I mean to really make love to each other). The result is great sex.

If you have never felt the energetic flow that comes from truly loving another person from the depth of your being, this may all sound like a fairy tale. Perhaps you have never been close enough to a woman to create the primal rush of masculine love throughout your body. Love is the magic potion that makes everything brighter, including you. You can't have truly great sex without honest-to-goodness, nothing-held-back love. This does not mean you can't have good sex with a woman before you fall in love with her. It just means truly great sex will have to wait until your love for her is flowing freely in your veins.

To be clear, in this context, to love someone does not mean you are ready to propose marriage or sell up and move to Moscow to be with her. It means that you care for her, that you have good feelings towards her, that you are sufficiently invested in her that you hope to see her again and explore some kind of relationship. You (or she) may later decide that you are not right for each other, but that is OK as long as you had integrity and good intentions during your sexual interactions.

Creating Pleasure

You no doubt have built something during your lifetime (e.g., a coffee table in the shop at school, or a garden in your backyard). Whatever it was, you felt deep masculine pleasure from doing the job well. Another source of masculine pleasure, one you may not have noticed (although you have certainly have felt it), is creating pleasure for your woman. Like the feeling of a job well done, pleasuring your woman generates pleasure for you. Perhaps it was a beautiful, candle-lit dinner with her. Maybe you created a sensual seduction scene that she loved. Maybe you tied her up and spanked her just how she likes it. Maybe you worshipped her as a goddess in a temple that you created for her (some white chiffon drapery in your bedroom and soft red lighting can work wonders). It could be a special gift that only you can give her—you: a fully present, nothing held back, all-in, *you*.

Whatever you do, you know that when your magic works, you (and your partner) feel wonderful, light, stress-free, blissed! This feeling is pure masculine magic, and you don't need an orgasm and ejaculation to feel it. You can bring your lovemaking into the realm of beauty and flow, where you and your lover generate magical pleasure simply by being with each other, with or without intercourse.

On the other hand, if your focus during a sexual interaction is *your* orgasm, you won't be fully connected to your woman and quite likely will be oblivious to what she is feeling. You probably know what I am talking about. You and your lover are engaged in a wonderful sexual encounter. Then, when you least expect it, you think, "It's getting late - we need to get to sleep!" and *WHAM*, just like that, you are no longer present and no longer connected to her. You are now in a solo performance where the script calls for you to orgasm… soon. What is going on?

When this happens in your lovemaking, what began as a loving interaction is only one step away from empty sex. If it happens to you (and it happens to everyone at times), snap yourself back to presence and consciousness by focusing your attention on her. Sense what she is feeling. Be aware of what feels good to her, and what doesn't. If you are able to gaze into her eyes as you interact (pick one eye and, without staring, gaze into it), both of you will likely regain a powerful connection with each other. Phew! That feels much better.

Your orgasm will come when it's ready. If you try to force it, you will likely go 'into your head' and any hope of an orgasm will disappear. So focus on her, and, even if she has already had a dozen orgasms, your orgasm will follow in due course. If your orgasm doesn't come, don't think of it as a failure. It's not a problem. It will come tomorrow or the next time. Many books talk about 'achieving' orgasm. Let's get this straight, having an orgasm is not like climbing Mount Everest; it isn't an *achievement*! Stop thinking that an orgasm that doesn't come is a failure. You can go to sleep and dream of the next time and how good that will make you feel.

Unlike males, women generally have an almost infinite capacity for sex and orgasm. As I discussed earlier, pleasuring your woman to orgasm will deepen your connection with her because an orgasm stimulates her desire to bond with you. Whether you inspire her to orgasm through oral or digital stimulation or intercourse, the effect on her will be similar. I know many women who have learned to orgasm by simply breathing in a rhythmical and deeply resonant way. I know that sounds improbable but it is not at all difficult for most women after a little training. While a male's capacity to orgasm is different from a woman's, I am happy to report that males can also orgasm by breathing in a similar way (with or without orgasm). This is a very cool thing to do, a true delight, but the 'how to' is a story for another book.

Talk

Before your interaction begins, talk to your lover about what she likes and dislikes. You will learn a lot, and the discussion might be incredibly erotic. Don't skimp on the details. You want to know every nuance of what she desires. As she talks, she will feel the sweet intoxication of anticipation.

Tell each other about your edges and boundaries. An *edge* is an activity you find intriguing but that you have not yet tried (e.g., you'd like to experience making love while blindfolded but you have never tried it). Telling a lover about an edge may allow you to challenge it. Successfully challenging an edge can be a wonderful experience. (You should always be thinking about challenging your edges; every edge you eliminate broadens your range of possibility.) A *boundary*, on the other hand, is a limit you are not interested in challenging. Therefore, boundaries tend to be longer lasting. Because you are still in charge of your life, you can expand or contract a boundary at any time. You can also create new boundaries. Remember that your partner has her edges and boundaries too. Honor her boundaries until *she* moves them and honor her edges until *she* decides to challenge them. A woman should honor your edges and boundaries too.

Plan

Being the choreographer of a sexual interaction means that you place all the items you might need (condoms, towels, toys, lubes) where you can easily reach them. There are many kinds of lube—silicon-based, vegetable-based, or water-based. Some are chemically contrived, and others are organic. One of the cheapest and best lubes is coconut oil, which is plentiful and readily available at your supermarket—and you can fry your breakfast in it! Whatever lube you use, make sure it's close by when you need it.

Try to set a room temperature that works (not too hot or too cold), and experiment with various lighting alternatives. A red or orange glow from lights or candles does wonders for the atmosphere in a room. It helps if your room is clean and tidy, and the bed has clean sheets and pillow cases. If you like music in your space, choose something soft and sensuous; consider asking her what she would like (not too loud, please). Consider timing. Does she have a last train to catch? Does she have to be up early for work? Do you? Create a welcoming atmosphere. Welcome her to your space with food and something to drink (providing food and drink for your lover is a primal, masculine rite). Go easy on the alcohol; stone-cold sober is best. Ask yourself whether you really want to make love to a woman who needs to get liquored up before having sex with you. Whatever you decide to do—something you think would be pleasing for both of you—do it with care and planning, and you'll be fine.

Once the interaction begins, be conscious of your lover and yourself at all times. To give her pleasure, you must figure out what she wants and how she'd like it. Some women need lots of time to warm up, while others are so quick you must be careful not to overstimulate them. Be aware of how she is responding to everything you do. Listen to her words. Sense her mood. Look at her smile. Stay conscious of her emotional and physical condition to gauge whether what you are doing is right in the moment. Allow yourself time and awareness to feel your own emotional and physical responses to what is happening as well.

With all the advice in magazines and books (including this one), it's easy to get into your head and destroy the joy of sex by wondering; *am I doing it right?* Sex can be messy and lead to strange contortions, flailing arms, and unintended bodily emissions. In other words, sex can be funny as well as fun. Try not to take yourself or sex too seriously. It's okay to be playful before, during, and after sex. Sex is pleasure, not a military maneuver. When it's all over, and you are relaxing in each other's arms, enjoy the postsexual high. Ahhh—that feels *so* good!

Anticipation

As I mentioned earlier, the anticipation of sex feels wonderful, especially for a woman. It lightens her mood, exercises her mind, energizes her body, and soothes her soul. You can feel all these sensations too. Few drugs bring about such profound changes in how you feel with no side effects and across such a broad range of body parts (brain, nervous system, heart, and more). Spontaneous sex is great, but don't overlook the beauty of a well-planned encounter with lots of notice to your lover about "something" to come later (let her ponder the possibilities). For example, if she knows in the morning that you are going to interact with her in the evening, she will be excited all day! Her anticipation feeds on itself as she becomes more and more aroused.

Romance

Romance (flowers, lighting, music, and more) requires a special effort and is a powerful aphrodisiac for a woman. When she knows that you plan to romance her, she will eagerly anticipate whatever you have planned. Romance is also a major source of bonding for a couple. For you, the bonding begins with the care you put into creating the romance and continues with her response to your creation. For her, it is admiration of your thoughtfulness, your care, and your masculinity. Romance lubricates the locks on her sexuality. Don't underestimate the power of romance in a long-term relationship. It will become ever more important as your relationship matures. Especially after many years together, your woman will appreciate romantic gestures, such as breakfast in bed, roses on the dining table, or a playful pat on the bottom as you pass her in the hallway (there is a lot of romance in a loving touch). I am sure you can think of many other ways to be romantic. So, here is a tip. Throughout your relationship, stay connected to your woman by touching her in ways she likes, by talking to her about whatever matters, and some things that don't matter. Be spontaneous and unpredictable. Do whatever you can to keep the energy of the connection at a high pitch. Avoid boredom, routine, and pattern sex as if your life depends on it because your life as a happy, loving, connected couple *does* depend on it! Here is an especially romantic evening:

Tomas called Heidi from work at 9:00 a.m. and told her to be ready to leave the house at 5:00 p.m. She should dress elegantly and did not need to bring anything with her. He did not tell her that he had all the clothing and toiletries she would need for a night at a hotel. After he checked in at the hotel, Tomas placed Heidi's clothes and toiletries carefully in Room 14. He sent a car to collect Heidi and told the driver to keep the destination secret from her. When the car arrived at the hotel, Tomas was waiting for it (he had tracked its journey on the Uber app) and greeted Heidi with a passionate kiss. He then led her to a courtyard, where they listened to a performer sing love songs under the stars.

After dinner, Tomas walked Heidi around the grounds of the hotel. As they approached Room 14, Tomas pretended to notice that the door was not locked and pushed open the door so they could *peek* inside. They were giggling as they entered (he managed to calm her worries about entering someone's room). They looked around the room, but when Heidi saw her favorite dress hanging in the closet she figured out that this was their room for the night, and that their evening of pleasure was about to become a lot more interesting.

Heidi never asked Tomas any questions about what was in store for her. She had trusted him and basked in romantic anticipation throughout the day as the mystery unfolded. Her trust in Tomas is, in many ways, her greatest gift to him. Treating Heidi like a goddess is his greatest gift to her.

Try doing something like Tomas did. Plan a super-romantic interaction with a dash of surprise and a hefty dose of excited anticipation. You do not have to spend a lot of money to create romance, but you do have to spend time and effort (music, candles, food, care, tenderness).

Man and Sex

Your lover, like many women, may want to control an interaction so she can set the pace and the agenda. For example, she may want to push her tongue down your throat at the first kiss. This is a sign that she doesn't trust you to interact with her in a way she finds pleasing. Unless you have agreed in advance that you will be submissive to her, show her that *you* are choreographing the interaction. If she does the deep-tongue dive, look into her eyes, and gently ask her to close her lips. Then deliver the slowest, gentlest, most tender kiss she has ever had (see "Kissing," below). Most women will be happy for you to lead the way, once they trust that you know what you are doing. Treat her like a goddess, show her that you know how to drive a sexual interaction and that she is safe with you, and then watch as she allows herself to become a goddess (a warm, juicy, feminine goddess). Of course, your partner can participate in any way that works for you both. Just drive the interaction forward as you planned, while she luxuriates in the beauty of the interaction. All of the doubt about who is leading the interaction can be resolved in advance by having a conscious discussion about the interaction before it begins. She can always lead the next interaction with you.

If your interaction falls flat, don't get into your head about it. It's bound to happen from time to time. Remember, many leading ladies had to kiss a lot of frogs before finding their prince. Of course, if your interactions with your leading lady often fall flat, you have some serious talking to do. If you make a "mistake" during an interaction, remain centered, and signal your recognition of what happened. Perhaps you said something stupid, or became distracted, pressed too hard, or went too fast. A mistake may sting for a while, but the effects soon wear off if you stay out of your head by focusing on your partner and on what you are feeling. Deal with a significant mistake by offering a sincere and well-expressed apology, in the moment and again, more fully, later.

Woman On Top

You may delight in being the receiver from time to time, with your woman driving the interaction. This approach is often generically called "woman on top," even though she may not be physically on top of you. It simply means she is leading the interaction. Remember that when she is leading, her focus is to bring you pleasure. Your focus is to receive and allow her to pleasure you in whatever way she chooses, within the boundaries you jointly set.

There are several benefits to having the woman physically on top of you. For example, you can maintain better eye contact (a valuable addition to the sexual energy). In addition, you will be able to see more of her as she moves, and that can be highly stimulating for a voyeuristic male. Of course, a woman may also enjoy being on top and in control of her movements. Doing so, can result in sensations you may not have felt before. In addition, in the on-top position, she may choose to have her back to you, so she is facing your feet instead of your head. Mmmm—interesting!

If you agree to have your lover leading the interaction, relax fully into your role as receiver. Let her choreograph the action, and resist the urge to tell her what to do, which is almost impossible to do without sounding critical. If you don't like being the receiver, talk about that later, and determine whether some modification to the choreography might improve your experience.

Kissing

Television and movies are killing the art of kissing. The sloppy, deep-throat dives with lots of head thrashing that you see on the screen are no way to kiss your lover. To up your kissing game, try the following, and see if it works for you:

Ask your woman to keep her eyes open. Without staring, focus your gaze on her left eye as you stand about 12 inches apart. As you gaze at her (still focused on her left eye), move slowly closer to her but not so close that her face becomes blurred. Notice the different colors in her eye. Look beyond her eye to sense what she is feeling. It's okay to blink and to move your gaze to her other eye but don't switch too often or you will break your powerful connection with her. Once you are sure she is ready, put your hand in the small of her back and draw her gently toward you. Remain loose and easy. No crotch-grinding! Put your other hand on the back of her head, and move her head a little. This action shows her that you are driving the kiss, so she can relax.

When your lips first make contact with hers, move them slowly and lightly across her lips. If she opens her mouth, ask her to close it. After a few minutes of the lightest contact between your lips, flatten your tongue and move it slowly across her lips from left to right. Kiss her nose and the skin around her lips. Bend her head forward, and kiss the middle of her forehead. Ask her to close her eyes, and kiss her eyelids. After some time, softly use your tongue to part her lips, but overcome the urge to force your tongue into her mouth—take your time; there is no rush. If she tries to take over the kiss, back away a little. Don't allow her to take control. If she continues her effort to control the kiss, just say, "Easy. Relax."

Eventually, begin to explore the inside of her mouth. Don't press, don't rush, and don't stop the exploration for at least five minutes—slower and longer is better. As the passion takes over, use your hands to move her head. Later, take your hands away and let your bodies lean into each other. After such a beautiful kiss, she will be anticipating your next move. Keep cool. Be gentle. Feel the passion rising.

Talking Afterward

It's good (and sometimes highly erotic) to talk about your interaction afterward. The Inquisition ended centuries ago, so try not to become an inquisitor. Begin by describing your experience: "I really liked it when you …" "It felt wonderful when I …" "I felt strange when we …" If your comments don't elicit a reaction from your lover, ask her how she felt, recognizing that she may be self-conscious because she is not accustomed to talking about sex. If she is reticent, ask whether anything you did was particularly pleasurable or unpleasant. Take the initiative, and ask her whether she would like more or less of something you did. Ask her how she felt about the foreplay, the location, the temperature, the lighting. Take your time as you build up a picture of what works for her and for you. Over time, she will become more comfortable talking about sex.

Don't ask her about your sexual performance or comment on hers. You want information, not a grade. Don't ask how many orgasms she had; stats are for baseball, not lovemaking; and do you really want her counting while you make love to her. If the experience was anything less than wonderful for *her*, ask her why (and encourage her to be honest). If it was anything less than wonderful for *you*, let her know why. Knowledge will allow you to make a correction. Good sex does not a relationship make, but bad sex can surely kill one. The best way to learn how to be a better lover is to be present and conscious during your lovemaking. The next best way to learn is to talk with her about your lovemaking. If you were 100 percent present while you made love, you probably won't hear anything you don't already know.

Speaking about sex can be difficult. There is always the danger that any comment, no matter how well meant, sounds like criticism. You want the straight scoop, even if you disagree with it. So before you talk, agree to be forthright, and agree that you won't react negatively to what you hear. Don't put the relationship on the line during the talk. There will be plenty of time to assess the state of the relationship afterwards. You must be totally honest but your honesty must be dispensed with a hefty dose of humility. Let's face it, if the interaction did not go well, it was not all her fault. If your performance during the interaction becomes the focal point of criticism, you will just have to listen carefully to what she says and be stoic. No matter how bad it makes you feel, you want to hear the unhearable even if she says,

"My name is Cindi. When you called me Susy, I almost threw up."

You also have to speak the unspeakable ("Sex once a month is not enough"), no matter how bad it makes your partner feel. You both need to hear the truth—all of it. You don't want any lies or half-truths to make you feel better. Talking about sex with your lover might take more courage than a cliff dive, but a plunge into the depths is a sign of your sexual maturity. If you can't talk about sex calmly and openly, you probably should not be having sex at all, which may mean your relationship has run its course. If so, it's time to leave.

Healing Sex

It may seem odd that sex can be a force for healing. Maybe you have not thought of sexual energy as healing energy, but you can be certain that it's especially healing (for you or your partner or both of you) when you are an attentive and conscious lover.

It's not easy for a male to comprehend how a woman feels when he is pursuing her for sex. Virtually every woman I know has a horror story about what some men have said or done when trying to engage them for a sexual interaction, whether in a bar, at work or at a party. I have heard many first-hand accounts from women who were abused, raped, or otherwise molested by family members, boyfriends, or random men. Probably every woman in the western world has felt pressure to doing something sexual that she did not want to do. Many who felt such pressure yielded to it, even though it made them feel bad at the time.

Given this background, women need much healing around men, and powerful, loving sex can provide that healing. If you have an opportunity as a Man to provide some of that healing for a woman, please do not *try* to heal her. Unless you have special training in healing sexual trauma, you are more likely to hurt her than help her. To provide your healing energy, you don't have to *do* anything, except be a Man—protect her, care for her, and keep her safe. Approach her slowly, carefully, respectfully and your protective masculinity will allow her to express her feminine power in all its glory. Therefore, whether you plan something as simple as a date or as significant as your first sexual interaction, consider how your woman feels, and take care to maintain your center as you accommodate her fears and satisfy her desires. Your number-one priority is *her* safety and comfort (not your orgasm). If she trusts you to keep her safe, she will be able to feel your healing energy and gain respect for you as a lover. When you put her feelings and safety above your own desires, your desires *will* be satisfied without you even trying to "get something" from her. None of this means that your interaction should be dispassionate. You still want to bring your passionate, powerful, present love-making to her. That is how you can help her to heal.

A First Time

Exhausted passion. Matted hair.
Her sleeping eyes speak no story.
There is no need.
Her body tells all.

You can only have a sexual interaction with a new partner for the first time *once*. Don't screw it up by blundering in without preparation. You don't need a fifteen-page script, but you do need to have a sense of the interaction's choreography. Therefore, think through the coming interaction, adding as much detail as you can (time, place, dress, approach, development, structure). There are workshops in which you can learn about yourself and how to be a better lover. Try those. What do you have to lose? When you have elevated your game and become a consummate lover, not only will you please your woman, but you will feel better about her, yourself, and (this may sound crazy) everyone else. Life is just better when you feel good about your sexual maturity. What follows is just one way you might create a memorable first interaction:

Shirts and dresses strewn
in hills of cotton,
Lay in their corner gloom,
cold and long forgotten.

A month ago, you met Randi at a Starbucks when she sat next to you on a sofa. Sparks flew immediately, and you've dated six times. Last night, you made her dinner at your house and said, "Randi, I am really attracted to you, and I feel our relationship is strong. I want to start exploring a future together. I'd like to become sexual with you and discuss how that might happen. I would like to know how you feel about that." As you spoke, Randi's eyes sparkled more than usual, and a shy smile stole across her lips. She said, "Yes, I agree. I think we are ready. Let's talk about it."

After dinner, you both revealed to each other that you had no history of STDs and had not had sexual contact with anyone since being tested a few weeks ago. (If you do have a history of STDs, this is the time to reveal it.) You agreed that you would be sexually and emotionally exclusive to each other and agreed to let the other know *in advance* if one of you wanted to change that status. Because Randi was on oral contraceptives, and neither of you had an STD, you agreed not to use condoms. You discussed your boundaries ("No tongue in my ears please" for her, and "Please don't touch my left thumb because of a recent injury" for you). You told her that you would not drink alcohol before the interaction; Randi said she might have one glass of wine. You both wanted to be sober for this interaction. You invited her to arrive at your house the next day at 6:00 p.m. (whereupon Randi's anticipatory clock started—tick, tick, tick).

In preparation, you thought through the upcoming interaction. You cleaned and tidied your house. You added fresh flowers, lit a dozen candles in your bedroom, and selected some soft music. When she arrived at your house, you sat on the sofa again and told her about your feelings for her. You were calm and caring and told her what you find so appealing about her. Sharing your personal thoughts strengthened your connection, and Randi was pleasantly surprised at how well you already seemed to know her. You both agreed that you would ask permission before removing each other's clothing or touching each other in a sexual way.

Eventually, the time felt right, so you asked her to stand and take off her shoes. You led her to your bedroom. You were both still standing as you gazed into her eyes and gently kissed her. With your hands moving slowly over her clothed body, you continued to look into her eyes. You did not rush (slow is good; slower is better). After about fifteen minutes, you asked, "Randi, may I take off your blouse and skirt?" She whispered, *Yes*, and you continued kissing her while slowly removing her outer layer of clothing. When Randi did not reciprocate by undressing you, you asked her to unbutton your shirt and loosen your belt—this might be a good way to show you are leading the interaction (i.e., that it's not just happening). After that, she needed no further encouragement to undress you, which she did after asking you if it was okay. You asked whether the temperature of the room was alright, and when she said she was a little cold, you turned up the thermostat. You laid her down gently on the bed, and continued to kiss her while gazing into her eyes and stroking her body with your fingertips. When you asked if you might take off her bra and pleasure her breasts, she immediately said *Yes*.

You were fully conscious and aware of how Randi was responding to your touch. At times, you increased your pressure and increased the passion, and at other times, you slowed down and became more gentle and tender. You never forgot that Randi was your companion on this journey of discovery, so you asked occasionally how she was doing and whether the speed and pressure of your actions were right for her. Because you had discussed earlier how to give feedback in a positive way, she replied, *a little less pressure please*. She did not say, *you are pressing too hard* which would have sounded critical of you.

After you had stimulated Randi's breasts for twenty minutes, you asked if you could remove the rest of her clothing and if it was okay for you to pleasure her genital area. She again gave you an enthusiastic *Yes*, but you continued to massages her breasts and did not remove her clothing for several minutes, during which time she was anticipating your next move. When you tenderly took off her remaining clothes, you positioned her on the bed in such a way that you could lie between her legs. From that position, you whisper-touched her labia, while looking carefully where you were touching her. You noticed the complexity of her vulva, especially the color and texture of her labia.

Some women enjoy you gazing on this private part of their body. When I asked them why, none of them could explain how they felt (which is not surprising— I can't explain why I like the taste of chocolate). My theory is that a woman admires a partner who can take the time to know her and her body, and resist the urge to mount an immediate assault on her vagina when it's right there in front of him.

If this is how you behave with a first time partner, she will know your interaction is going to be deliciously different from what she expected, and what she has experienced before.

Although you had been stroking Randi's labia with your fingertips and your tongue for ten minutes, you did not touch her clitoris glans because you knew it would wait for you (and stimulate itself in the meantime). You softly stroked her vestibular bulbs, which were swollen by her arousal. You pressed inward on the bulbs and asked whether your pressure felt good. Randi found this touch highly arousing and later confided that nobody had ever done that to her before (she had not even done it to herself). Eventually, you used your tongue to slowly and tenderly stimulate her clitoris glans. After fifteen more minutes, you asked to enter her with your fingers, which brought a breathless, *Oh my God, yes*, from Randi.

She was wet with her natural lubrication, but if she had needed it you would have added lube to your fingers before entering her. With your fingers moving slowly and gently inside her, she moaned when you used your tongue to pleasure her glans at the same time. As you stimulated her G-spot, her sounds and movements told you that she was becoming ever more aroused. You also thought to ask her how your touch felt; her breathless reply was, *I love it. Please don't stop.*

When the time felt right, you asked her whether she was ready for you to enter her with your penis, and Randi begged, *I want you inside me. Now!* You entered her slowly, (your penis is not a battering ram) and began to move slowly and rhythmically, with your penis just an inch or two inside her. This motion may be particularly stimulating for both of you, as your penile corona puts pressure on her G-spot and her vaginal muscles squeeze your penis, putting delightful pressure on your frenulum. Later, you eased your penis deep inside her (*easy* because you wanted to make sure her vagina was relaxed enough to accept the entire length of your penis). The whole time, you maintained eye contact with her, elevating the experience and the connection for you both. Several times you had to pause in your movement because you were so stimulated by the beauty of your interaction that you were close to ejaculating. The slow lovemaking had Randi in ecstasy throughout and gave her several long and intense orgasms. Your own orgasm followed in due course.

After you withdrew, you held her close and told her how you felt. She reciprocated by telling you how much she appreciated your care and tenderness. You slowly brought your interaction to a close by looking into each other's eyes as you lay side by side; this is the *golden time.* Thousands of poems have been inspired by this post-coital feeling. Enjoy it!

If this interaction sounds like something you would like to do with a first-time partner, why not adopt it as a baseline for future interactions with her and try to build on the beauty of what you created in your first interaction. When you get to know each other better, you will be able to enhance your sex life with infinite variety. Go for it!

Odds and Ends

1. Sex with a new partner is not a cure for the heartbreak of a failed relationship so don't initiate sexual interactions with a new lover until you are clear of the emotional and spiritual debris of a past relationship. If you are not clear, you will contaminate your new relationship with the wreckage of the old one, and risk spoiling a promising new relationship. Forgive your former lovers, as I described earlier, and forgive yourself for any actions that you don't feel good about. When you are truly clear of all past relationships, your new relationship has a much better chance of growing stronger.
2. To keep the feeling of new sex fresh, make love to your woman 24/7 with your eyes, your voice, your heart, your touch, and everything else you have to offer. To keep her fire burning when you are not together, send an occasional email or text, or make a telephone call (leave a message if she does not answer). When you are together, touch her, compliment her, hold her, and share yourself with her. When you make love to your woman like this, your relationship can remain juicy for many years to come.
3. Standing in your power means doing the right thing at the right time, all the time. When you commit to protect your woman against all comers and that you will always have her back, she will admire you for it.
4. Exercise your masculine power well, and you will unleash the wild woman she only lets out when she is with a Man, because she knows he can handle it. Your lover's wildness won't overwhelm you when you stand in your masculine power. Wild-goddess sex can fry a man's brain, but you are a Man, so you can stand the heat!

There is a lot to think about here. Some of it may seem calculated, but I say, fear not! A woman will appreciate that you care enough about her to consider all these things. A bonus is that the discussions in advance of your first sexual interaction will be erotic and will stimulate her anticipation. Make a magical, loving connection to a woman, and savor great sex, nature's wonderful gift, perhaps for the very first time.

18

HOW INTERACTIONS GO WRONG

KNOWING WHERE SEX MIGHT GO wrong is a critical element of a lover's repertoire. Here are some examples of how that might happen:

Stormy Weather

She'll let you in her car
to go driving around.
She'll let you into parts of herself
that'll bring you down.
Secret Garden
Bruce Springsteen

A woman is, in some ways, like the sky. Imagine that you are a glider, flying in her sky. You love the beauty and tranquility as you soar silently above the earth. Her sky is cloudless, with gentle breezes that waft you toward a sunny horizon. Then, in the next minute, her sky is all darkness and squalls, twisting your psyche while scrambling your brain. What to do? Reread the vignette of Helen and Steve fighting in Chapter 7. When your woman is stormy, do what Steve did then. Let her blow herself out, while you remain a steadfast rock. Losing your cool will only make everything worse.

People use speech to intimidate, control, and insult each other. Because they have spent so much time together, partners know just where to stick the dagger to antagonize their partner. Your attempt to control your partner will wreak havoc on your relationship. While the damage from one attempt to control her may not be fatal, your attempts will accumulate and eventually doom the relationship.

As Mr. Springsteen so eloquently states (above), a woman can take you down, even while she is professing undying love for you. If you want to zig when she wants to zag, and you both feel strongly about the "right" choice, your differences may lead to a confrontation. This is especially so when points of principal are at issue: hint, they rarely are. If you do feel that a point of principal is at stake, as Marcellus Wallace said to Butch in Pulp Fiction "That's pride fucking with you." (credits and apologies to screenwriters Quentin Tarantino and Roger Avary). When your woman flies into a rage, she may seem intent on destroying everything in her path. As a centered Man, you don't follow her lead because you know there is no point in arguing if you are no longer trying to find a solution. Be the rock, and you will still be standing when her tidal wave dissipates on the shore. Remember: Your lover may strike with exquisite precision, but you don't have to *lose* to her. When a conflict arises, simply stand in your power, and allow your partner to stand in hers. As Steve demonstrated in his approach to Helen's fury, if you let go of needing to *win*, you can make sure you don't lose (with the added benefit that your partner won't lose either). A relationship is not a race or a game. There are no prizes for winning an argument with your lover, girlfriend, or wife. In fact, the opposite is probably true; every win costs you way more than you can possibly gain.

Here is a way to use your sacred space (your version of The Yellow Chairs) to resolve issues that come between you and your woman:

Once in your sacred space, stand in your power with good intentions, kindness, and understanding. Stay focused on the issue. Leave everything else for another time. Speak calmly and quietly. Start by focusing on her point of view, and try to understand it. Do your best to explain your point of view calmly and graciously. Note points of agreement and difference. Discuss those. If the discussion strays off topic, gently suggest a return to the issue at hand, and deal with the other stuff later. Try to offer alternatives, so that your respective *preferred* outcomes are not the only ones up for discussion. Above all, don't put your relationship on the line with threats or ultimatums:

If you don't _____...
if you do _____...
if I can't _____...
then I am leaving you.

During a conflict, when temperatures are high and blood pressures are at bursting point, is not the time to make threats.

If you can accept her choice, and do so with good grace (i.e., no sulking afterward), go with it. Don't back down in anger and then resent your choice. Even if it seems like you lost the argument, hold out the olive branch afterward. You won't lose anything by being a peacemaker. You can't measure the quality of your relationship by how many decisions went your way. A relationship is not like boxing; you can't knock her out or win on points.

If you fight, the fight is not over until you make love. Makeup sex is real; the bonding chemicals work their magic to bring you back together as a couple. Begin making up by gently "spooning" each other, with the partner who most needs tenderness as the inside spoon. If you can't bring yourself to make up, it's because you are carrying meaningless, caustic junk around with you. Get over yourself, and shed the junk; it's of no value to you. However, if you constantly find yourself "losing" (e.g., you feel that your woman always wins), then you have to figure out what is going on with *you*. Maybe your train has stopped. Maybe you have lost your train. Don't blame her. Become a Man, and you will be fine.

Bad Sex

If you feel that your lovemaking isn't going well, then you will probably assume that your partner is a *bad* lover. A typical conversation may go like this: "It's not my fault. You never do it the way I like," or "I am trying, but you just lie there." Blaming your partner won't help. If she has a problem with sex and sexuality, work on that problem together by discussion, counseling, exploration, or workshops. If your long-term relationship is suffering from sexual dysfunction (not enough sex; too much sex; the children will hear sex; unacceptably kinky or sado-masochist sex, etc.), you may both find it difficult to discuss what is going wrong. The question is what are *you* doing to cause these difficulties. Realize that you have to know the answer to that question, or you will never be able to have a constructive discussion with your lover. It's not all her fault, so don't blame her. There is no place for blame in a loving relationship. Focus on finding out what is happening to each of you and what you can do together to change it.

A common theme I hear is, "If I could only find a woman who was less complex, easier to understand, and knew how to treat me, everything would be okay." Recognize that a woman is a package deal—and a complex one at that. Of course, men disappoint their women too, though a woman may phrase the problem differently: "You never listen to me." Whatever the problem, unless you fix it, your relationship is essentially over (even though you may never actually break up). You must talk to your lover about what is happening, and she must be prepared to listen and talk too.

Paradoxically, long-term couples find it more difficult than new couples to talk about sexual problems. Early in a relationship, when couples are still working through the mechanics of sex, the issues and problems are easier to talk about and solve. Long-term partners, on the other hand, see such discussions as an existential threat to the relationship, so even talking about a sexual issue is almost impossible. Therefore, try to initiate a discussion with your partner as soon as you sense a problem. If you wait months or years, your relationship is doomed to oblivion or purgatory as the acid drip of unresolved sexual issues dissolves the glue that holds you together as a couple.

When you talk, do so in your sacred space. Focus on your role in the problem and say, "This might be a difficult conversation, but I want to talk about our sex life. I want to know whether having sex with me is good for you. Is there anything I can do to make it better?" You may let her know that you are aware that you have not been present, fully connected, or wholly engaged with her during your lovemaking recently. Tell her you would like to get back to how sex used to be when your relationship was new. Speak the unspeakable about *yourself*. If she hangs in with you while you talk, invite her to do the same. A basic starting point may be deciding that there is a problem to talk about. Often, only one partner thinks there is a problem, while the other is happy with the status quo. If you can, offer your ideas for a solution to any problem you identify, and ask her if she has any ideas. However long the problems have existed, you were as much a part of creating them as she was, so focus on solutions. If she does not agree that there *is* a problem, or she is adamant about not changing, you have more major issues to talk about. If changing the way you have sex is your bottom line, and sex as you currently do it is her bottom line, then the relationship is over, whether you split or not.

David Deida's books describe how to reorient your approach to sexuality to incorporate a more spiritual element (see Resource section). Becoming a more spiritual lover might help you save your relationship. If you don't think your relationship is important enough to try to save it, then it's already over. Once you embody the spiritual approach that Deida espouses, women will find you more appealing (sexually and otherwise), although they may not understand why (and you don't have to tell them why). A bonus is that once you have a spiritual connection with your woman, talking about sex is much easier.

Taste

A woman's vaginal taste (and smell) is all her own. Her taste and smell may change over time, depending on what she ate recently, where she is in her menstrual cycle, and her overall health. If you find your woman's taste or smell distracting during an interaction, it's okay to forego oral pleasure. If you go ahead and have a sexual interaction even though you detected an unusual odor, when your interaction is complete, you can let her know what happened (don't say she smelled *bad*). If her taste and smell change for the worse, it may be because she has an infection that a trip to the doctor or even an over-the-counter preparation can quickly clear up. You owe it to yourself and your partner to identify the problem and take care of it.

Stuart often began lovemaking with his wife, Kim, by stimulating her orally. Over the course of a few weeks, he noticed Kim's vaginal odor had not only changed, but it had become so unpleasant that he lost his desire for sexual activity of any kind. When they discussed the odor in their sacred space, he said, "Kim, you have always tasted sweet to me, but in the last few weeks, I have noticed a significant change in your vaginal odor. I think you have an infection of some kind. Let's go and see your doctor."

Her ob-gyn, told Kim that she had an infection as a result of her *bad* vaginal florae growing unchecked because her *good* florae were severely depleted. The doctor prescribed a vaginal probiotic to stimulate the good florae and boric acid suppositories to increase the acidity of the vaginal fluid to weaken the bad florae. The treatment cleared up the odor in a few days. Kim also treats herself with the probiotic and the boric acid if she is travelling, is under stress, or if she is sick (because travel, stress and sickness weaken her immune system).

Kim was impressed that Stuart could tell her what was going on with her own vagina. "That," she said to him, "was really romantic for me. It turned me on that you knew about vaginal florae and that you came with me to see the doctor."

A healthy woman's vaginal secretions are an aphrodisiac for a healthy male. So take the time to enjoy the flavors your partner offers you. You will soon become accustomed to how she tastes and will know immediately if her florae are out of balance.

Sexual Appetite

You must find a level of sexual activity in which neither you nor your partner is overwhelmed by sexual demands from the other, while satisfying your own sexual needs. Because everyone's needs are different, navigating the deep waters surrounding sexuality can be treacherous. I have been appalled at the number of otherwise healthy men and woman in long-term relationships who have not had sex (at least with each other) for months or years. In each case, intimacy has ceased. Except in cases of injury or disease, a relationship without sex is a business arrangement. Couples who are not sexually active with each other are nevertheless satisfying their physical desires, maybe by working all the time, watching sports, or quilting! It might also be massage parlors, pornography, or an affair. Sadly, the rate of cheating spouses suggests that affairs are a common escape when a relationship loses its juice.

Unlike most other species, a woman can have sex with you at any time and, as a general proposition, the more sex she has, the more sex she will want. I know many women who are willing to be sexual with a male who knows who he is, what he wants, and how to ask for it, even when there is no existing relationship. Therefore, if you are struggling to find a woman to engage with sexually, it's not because women lack the capacity or desire for sex. Could it be your confusion getting in the way? When you are a Man with a train, women will want to get on board. No matter what shape or size you are, if you are a Man, there are good women looking for you.

In the next few paragraphs, I will give you some broad outlines of things to try if your lovemaking is not following the script you have written in your mind. If you have a significant or continuing erectile dysfunction (ED), please consult your physician and read The Penis Book, by Aaron Spitz. The book offers a wealth of information which will help you choose the right physician to help you. Rest assured, there are many cures for ED, and even if there is no cure for your particular condition, there are numerous treatments to reduce its severity.

Express Delivery

You may have noticed that the excitement of a new lover is sometimes so great that, to your utter dismay, and long before you have satisfied her, you ejaculate. Your express delivery may arise for several reasons. A new partner can cause an express delivery because the excitement of being with her is just too much. It might also be because it has been a long time since you ejaculated. Or that you are not sexually experienced. Or that you have a condition that causes you to ejaculate very quickly. Don't worry, even if your accelerated completion leaves her unsatisfied, she will forgive you. She knows that this happens, but she will expect you to slow down fairly soon. The combination of a slow-to-orgasm female and a fast-to-orgasm male may be especially challenging for new partners. What to do?

Relax. More frequent sex reduces the tendency to ejaculate quickly. If you are a young man with little sexual experience (thanks for reading this book), more experience with a variety of women or more experience with this new woman will slow your express delivery soon enough. Relax; you'll be OK.

If you are ejaculating too quickly for your liking (or hers), try to be calm about an upcoming interaction ("uber-cool" is good). Focus on the romance of the situation, the setting, the ambience, and especially on your lover. During intercourse, if you feel the urge to ejaculate building, slow your thrusting or stop completely. Pausing in this way is a fine art and a great arrow to have in your quiver, especially if you are quivering about ejaculating too soon. You can pause with your penis inside your partner, but if you are super-sensitive, pausing while you are withdrawn will work better. Just withdraw until your sexual energy subsides (a minute or two), and then continue. You can pause many times during a single interaction. Pausing won't interfere with your partner's pleasure overall, and she will be delighted that you are skilled enough to know what to do. If you know she is about to orgasm when you feel the need to pause, fear not. You can pause, or keep thrusting and orgasm together. When you withdraw, if she loses her orgasmic energy, she will quickly recover it when you re-enter her. If you think that the motion of withdrawal itself will result in your ejaculation, stay connected and whisper in her ear (e.g., "Don't move. Don't even breathe"). You may feel the pulsing of an orgasm in your genitals, but if your withdrawal was early enough, you won't ejaculate. Congratulations—you just had an orgasm without ejaculating. Now you can start re-building your sexual energy again. After your non-ejaculatory orgasm, it will be a while before your next orgasm (it really is like starting over). If you continue with intercourse, and later feel the desire to orgasm building again, decide then whether to ejaculate, or pause and repeat the cycle. If you think this is impossible, think again. Orgasm without ejaculation is not difficult or even uncommon for a skilled lover.

Even if you are not having a problem with the timing of your ejaculation, try pausing sometimes to allow yourself to slow down your orgasm/ejaculation and prolong the beautiful interaction you and your partner are enjoying. Once you become adept at pausing, you can have sex for hours.

Finally, if you have taken the time (at least an hour) to pleasure her in all the ways I describe in this book, it will have given you time to calm down (you will also be in your head a little as you try to keep it all straight, so you won't have time to think about your performance). Focus on giving her pleasure and your orgasm and ejaculation will probably be fine.

Condoms will reduce the intensity of your sensations. Therefore, if successive pauses are not slowing you down enough, use a condom, or try a thicker condom. Condoms with ribs and other shapes embedded in their structure tend to be thicker and will probably slow down your ejaculation for a while. The combination of a male *and* female condom (more about female condoms below) will slow down your ejaculation even more. If you have the female condom in place, when you are ready, slip on the male condom. The combination of both may be enough to achieve the desired delay. You can also try desensitizing creams. I have never tried a desensitizing cream, so I have no idea whether they work or what effect they have on your partner; she may not want to be desensitized. Realize too that the cream is a chemical substance of unknown composition that will enter *her body* via absorption through the vaginal wall. Therefore, you ***must*** discuss with her your intended use of a desensitizing cream *before* your interaction begins (this is what informed consent is all about). Numerous advertisements in the daily newspapers offer medical treatments for erectile dysfunction. I have not tried these treatments, so I can't comment on them. What I can say is that there are many false promises made for products in the sexual products arena, where snake-oil salesmanship is alive and well.

The only "deferral" mechanism I have ever used is nonmedical, nonsurgical, and non-mechanical. It requires little in the way of imagination, just some basic arithmetic (and being bad at arithmetic won't hurt you a bit). All you have to do is follow these simple steps during intercourse—and remember, you heard it here first:

Picture the number 1,000 in your mind.
Subtract 7 from 1,000, and you get 993. Easy?
Now subtract 7 from 993 to get 986. Still easy?
Thereafter, keep subtracting 7 from your result each time.
Tip: It helps if you picture the resulting number in your mind as you do the math.

If you are highly numerate or just want a wild alternative, try subtracting a bigger number (17 instead of 7, for example), and if you are just crazy good with numbers, start incrementing the subtracted number (so you first subtract 1—999; then subtract 2—997; then 3—994; then 4—990). Now we are on the bleeding edge of what is arithmetically possible (unless you want to work on the value of π to a hundred decimal places). If you want a simple and reliable method to delay your ejaculation without anyone knowing about it, try the arithmetic route. I have used this method a handful of times in my life, and it worked each time.

You may ask how counting backward from a thousand is compatible with being fully present in your sexual interaction. The answer, of course, is that you can't be fully present with your lover if you are doing mental arithmetic. Once the immediate impulse to ejaculate passes, you can easily regain your presence. Eventually, you will be able to forget all about counting and double-thick condoms.

Plug-In/Plug-Out

When your Mozilla Firefox plug-ins don't work, you may be disappointed. If your personal *plug-in* doesn't work, you may be devastated. If you have never lost an erection at a critical time, congratulations. If it has happened to you, it was not the disaster you thought it was at the time. All kinds of factors play into what happened, such as how much alcohol you had consumed, your overall health, how tired you were, your degree of connection to this woman, and more. You may be surprised to learn that even though you are a major league stud, if you hold an erection for a long time (say during 3 or 4 hours of foreplay), just when you think your rocket is ready for blast-off, you can lose your erection. Don't sweat this one. It happens, and your erection will come back if you give it a little time without getting in your head about it.

During a long period of sexual activity, your erection may rise and fall multiple times. Don't worry about this either. Your erection will come back. If it does not return all by itself, try this:

- Accept that your erection will return and stop thinking about it.
- Take a break, but don't drink alcohol.
- Focus (really focus) on your woman's pleasure—kissing, cuddling, fondling, squeezing.
- Give her oral sex; her vaginal taste and aroma are powerful stimuli that, like a stiff breeze at sea, can blow your vessel out of the doldrums.
- Talk about sex and erotica.
- Change the vibe (lighting, music, temperature).
- Become 100 percent present.
- Ask her to pleasure herself, and pleasure yourself while you watch.

If you have been drinking alcohol for hours, or you are simply exhausted, it's probably better to wait until you feel better before trying again. If nothing works, don't dwell on it. Be loving and gentle with each other. Look into each other's eyes. Talk softly about your connection and your interaction so far. If you have time, try again later.

If you are a woman, please be aware that when your man loses his erection at a critical moment, nothing you *say* will help him! Unfortunately, *anything* you say will sound condescending or even agonizing to him. Worse, your comments will likely start him thinking with his head, and that will be the last you will see of his erection for a while. If you can spend the night with him, go to sleep. He will be fine and probably will greet you with a fine erection in the morning.

Condoms, Cock Rings, and Chemicals

A lost erection is more likely to occur during the time you are fumbling to put on a condom than at any other time. Putting on a condom should take no more than fifteen seconds, but if you drop the condom, or try to put it on upside down, or just take too long, your erection may wither on the vine. If this happens to you more than once, try the following:

- Recognize in advance that you will need a condom.
- Know whether your partner is allergic to any condom material. When you are at the height of passion and you are putting on a latex condom, is a dreadful time to discover she is allergic to latex. The best time to ask about allergies is when you talk about boundaries and permissions and agreements (you did have that talk, didn't you?). It may even be a deliciously erotic conversation. A side benefit of discussing condoms in advance is that she can stop worrying because she knows you plan to use one.
- Practice putting a condom on, until you can do it in the dark. Practice will only cost you a few dollars, but it will make all the difference when it counts.
- Before you begin your lovemaking session, place several condoms close at hand, have at least one of them open with the right side up so you don't fumble when you need it (a fumble on the football field is bad; when you are about to have sex, it can feel like a disaster). If you don't know which is the right side up, remember—if the brand name is up, the condom is usually the right way up too.
- When you are *both* ready (she is ready for you to enter her, and you are ready too), reach for the condom. Slide it on smoothly. Have the right kind of lube handy, and unless she is already awash in lubrication (natural or otherwise), put a little lube on the tip of the condom. If you are using a latex condom, don't use a silicone lube (the silicone "melts" the latex).
- With the condom in place, enter her immediately—realize that while you put on the condom, the action stopped

for her too. Just enter her slowly; this is no time to be a battering ram. Think immediate but slow.

- When you ejaculate, withdraw within thirty seconds because as your erection fades, the condom will slip off, which defeats the whole point of the condom. Oh, and if the condom has slipped off, it will be inside her. Don't ask her to go fishing for it. Going to get it, while you preserve her dignity, is a delightfully lighthearted moment. Nervous giggling is encouraged!

If you frequently lose your erection, or you want your penis to feel harder, try adding a "cock ring" to your bag of tricks. Slide the ring onto the shaft of your erect penis, and push it down to the base. It will give you stronger and longer-lasting erections.

I promised to tell more about a female condom. That there is such a thing as a female condom is a well-kept secret. It's much larger than a male condom and goes inside her vagina. A ring at each end holds it in place. The outer ring covers most (or all) of her vulva; the inner ring goes over her cervix. They are comfortable, easy to use, and don't restrict the blood flow to the penis like a tight-fitting male condom. They are barely noticeable for both partners. Ask the woman to insert the condom herself so that she can position the inner ring properly over her cervix. Numerous women have told me that a female condom does not diminish their pleasure, and I can attest that they definitely feel better than a standard condom for the male. I bought some female condoms online at Walgreen's and tried them (the things I do for you!). They are a wonderful creation. The brand is FC2 or fc2. If you have not tried one, go here to take a look: www.fc2femalecondom.com.

Of course, we live in the golden age of Viagra and its magical progeny, which can give you a powerful erection within thirty minutes. The effect of these drugs lasts between a few hours and a long weekend. Although I did not need them, I tried them all and found them to work as advertised. They are especially helpful if you anticipate a long interaction (I hope you do) or multiple interactions over a short time. If you don't need a pill, great. If you do, they are there for you. You can get a prescription from your doctor after a simple medical check. There are foreign suppliers (think Canadian pharmacies) of these drugs, and their prices are lower. Although you may be able to order them online without a prescription, have a medical doctor check you out before using these drugs because they all affect your blood flow. Blood flow causes inflation, which may not be good for the economy, but is a very good thing for a penis. I have tried pills from several of these foreign suppliers, and they work as well as the brand names (according to the packaging, they contain the same active ingredients as the branded pills). I can't vouch for the quality and long-term safety of these products, so either pay for the branded US versions, or try the foreign versions at your own risk.

Important Warning
Don't ignore the warning against having an erection that lasts more than four hours.
If you ignore a persistent erection, you may suffer a painful and, possibly *permanent* bending of your penis (by ninety degrees or more!)

If your erection lasts four hours (and I would not wait that long), get thee to the emergency room ...Now!

Permanent Loss of Erection

Many men have lost the ability to achieve an erection due to medical problems (prostate surgery being a leading cause), work-related injuries, or for other reasons. Whatever happened to you, life does not end because you can't have an erection. Thousands of other males have suffered the same fate. Sexuality can continue, with or without an erection. Consider Wesley's situation:

"My prostate surgery left me impotent. Even worse, I don't have any sexual urges left in me. Even if I see a beautiful, naked woman, I feel nothing. What I used to think was great porn, leaves me cold. I don't feel the slightest connection to a woman on a sexual level." Wesley asks, "Is that it? Is my sex life over? Is my wife destined to have a life with no sex? Will she cheat on me? Will she leave me for another man? Do I have to find her a surrogate lover?"

These are difficult questions for males who have been brought up from puberty to believe that their manhood and their erect penis are the same side of the same coin and that without an erection, they have nothing to offer a woman. The answer to all of these questions is a resounding *No*! I can hear you now: "That is easy for Clarke to say, but that doesn't work for me."

I encourage you to seek all the appropriate medical attention the healthcare system has to offer. I don't want to interfere with that process, which is between you and your physician. However, I do want to suggest that in addition to the medical route, you also consider approaching the problem from a spiritual angle as well. I have never heard this suggestion from any medical or sexual adviser, but if you are in Wesley's position, consider this:

There are many things you have done in your life that provided no immediate or tangible benefit to you, other than the sheer pleasure of *giving* to someone else (e.g., giving joy, or providing financial, physical or emotional support). For example, you gave a lot to your children with no expectation of a return, other than to watch them grow into mature adults.

In the same way, you can give sexual pleasure to someone even if you don't feel sexual pleasure yourself. Use your hands and fingers, or your lips and tongue to stroke, kiss, nuzzle, lick your partner. Try a variety of toys of all shapes and sizes too. Giving sexual pleasure to your lover will allow you to feel pleasure *in the giving*. The tenderness you share with your woman will be welcome, and your gift to her will be a powerful masculine act in its own right, even if you feel no physical gratification or sensation.

You can also try to remember what the sensations of sex felt like. Tune in to your memories of sexual pleasure, given and received, and you may find that you can give that same pleasure to your woman now, even if you feel nothing physically. Maybe you can trick yourself into feeling pleasure by remembering the pleasure you felt when you did the same thing before you lost physical sensation. You owe it to yourself and your woman (yes, that woman, the one who is standing by you) to give her everything you have. If pleasuring her sexually is too much in the beginning, you can go for a walk while holding her hand or put your arm around her as you sit on the sofa. Try touching her where you remember she likes to be touched. If you can no longer remember where that is, ask her where she would like you to touch her, and do it.

Your injury did not diminish your ability to be kind, so try some simple acts of kindness and see what happens. Kindness rewards the giver as well as the receiver. If you can no longer find it in yourself to be kind and thoughtful, please seek counseling to find out why. It would be unusual to lose those empathic qualities because of an injury or surgery. If you have lost empathy, you may be hanging on to a new story, which is another version of "poor me." As I described earlier (Chapter 11), you need to give away your story for many reasons, not the least of which is that your partner deserves all of you. Even though you have lost your erection, you can still be a good partner and live a good life, but only *you* can make that happen.

If you have been making progress and want to try something else, try to master the art of touching her non-sexually. When you have mastered that, massage her breasts for at least fifteen minutes to begin, and work up to forty-five minutes. Kiss and nuzzle her nipples. Ask for feedback on how much pressure she likes because you may not be as in tune with what she is feeling as you were before your injury. Once you are comfortable massaging and kissing her breasts, and especially if she is turned on, you can pleasure her genital area.

Before you do that, go back, and read the section on how to pleasure a woman in this area of her body. Seek all the feedback she can give you, and don't be upset or triggered if what she says sounds critical of you when you are doing your best. She is doing her best too, so explain how to give feedback in a positive way as mentioned previously ("A little slower please. Oh, that's good," or "A little less pressure. Yes, that's perfect").

I hope that your efforts to retain a powerful connection with your lover, in spite of losing the physical sensations of sex, lead to a continued or renewed connection with her. She deserves to be sexually gratified, and you can do that for her, no matter what you feel yourself. If all else fails, and you are able to get your head around it, consider helping her to find a substitute sexual partner. If you do decide to find a substitute sexual partner for her, don't become jealous or hold it against her if she avails herself of your offer. She will not leave you for this other male, as long as you are a Man; and finding a sexual partner for your woman would be the act of a very powerful Man.

Too Long to Orgasm

You may not know that many women worry that it takes them too long to orgasm. Their worries stem from several assumptions, as well as some practical observations.

- You will orgasm first, lose your erection, then roll over and go to sleep.
- You will become tired and quit, leaving her unsatisfied.
- You will think she is not enjoying you or your lovemaking.
- You will assume you are incompatible lovers and abandon her.

There are variations of these concerns, but they stem from the same phenomenon; some women take a long time to orgasm. What can you do to help your woman with this?

It should come as no surprise by now that women are not all the same; there are millions (probably billions) of different female genital anatomies. A woman's anatomy affects both how she likes to be pleasured and how long it takes her to orgasm. All other things being equal, if her G-spot is near the introitus (i.e., near the front of her vagina) and her clitoris glans is relatively exposed, she will be quick to orgasm. In some women, the G-Spot is deep within the vagina and a clitoral hood covers their clitoris glans. Both of these conditions will tend to make her slower to orgasm. Even though some women take much longer to orgasm than others, they are all good, and if you understand the differences, you won't be patting yourself on the back when your woman orgasms in the first minute of intercourse, or beating yourself up because, although you did *everything right* (and if you believe that, I still have that lovely tower in Paris for sale), it took her too long to orgasm.

Once you know what to expect it will be easy to accept that your new lover is different from your previous lovers (snowflakes, remember?). Your knowledge will also help reduce your lover's fears around her sexuality. If your woman is particularly slow to orgasm, discuss with her how you might help her to orgasm more easily (not necessarily more quickly). For example, using toys to stimulate her before intercourse begins may be perfect for her. Once you have started to have intercourse, try different angles of entry, or a side to side motion. You could try talking to her during intercourse. For instance, create a sexy vignette and whisper it into her ear as you make love. Tell her how much you love her and what you love about her. Don't forget that much of the pleasure a woman feels comes from her mind. Feed her mind something juicy and she may orgasm sooner than she ever has before.

Feel into her pleasure to determine what it is you do that gives her the most pleasure; if you are not sure, ask her. It takes time to learn about a new lover. Don't expect to learn in a single interaction how fast she would like you to move, how much pressure she likes, what image she likes in her head. Be patient and enjoy the discoveries together. As a conscious lover, you will still be learning after decades of sexual activity. You can always learn more about your lover, about yourself, about new sexual techniques, and about the myriad variations that makes sex with your lover so wonderful. Remember, if you are having pattern sex, you will likely become bored. Once sex lacks the emotional impact and the physical excitement needed to keep a long-term relationship juicy, you are already a statistic in Ms. Haag's book.

Female Ejaculation

A woman may ejaculate during an interaction, even if the man has not entered her; foreplay (or even the anticipation of sex) is enough to make some women ejaculate. For a male, a woman's ejaculation can be a delightful surprise or a horrifying shock, depending on whether he has seen it before, and how prepared he was to handle it. So let's talk about female ejaculation so it won't be such a surprise to you when it happens.

The ejaculated fluid has many names, but I am going to call it amrita; a Sanskrit word for "nectar." A woman may ejaculate amrita before, during, or after she orgasms and may even start oozing amrita as soon as you begin to stimulate her. What follows is a description of a male's first experience of amrita:

Jody and Aaron met on an online dating site. They met once and shared a wonderful evening that ended with a lingering kiss. On their third date, they shared a delightful dinner at her house, with lots of shared intimate information. After dinner, they became more intimate, kissing and cuddling on the sofa. After an hour or so, they moved to the bedroom to make love. Aaron was surprised when

Jody grabbed three thick towels and placed them on the bed. He had no idea why she had done that. They stood toe to toe at the foot of the bed, pleasuring each other for another fifteen minutes as he slowly undressed her. Aaron had never seen or even heard of female ejaculation, so he did not make the link between sex and the towels. He did notice that Jody had placed the towels where she was about to lie down, but he didn't ask her what they were for because he didn't want to appear naive.

Aaron was not an experienced lover, but he knew enough to go slow. (Go, Aaron!) When he lay Jody down on the bed and tenderly pulled off her panties, he was shocked to find that Jody immediately started to ooze a thick, pale fluid (the amrita) that flowed like slowly moving lava from her vaginal area. To Aaron, the amrita tasted almost as sweet as honey, with the consistency of heavy cream.

He positioned Jody on the bed, lay down beside her, and continued to pleasure her. As he did so, he noticed that the flow of this strange fluid had increased, and that the consistency gradually became thinner, more like olive oil than lava, and later as thin as milk. After half an hour of pleasure, the towels were soaked. Aaron had never seen anything like this, and he was unsure what to do. Jody reassured him that it was all okay. When Aaron entered her, the flow of amrita stopped as abruptly as it had begun.

Three other observations:

Sheena ejaculates only after her partner withdraws. Her eyes roll back into her head, and she ejaculates between four and six ounces of amrita. The amrita comes all at once, and she signals its impending arrival with a howl, like a wolf baying at the moon. Her amrita is a sweet-tasting, clear liquid that is considerably more viscous than water but much less viscous than Jody's creamy lava.

Tami and Vonda gush large quantities of watery amrita throughout a sexual interaction. They both use a large, waterproof pad with a rim designed to save the bedding or carpets from staining. Their amrita seems to have no end. Tami's is sweet, and Vonda's is salty.

Katey is like many women. When she feels the urge to ejaculate, it feels like she wants to urinate. She used to hold it back by tensing the same muscles she uses to hold her urine until she can find a toilet. Once she learned to empty her bladder *before* sexual activity began, she became comfortable just letting her amrita flow naturally and freely. The quantity she ejaculates is small (about an eggcup full), and its taste is salty.

Many women ejaculate amrita, but in such small quantities, it's hardly noticeable. If you are touching the inside of your partner's vagina and detect a sudden change in the texture or consistency of her natural lubrication, it's probably because she released some amrita. In some women, amrita oozes out slowly, while in others, it comes out in a projectile stream (hence the coarse vernacular *squirter* to describe a woman who ejaculates in this way). If your partner ejaculates amrita in large quantities, simply put a pad or towels under her in order to protect whatever you are lying on. Use as many towels as you need. Pads are available online (see the Resource section).

It's shocking (to me, at least) that medical science still has no generally accepted understanding of amrita or female ejaculation. Some physicians say that the Skene's glands secrete amrita. Others have pointed out that only the bladder could contain the amount of fluid some women ejaculate, so it must be urine. There are numerous hypotheses as to what is going on, including some misleading information (some hypotheses are opposites of each other so at least some of them must be wrong). Even if it contains some urine, amrita is certainly not *only* urine, as its color and consistency are totally different from urine. Neither is it the same as the other secretions that lubricate a woman's vagina, because its texture and viscosity are not at all the same. Until some enterprising student in search of a PhD comes along to make a careful study, the source and composition of amrita will remain indeterminate. Wherever it comes from, amrita's taste is somewhere between salty and sweet, not particularly yummy but not unpleasant either. Amrita is often a fairly clear fluid, but as Aaron discovered, it may be thick and creamy. Its purpose is unclear. If you come across amrita when you are not expecting it, have no fear. It won't hurt you. And whatever you do, don't shame your woman because she is releasing amrita. For her, it is a natural expression of her sexuality.

Life's Distractions

Modern life is so full of attractive distractions that it's hard to concentrate on anything for long. Society's devotion to electronic media seems to have backed people into a place where sex is the last item on the agenda. The story goes, "If I don't have to get up early, the laundry is done, and *The Late Show* has finished, then I will consider sex with my lover." Even if sex makes the cut, it often turns out to be a rush job because you are both tired. How did we ever give up sex in favor of TV and iPhones? It's a mystery, for sure!

In addition, it's too easy to become swamped by the constant need to be connected to everyone through Facebook or your phone. Try this: Go to Facebook once a day, at most; keep the ringtone on your phone turned off most of the time; turn the device off completely at eight o'clock every night when you are at home; and never check your phone when you are with your woman. Never! Be with her, not your phone.

Work, of course, consumes much of a person's day, but if you let work dominate your life, make a mental note—there is no prize for having the least amount of fun in your life. The only way to keep your sex-life alive, is to set aside time for it. Make a date. Have date-night once or twice a week, at least. Be spontaneous and make love at odd times. If you *have* to work, find the time to keep your relationship healthy by jettisoning something else that you spend time doing; like TV. Do whatever it takes to stay juicy or become a statistic in Ms. Haag's book; your choice!

19

THE END

IF YOUR RELATIONSHIP IS STRUGGLING, and it looks like one of you might quit, what can you do? The best course is to discuss what is happening. Talk about your relationship right from its humble beginning. Agree to keep the relationship intact as long as you both agree it's still working. Agree that if either of you ever feels the relationship is no longer working, you will talk to see if it can be repaired.

How do you know that your relationship is over and it is time to walk away? The end comes when you have gone as far you are willing to go to satisfy your partner (you have reached your bottom line), and your partner is still not satisfied (you cannot satisfy her bottom line) or, of course, the other way round. If one partner in a couple wants out of the relationship, what the other partner wants is irrelevant. At that point, all that remains is to part gracefully.

When the End Comes

When the time comes to end the relationship, state your truth ("I'm leaving") with absolute honesty, and don't back off. You want to leave in the best possible way:

- Make the time and space to tell her that you are leaving.
- Stay calm and centered as you deliver the message.

- Don't waver from the "I'm leaving" message.
- Don't raise your voice or be abusive, no matter what she says or does.

The time for rationales, complaints, stories, and explanations is past. Clearly state your terms of departure, which will vary depending on the history and current mood of the relationship. For example:

- I am leaving as soon as we stop talking.
- I will return tomorrow for the things I need immediately.
- I have a key, but I will notify you before entering the house.
- I will return for my other things later.
- I will only take things that are mine.
- I won't remove anything of *ours* without your agreement.

The delivery of the "I'm leaving" message does not have to include any details beyond those I noted above. Discussing where you are going and what you are going to do will prolong the leaving speech for no benefit. Later, divide the assets calmly and fairly. If children are involved, you will need lawyers and courts to protect their interests. If you have the means and alimony is an issue, try to negotiate a settlement, even if it costs you more now. A settlement will save you the angst of signing an alimony check every month. Support your children emotionally, physically, and financially. They need you to be there for them more than ever. Your son still needs you to show him how to become a Man, and that will be difficult if you are fighting with his mother. Don't forget that you are your daughter's role model for how a Man deals with adversity, especially in situations like the separation. She needs to see you behave as a Man so she can calibrate (on the Man scale) the quality of males she meets in future.

Lawyers are expensive and will frequently cause a fight over something you could have resolved without their interference. At every step, the high road is cheaper than paying two attorneys.

20

EXERCISES

What follows is a short series of exercises to give you a greater understanding of yourself. You can attend workshops or other courses (see Resources) if you want a more immersive experience doing exercises similar to these and others (including, perhaps, much more challenging exercises under supervision). These exercises may seem onerous, but don't let that stop you from doing them. Each takes about one weekend, and a weekend devoted to discovering yourself is worth the effort. You can do all these exercises by yourself, but if you know people who have already started to discover themselves ask them to join you and share your journey of discovery. Try to do these exercises more than once. Maybe even annually. As you do the work and continue to grow, you will discover more and more of your past, and it will be good to deal with it by forgiving everyone involved (including yourself) for what happened.

Who Are You?

1. Write a description of yourself in sufficient detail that people who have never met you would feel they know you. Don't limit yourself in what you write. Only you will ever see it. At a minimum, write about the following:

    - What you look like: hair, face, hands, belly, skin, teeth, scars, and so on.

- Describe your thinking style: concrete, abstract, spiritual, emotional, unfocused.
- What you like to do, and why.
- What you don't like to do, and why.
- Who you like to do things with: at work, at play, at home, in social settings.
- What you like and what you don't like about each of your friends.
- When you last learned something new; what it was, and how you felt afterwards.
- When you last went somewhere new: what it was like, how you felt, who was with you, who you met.
- What you watch on TV and how many hours a week you watch TV (don't guess, measure it).
- What you do on social media; list all.
- What your beliefs are (list all the ones you can think of).

2. Pick the 20 people who know you best and write down what you believe they think of you.
3. Do the same in reverse. Write down in detail what you think of each of these 20 people.
4. Pick 20 people who have been meaningful (positive or negative) in your life. Write down what you consider to be special about them and describe their roles in your life and what they did that was meaningful for you.
5. List at least 10 people who support you now (financially, spiritually, physically, and so on). Write down what is special about each person and what he or she does to support you. If you can't think of anyone to put on your list, ask yourself why that is the case, and write that down instead.
6. Describe all the times in the last 30 days when you were kind to someone, and all the times someone was kind to you; note who was involved and the circumstances. If there are no such times, go back a year, or however long it has been since you

gave or received kindness. If you can't think of anything to put on your list, ask yourself why that is the case, and write that down instead.

7. Write down the names of 20 people with whom you have had a close relationship, that was not sexual or romantic, in the last 10 years. They may be coworkers, friends, or family. Write down what you like or love about them. Write down what you do not like or love about them. If the relationship has ended, write down why it ended.
8. List 20 women with whom you have had some form of sexual relationship (heavy petting counts). Write down how you met and why each woman was important to you. Describe your lovemaking—what was good about it; what was not so good. Describe how you talked with your lover about your lovemaking, especially how you dealt with any issues (sexual or otherwise) that arose between you. In particular, write down how each woman made you feel. List all the memorable places you went together and what you did there. Write down who suggested you go to each place.
9. If you have not been sexual with 20 women, write about those you have been sexual with. If you have not been sexual with any woman, write down why that is.
10. If any of the relationships you listed above ended, write down why they ended and what your role was in ending the relationship. Write down whether you are still friends with your former relationship partners. If you are no longer friends, write down why not.
11. Write down where every train you are driving is going and how you are going to get there. Add your assessment of how each train is doing on its journey (e.g., is it going full speed, derailed, or stuck in a siding).
12. Identify where you want future trains to go. Write down why you are not already driving a train to these destinations (I don't have time; I need a car and can't afford one, etc.). Make

a plan to start your train down the track to at least one of the places you identified above. Then implement the plan.

Take the time to study all of your writings above and note any similarities between each writing. In particular look for similarities in who the driving force was in each relationship, interaction, or activity. Also, look for similarities in what you liked and didn't like about the other people (romantic interest or not) and what you liked and didn't like about your own actions.

Forgive

If you are not clear about forgiveness, reread Chapter 7. It's pertinent here too. Write down every person you need to forgive and make sure to forgive them in a ceremony as I described (also in Chapter 7). If necessary, forgive yourself too.

Exercise Your Center

Pilots repeatedly practice what to do if their airplanes suffer a malfunction, which is how they are able to maintain their cool when most people would panic. Take a leaf out of the pilot's handbook, and write down what you are going to do next time you are in danger of losing your center. Write down how you will maintain control of yourself so you don't lose your center and how you will regain your center if you lose it. After you are finished writing, speak what you wrote aloud to yourself, but even better, speak it to a friend, or a group of friends. It may feel weird, but don't let that stop you. See if you can find friends who will do the same and join you to share what you wrote in a group setting.

Firming up your approach to challenges that might arise will enhance your ability to remain centered when challenges do occur. Here is an example of what you might write:

Currently: What often happens to me is that other drivers cut me off. It usually happens when I am slowing down as I approach a traffic light (I like to come to a stop slowly so the ride is smooth). Inevitably, some crazy person swerves around me and cuts into my lane right in front of me. So I lean on the horn, and the driver (so far, it has always been a male) waves his arms about and flips me off. A couple of them have even gotten out of their cars and banged on my windshield. I am just trying to stop them cutting me off, but they seem to think it's all my fault. I am ready to explode when this happens and I have chased a couple of cars but, so far, I haven't done anything. I never got out of my car. I haven't even opened my car door.

From this day forward: I am not going to lean on the horn when someone cuts me off. I won't make faces or flip off anyone either. I am going to remain calm, keep my center, and relax. I will just be happy that I am not hurt. I will accept that there are bad drivers on the road, and there is nothing I can do about them except be vigilant and avoid them. If I feel my anger start to rise from my lower abdomen, I am just going push the anger back down where it began and stay centered. I might allow myself a quick eye-roll and then calmly go about my business.

Write down what it will take to knock you off your center? Use the following samples to get started and write down what your reaction would be in each scenario:

- Stuck in traffic when you are late for a date.
- Forgot you had a job interview and slept in.
- Lost a hundred-dollar bill.
- Football team lost a big game.
- Lost your job.
- Wife left you for another man.
- Girlfriend became desperately sick (or pregnant).
- Lost your house because you couldn't make the mortgage payment.
- Crashed your motorcycle and were severely injured.

- Father died.
- Discovered you have only six months to live.

Write down how you would react to these and other challenges. Talk to your friends about how *they* think you would react (this will be a valuable insight into what they think of you). Doing so will solidify your thoughts on such challenges and make it easier to take the right actions if challenges happen.

Parents

Describe your relationship with your father:

> How did your father and mother relate to each other?
> How did you and your father relate to each other?
> What was your father's relationship with men at his work and in social situations?
> Describe all the activities you and your father did together.
> Who else shared in the activities you did with your father? How did that feel?
> How did your father punish you? When did he last physically punish you?
> How old were you when you first defied your father to his face?
> Describe each incident in which you defied your father. How did that feel?
> Describe your father's reaction each time.
> Describe the relationship you had with your father once you were independent of him.

Describe your relationship with your mother:

> How did your mother relate to your father?
> How did you and your mother relate to each other?
> What was your mother's relationship with other women?

Describe all the activities you and your mother did together.
Who else shared in the activities you did with your mother? How did that feel?
How did your mother punish you? When did she last physically punish you?
How old were you when you first defied your mother to her face?
Describe each incident in which you defied your mother.
How did that feel?
Describe your mother's reaction each time.
Describe the relationship you had with your mother once you were independent of her.
If you are not independent of your mother, write down in detail why that is.

Exercises in Tenacity and Commitment

Choose three items from the list below (you can do more later). Many of these items will require training and much practice if you are to succeed. I recommend that you use qualified coaches to supervise your training and practice.

1. Swim one mile in a lake or in the ocean. There is no time limit. Pause to rest as needed. Have a safety boat with you in case you get into trouble.
2. Bicycle 100 miles. No vertical limits but an overall time limit of 15 hours. No rest except for six 20 minute breaks.
3. Run a half marathon – 13.1 miles. No walking. An overall time limit of 2.5 hours.
4. Walk for 12 hours without stopping except for a 10-minute break every two hours. No distance requirements but you will have to carry your own water and food as needed.
5. Climb a mountain or hill with a vertical rise of at least 5,000 feet from where you begin to the top. No time limit. If the biggest mountain in your area is only 2,500 feet high, climb it twice one right after the other. If you need food and shelter, take those things with you.
6. Organize a 3-day trip with at least 7 other people to accompany you. You can go sailing, camping, cycling, walking, in fact, any kind of group physical activity will be fine (sex does not count). The important thing is not what activity you do, it is that *you* organize it all. You find the people (bearing in mind their personalities and compatibility); you find the location (and scout it in advance as necessary); you set the dates of the event (considering weather); you get buy-in from everyone in the group (to your idea and your leadership – you must handle anyone who wants to push you out of your leadership role); you make sure that all of the needed items are taken on

the trip (if you are camping don't forget the food, the stove, the matches, the water, the tents, the sleeping bags and so on); in short it is your job to make sure it all goes smoothly, that everyone has a good time, and that you get home safely. You can delegate but you MUST be the responsible leader.

7. Learn to play a guitar (or any other musical instrument), well enough to sing and play one song at a party within six months.
8. Learn to juggle three balls for at least five minutes. You have 6 months to learn.
9. Pick any sport that you know well enough to coach and commit to coach that sport for a minimum of 3 years at any level you choose.
10. Find at least one child to mentor. All kinds of philanthropic organizations can pair you with a child. Commit to be a mentor for a minimum of three years.
11. Write your life story in as much detail as you can. Recount events that happened to you, no matter how insignificant they may seem. Describe all of the people you can recall, what they were like, what they did with you or to you, what you learned from them, and how they affect your life now. If it is less than 100 pages of small writing, typed or handwritten, find more events and people to write about. Don't worry about grammar and editing. Just put what you know on paper.
12. Take singing lessons for a year, then perform three songs at an open mic night, or with a band, or in karaoke.
13. Subscribe to a daily newspaper and read it every day. Los Angeles Times, Washington Post, Chicago Tribune, New York Times, Wall Street Journal are all good. Local papers may be good too. Read the newspaper from cover to cover and learn about world and local events every day.

14. Visit a foreign country where you do not speak the language and get to know someone from there.
15. Make a short list (5 things) you have always wanted to do but were afraid to try. Start doing at least one of these things within three months. Then do the others over the course of the next few years.
16. Join a tennis club, golf club, bowling club, rowing club, sailing club, soccer club, rugby club, lacrosse club (actually any kind of club provided you have not done this activity before) and participate.
17. Help in a soup kitchen for the needy one night per week for one year.
18. Take a spiritual sexuality class.
19. Join a tantra meetup group or an ecstatic dance group or a contact improve group (search on the internet for such groups in your area).
20. Keep thinking about new things to do, then go do them.

21

RESOURCES

Group Activities

Men's Workshop: I created the Men's Workshop with the goal of providing men a way to set their inner Man free. Please contact me at freemyinnerman@gmail.com if you want to learn more about the Men's Workshop.

Quodoushka ("Q" for short) is a group of spiritual sexuality workshops. To access their website, go to www.quodoushka.org for a full schedule of Q events. I have found the Q's to be a source of great personal growth; one of the workshops offers powerful a way to eliminate shame and guilt and to extend forgiveness to others who have hurt you. Q's have been controversial, as teachings about sex and sexuality tend to be. If you are on a quest to learn and grow, I suggest you contact Amara Charles personally (see below) to determine whether they are right for you.

Teachers

Amara Charles: one of the leading teachers of the Quodoushka workshops, with decades of experience. She is insightful, shamanic, and a gifted, passionate speaker. Amara led the commitment ceremony for Karen and me. She offers numerous other workshops some of which are designed to be for women only (Shakti Queen). Some of her workshops are done on line. Access her website at amaracharles.com.

Kristin Viken and John Kent: In addition to teaching Q's, John and Kristin offer a 12-day workshop designed to liberate participants from the grip of their armor that over the course of their lives has become so thick, and so high, that they can no longer feel many of the good things in life. They do this by giving attendees the tools to jettison their baggage and better understand themselves. Access their website at shamanicdearmoring.com

Mukee Okan: I am sad to report that Mukee Okan died before I finished writing this book. I miss her greatly. Mukee created a documentary called *The Pussy Talks.* As the name suggests, the focus is a woman's relationship with her genital anatomy. You can download *The Pussy Talks* for a nominal fee from her website: thepussytalks.com. A fun way to watch The Pussy Talks is with a group of friends. Invite them to watch it with you, share a glass of wine, then enjoy the delicious discussion after the viewing.

Mukee also created *The Cock Tales*, which, as you might also guess from the title, deals with the relationship males have with their genital anatomy. I am not sure whether *The Cock Tales* is still available. At the time of writing, it is not available on her website. Access *The Pussy Talks* documentary at thepussytalks.com

David Deida: David is one of the most prolific writers and teachers on the subject of men and women and the relationship between them. He also has covered sexuality on a broad front. You might also try one of his multiday intensive workshops, especially if you are new to spiritual sexuality. You will find some of what you are seeking there. Access David's website at deida.info

Michaela Boehm: Michaela provides a wide range of sexuality classes with a broad range of activities all over the world. Access her website at michaelaboehm.com/workshops

Alison Armstrong helps women and men to understand each other through her PAX programs. I highly recommend Ms. Armstrong's teaching for both men and women. Her lectures and classes offer some real nuggets. Access her website at understandmen.com

Access her website at understandmen.com

Laurie Handlers: Laurie is a Tantra teacher that I know well. I have done several classes with her and two radio shows. Laurie's Sex Magic class helped me let go of some past 'stuff' that was affecting my daily life. She also teaches ISTA all over the world but I have not done that class. Access Laurie's website at butterflyworkshops.com Information on ISTA training can be accessed at info@schooloftemplearts.org

Activities

Rites of Passage: There are numerous commercial enterprises offering rites of passage in the US. Search for them on the internet. One that offers a wide range of activities throughout the year is The School of Lost Borders. It can be found at schooloflostborders.org. I have no personal experience of any commercial enterprises offering rites of passage.

Salons: My Salons are in Phoenix, Arizona. Of course, it is impractical for you to come to my Salon unless you live close by. So, consider starting your own Salon series, which you can do without much difficulty. Here are some of the Salon rules:

1. Everyone's comments and opinions are as valid as everyone else's comments and opinions.
2. Telling anyone they are wrong is not allowed.
3. Teaching (or telling someone what they *should* be doing) is not allowed.
4. Participants speak from the heart about *their* experience. Participants may ask questions about what someone said, but criticizing or analyzing another participant's commentary is not allowed.
5. No alcohol is allowed until the Salon ends.
6. What happens at a Salon stays at the Salon; confidentiality is critical.
7. Be brave and participate.

8. Be honest; be in integrity with yourself and with each other.
9. Care for yourself and for others.
10. No touching another person without permission.

I break up the Salon timetable with simple exercises related to the subject matter we are discussing that day. The exercises are usually done in pairs, but we have done groups of four from time to time. We talk about challenging things at a Salon, so I ask people who are in a relationship outside the Salon to do the exercises with someone other than their partner. This allows participants to deal with difficulties in their relationship without their relationship partner being involved or challenged. Salons typically last five to six hours after which we have a BYOB party. There is no charge to attend a Salon but I do ask that everyone bring whatever they want to drink (I provide water) and a dish to share for the party.
Tantra: Tantra classes are available all over the world and are a source of information and teaching, as well as spiritual practices. Be aware, though, that there is no body of knowledge that controls what is taught in Tantra. Anybody can call themselves a Tantra teacher, and there is no set body of knowledge for Tantric practice. Therefore, there is enormous breadth to what is taught in a Tantra class. What you learn will depend on your teacher and your fellow attendees (from whom you may learn much). You might search for a Tantra meet-up group in your area, and start there. Tantra groups are a low-cost way to get started on a spiritual path. A word of caution: While many Tantra instructors work for nothing or close to it, they are not being charitable. They often make up for gifting their teaching services with *sessions* during the classes in whatever practice they might offer—counseling, massage, yoga, or something else—and the sessions can be quite expensive. I don't have a problem with this because this is their livelihood after all. However, in my experience, the quality of what is offered and the subsequent results vary wildly, so buyer beware.

Active Meditation: There are many sources, but I found this one the simplest to understand and accept if you are not a practiced meditator: **activemeditation.com**

Orgasmic Meditation A community for connecting with others in sexual integrity: Their website is onetaste.us. The OM practice is one place to begin your journey to sexual integrity. Although the breadth of their offering is exceptionally narrow, and the pricing of their extended classes is outrageous, their introductory class and ongoing practices are inexpensive.

Facebook: Numerous Facebook groups profess knowledge of masculinity. They represent a generally free source of information. You'll find many different perspectives, some of which might make you think. A word of caution: Some of these ostensibly masculine groups are dominated by women. Beware of any woman telling you how to be a Man; she is trying to fix you. Women have no idea how to be a Man. At best, they can tell you how they think they want you to treat *them*. My suggestion would be to read the Facebook material of many such groups and decide for yourself which work for you. You can also try the following:

- Tai chi and other martial arts classes (most embody spiritual development along with the physical mastery of their discipline).
- Meet-up groups, of which there are thousands.
- Therapists, if you need professional help.
- Books by the thousand (a partial list is below).

Reading List: alphabetical by author; available online)

Margo Anand	*The Art of Sexual Ecstasy*
Robin Baker	*Sperm Wars*
Bayda and Bartok	*Saying Yes to Life (Even the Hard Parts)*
Stuart Mark Berlin	*Sexual Secrets of Tantric Kabbalah*
Amara Charles	*The Sexual Practices of Quodoushka*
Amara Charles	*Sexual Agreements*
Paulo Coelho	*The Alchemist*
Paulo Coelho	*A Manuscript Found in Accra*
David Deida	*Dear Lover*
David Deida	*It's a Guy Thing*
David Deida	*The Way of the Superior Man*
David Deida	*Wild Nights*
Joe Dispenza	*You Are the Placebo*
Easton and Hardy	*Ethical Slut*
Warren Farrell	*Why Men Are the Way They Are*
Helen Fisher	*The Anatomy of Love*
Robert Glover	*No More Mr. Nice Guy*
Pamela Haag	*Marriage Confidential*
Cynthia Hazan	*Human Bonding*
Anne Hooper	*Erotic Massage*
J	*The Sensuous Woman*
Sam Keen	*Fire in the Belly*
Dan Kiley	*Peter Pan Syndrome*
Hsi Lai	*White Tigress—Green Dragon* [or Jade Dragon]
Hsi Lai	*Sexual Teachings of the White Tigress*
Dr. Phil McGraw	*Relationship Rescue*
Moore and Gillette	*King, Warrior, Magician, Lover*
Kathleen Parker	*Save the Males*

Penney Peirce	*Frequency: The Power of Personal Vibration*
Jordan B. Peterson	*12 Rules for Life*
Matt Ridley	*The Red Queen*
Don Miguel Ruiz	*The Four Agreements*
Ryan and Jethá	*Sex at Dawn*
Lynn Saxon	*Sex at Dusk*
David Schnarch	*Resurrecting Sex*
Zhi Gang Sha	*Soul Healing Miracles*
Janis Abraham Spring	*After the Affair*
Aaron Spitz	*The Penis Book*
Neil Strauss	*The Game (Undercover in the Secret Society of Pickup Artists)*
Tristan Taormino	*Opening Up*
Rollo Tomassi	*The Rational Male*
Rollo Tomassi	*The Rational Male – Preventative Medicine*
Rollo Tomassi	*The Rational Male – Positive Masculinity*
Naomi Wolf	*Vagina*
Naomi Wolf	*Promiscuities*
Andrew Yorke	*The New Art of Erotic Massage*

Video and Podcast List

The Red Pill documentary by Cassie Jaye; currently available on Amazon.

The Vagina Monologues, a show written by, and starring, Eve Ensler; currently available on Amazon as a DVD, but also in a Kindle edition, paperback book, or audiobook.

I particularly like the eerily sensual *Mind Body Soul Series*, © 1999 New World Music Limited, www.newworldmusic.co.uk.

Rollo Tomassi contact information and blog therationalmale.com

Intelligence Squared Podcasts:
Jordan B. Peterson interviewed by Anne McElvoy on Gender, Patriarchy and the Slide Towards Tyranny
Stephen Fry and Friends on the Life Loves and Hates of Christopher Hitchens
Richard Dawkins, The Rational Revolutionary
Anne Marie Slaughter on What Next for Feminism
Pornography is Good for Us: Without it We Would Be a Far More Repressed Society.

Material Resources

For a pad that goes under your sheets to absorb amrita, try the NorthShore Champion Washable Underpad (available on Amazon). It's large and absorbent, and its structure means it won't make a crinkling sound as you move on it (such sounds can be off-putting at an intimate moment).
Female condoms - www.fc2femalecondom.com. At time of writing they were available at Walgreens online.
Lube:
LouAna Coconut Oil (never dries up, inexpensive, available at Safeway supermarkets)
"Extra rich Coconut 'miracle' oil" by OGX, distributed by Vogue International, Clearwater FL, USA 33579 (never dries up, spray bottle is a convenient dispenser)
Sylk, a natural plant based lubricant that has great staying power at sylkusa.com.